The Sum of All Heresies

The Sum of All Heresies

The Image of Islam in Western Thought

FREDERICK QUINN

OXFORD
UNIVERSITY PRESS

2008

OXFORD

UNIVERSITY PRESS

Oxford University Press, Inc., publishes works that further
Oxford University's objective of excellence
in research, scholarship, and education.

Oxford   New York
Auckland   Cape Town   Dar es Salaam   Hong Kong   Karachi
Kuala Lumpur   Madrid   Melbourne   Mexico City   Nairobi
New Delhi   Shanghai   Taipei   Toronto

With offices in
Argentina   Austria   Brazil   Chile   Czech Republic   France   Greece
Guatemala   Hungary   Italy   Japan   Poland   Portugal   Singapore
South Korea   Switzerland   Thailand   Turkey   Ukraine   Vietnam

Published by Oxford University Press, Inc.
198 Madison Avenue, New York, New York 10016

www.oup.com

Oxford is a registered trademark of Oxford University Press

Library of Congress Cataloging-in-Publication Data
Quinn, Frederick.
The sum of all heresies : the image of Islam in western thought /
Frederick Quinn.
   p. cm.
Includes bibliographical references and index.
ISBN 978-0-19-532563-8
1. Islamic countries—Relations—Europe. 2. Europe—Relations—
Islamic countries. 3. Islamic countries—Foreign public opinion, European.
4. Civilization, Islamic. 5. Public opinion—Europe. 6. Christianity and other
religions—Islam. 7. Islam—Relations—Christianity. I. Title.
DS35.74.E85Q45 2007
297—dc22   2007010412

9 8 7 6 5 4 3 2 1

Printed in the United States of America
on acid-free paper

For our children: Christopher Edward Vermilye
and Kristin Buch Quinn, Alison Moore Quinn, Stephen
Tanner Irish, Jessica Lee Irish and Stephen Metts,
Thomas Adams Irish and Grace Atmajain,
and Emily Anne Irish

"O brave new world that has such people in it."
—Shakespeare, The Tempest

Acknowledgments

The study of Islam became a fulltime subject for me in 2000 when I spent time in Abuja, Nigeria, with my late wife, Charlotte, who was writing a book on Islam in Africa. Sabbatical time at Oxford University in 2003 allowed me to draw on the resources of the Bodleian library through the friendly and efficient staff of Rhodes House, and also allowed for several long conversations with Bishop Kenneth Cragg, whose pioneering work on Muslim–Christian relations represented the Anglican Church's principal point of contact with Islam for nearly half a century. Oxford's Centre for Islamic Studies was a hospitable venue, and I profited from discussions with Professor James Piscatori, coauthor of *Muslim Politics*, and Keith Ward, Regius Professor of Divinity at Oxford University and author of numerous volumes on world religions. Jane Shaw, historian and Dean of Divinity at New College, was a lively interlocutor, as was Shirley Ardener, whose seminars at the Institute of Social Anthropology were a venue for scholars from all over the world to exchange ideas.

In Utah, an opportunity to deliver the Stirling McMurrin Lecture on Religion and Culture in October 2003 allowed me to initially lay out some of the ideas elaborated in this book's concluding section. Conversations with John O. Voll, director of Georgetown University's Center for Muslim–Christian Understanding, and Norman Jones of the Utah State University History Department allowed me to test some of the ideas presented in this work. An invitation to teach courses on political Islam and global Islam through the University of Utah's Political Science Department and Middle East Center in 2004 and 2005 allowed further exploration of the topic. I am grateful to Ibrahim Karawan, Bernard Weiss, Peter von Sievers, and Hakan Yavuz for their kind assistance.

The assistance of Leonard Chiarelli, assistant librarian, the Aziz S. Atiya Library for Middle East Studies, University of Utah, was invaluable. Tree Brown Hayes, another librarian, was most helpful in the preparation of the manuscript and selection of illustrations, as was her talented graphics arts husband Jim, aided by Sahara, Marina, and Ogden. Cynthia Read, Executive Editor at Oxford University Press, has proven once again to be a wise and creative counselor, and Daniel Gonzalez, her editorial assistant, and Christine Dahlin ably and cheerfully saw the book through production.

Part of the book's final chapter was delivered at the Brigham Young University's conference on "Islam in the European Public Sphere," January 28–29, 2006, in Provo, Utah. I am grateful to Professor Wade Jacoby of Brigham Young University for his hospitality and assistance.

My article " 'Am I Not Your Lord?' Kenneth Cragg on Muslim–Christian Dialogue," which appeared in the *Journal of Muslim Minority Affairs* 26(1) (April 2006), is reprinted with permission of the *JMMA*.

Contents

The Sum of All Heresies

Introduction

Islam has become a major topic in international relations in recent years, triggered by the 9/11 disaster, sustained warfare in Iraq and Afghanistan, the spread of terrorism in the guise of Islamic jihad, and increasing global tensions. Behind these difficult East–West political encounters are a general lack of knowledge about Islamic history, beliefs, and politics and a sharply negative image of Islam often held by policy makers, religious leaders, and the general public. This topic in its emotional complexity—the image of Islam as it has developed in the West—is the subject of this book.

Some of the subject matter discussed in this work is porous—we are talking about images and attitudes about Islam in locations with changing topographies like the Orient and Middle East; and their inhabitants, variously described as Turks, Persians, Arabs, and Moors, can be equally elusive. Authors in various periods had different "Orients" in mind, most of them more cerebral entities than geographic realities. Todd Kontje used the concept of "German Orientalisms" to cover the multiple uses of Orientalist images in that country.[1] L. P. Harvey, in *Islamic Spain, 1200 to 1500* and *Muslims in Spain, 1500 to 1614*, highlighted the difficulty of using even such apparently obvious words as "Moor," "Spain," or "Morisco," and Maxime Rodinson's provocative study *Europe and the Mystique of Islam* and Thierry Hentsch in *Imagining the Middle East* argued for the interrelationship of "Occident" and "Orient" and asked if in the

West the idea of the Orient could exist as a reality independent of the writers who employed it.[2]

The "Orient" for Westerners originally meant countries east of the Mediterranean, with London, Paris, Berlin, or New York as vantage points, but this, again, was not a geographical concept, for the East could begin at Vienna's outskirts. "Asia begins at the Landstrasse," Count Metternich reportedly said, when European boundaries were once more being reshaped in the early nineteenth century.

Additionally, the Middle East is not the same as the Islamic world. The American naval historian, Alfred Thayer Mahan, first used the term "Middle East" in 1902 to designate the landmass between India and Arabia. British journalists and politicians preferred "Middle East" to "Near East" and quickly adopted the former term, whose use continues to the present, replacing another widely used Western term, "the East."[3] Political-military questions beginning in the Balkans were known as "the Eastern question" and Fitzroy MacLean's memorable account of diplomatic sleuthing from Yugoslavia to Soviet Central Asia was called *Eastern Approaches*.[4] In France, by the nineteenth century the Orient extended as far as Indochina and intellectually could include Confucian thought and culture; for the British the Orient usually stopped with India, where there was a strong interest in Hindu religion and mythology. And somewhere in distant mountains and valleys, German savants decided, an Aryan race once lived before decamping westward for the Nordic lands. Hence, these Eastern lands did not always equate with territory peopled by Muslims.

The term "Orientalist" in the nineteenth century was largely value-neutral, identifying those who studied the languages, literature, and archaeology of the Orient, but especially in recent years, in the writings of Edward Said, it was refashioned to mean Western political and cultural imperialism and domination of non-Western countries. Thus there is elasticity to the terms used in this book. "Islam" derives from an Arabic word meaning submission or peace, and believers are part of a worldwide community, the *ummah*. I use "Islam" primarily to refer to the religion and culture of Muslims, more than a billion people spread over the earth, with heavy concentrations in the Middle East, Africa, and Asia. A universal "image of Islam" does not exist. "All Islam is local Islam," it has been said and to an extent that is true. The Koran and Hadith are interpreted variously in local languages from Morocco to the Philippines and by local mosque congregations, each influenced by particular histories, geographical locations, and local economic, political, and cultural realities. When, in the wake of 9/11, an American congressman asked, "When you call 911 Islam, who do you get?" the answer was a multiplicity of responses. Muslims, like members of other faith communities, both affirm the universal truths of their religious beliefs and apply them in the unique settings in which they live and have their being.

My response to this problem is to use each term in the context in which it first appeared, admitting its imprecision. The book's focus is on the image of Islam as it developed in the West from the Age of Muhammad until now. It is not a traditional political history, although political history provides the scaffolding in which the study fits. For each topic, I have selectively used examples, but not all possible examples, to illustrate a theme. The book's narrative thus cannot be like that of an engineering manual, but more like a musical work of interwoven themes clearly announced at the beginning and restated with variations, all part of a carefully constructed whole, the unity of which is audible from a distance but not necessarily in each isolated instance.

The term "image" admittedly lacks precision, for the beliefs societies hold represent a cross-stitched network of meanings. By "image," I mean the mental representations of Islam that were recorded in various times, places, and forms by religious writers, political figures, and creative artists representing aspects of a larger reality. These delineations of Islam in turn were passed on to various academic communities and the public. Some such images were formed in response to a particular event, such as the Ottoman invasion of Vienna or 9/11. Others were held over a much longer term, as in the centuries-old biographies of the Prophet Muhammad that made their way through generations of readers. The Dutch sociologist of religions Hans J. Mol has usefully written of identity as "the place in which an individual, group, or society fits; the core group of beliefs, values, and ideas of an individual or society."[5] In this work, the focus is on how Westerners identified Islam in different centuries, not on how Muslim societies identified themselves; such an important study remains to be written.

This introduction is briefly about my own journey toward this book's subject matter. The book's central chapters discuss the history of emerging Western perceptions of Islam from the Middle Ages to the present. Material is drawn from religious writings, histories, travelers' accounts, literature and drama, and—as they became available—popular and classical music, the visual arts, and films. The bibliography points to many specialized studies on aspects of how Islam was portrayed in different centuries to different audiences.

Even after years of sympathetic Islamic–Christian dialogue, sharp differences remain, and there are few points of compatibility in the theologies of the two religious systems. Muslims find a trinitarian God incompatible with the Koran's idea of Allah; Christians find the treatment of Jesus in Islam to be woefully inadequate (i.e., no Crucifixion, Jesus as a lesser prophet than Mu-hammad, etc.). Differences of language, history, and culture only widen the gap and it sometimes appears that no additional door is left unlatched that will allow participants to move to a new place.

Yet there are grounds for hope; both religions (and Judaism) are based on love, peace, and forgiveness. Prayer, generosity of spirit, and good works are required of believers in their daily interactions with others, both members and nonmembers of these faith traditions. It is surely not in the creeds of the great Abrahamic religions that followers of the three holy paths hate, slander, and kill one another.

The task of finding common ground is urgent. One-fifth of the world's population is Muslim, and in America the rapidly growing Muslim population has been variously represented as being over six million people meeting in over three thousand mosques, Islamic schools, or meeting centers. Conflict, mistrust, and misunderstanding characterize the Muslim–Christian encoun-ter, and examples of cooperation are few as antiterrorism budgets mount, visa and emigration restrictions multiply, and civil liberties are curtailed. The pur-pose of this work is to help find grounds for an ongoing conversation among members of different faiths, by showing the historical roots of such misper-ceptions and the origins of such religious and cultural mistrust and hatred. Let me explain where I began this journey, one that many others have taken in different steps, reflecting the times and settings in which our attitudes were shaped about a world beyond our shores.

The World beyond Oil City: *John L. Stoddard's Lectures*

In the parlor of my Great-Aunt Sade's farmhouse in Oil City, Pennsylvania, in the 1940s was a four-shelf walnut bookcase with a curved glass front. It contained a set of Charles Dickens's works, a massive Bible with space in it to record the births and deaths of family members, and a complete set of *John L. Stoddard's Lectures*. Born in Brookline, Massachusetts, in the mid-nineteenth century, Stoddard had been valedictorian at Williams College in 1871, attended Yale Divinity School, and taught Latin and French at the Boston Latin School. He then made the customary tour of continental Europe, to which he ad-venturously added Greece, Asia Minor, Palestine, and Egypt and for the next twenty years he traveled across America giving lantern-slide lectures about the world he had seen. In 1897 Stoddard published his talks in ten handsomely illustrated and luxuriously bound volumes. Families across America pored over the illustrations on winter evenings. "His travels embrace nearly all the habitable parts of the world," a promotional flyer announced.

These printed lectures were my introduction to international life in an age before television. I looked at the crowded foreign streets, pointed towers, strangely costumed people, and postcard-view landscapes. Years later, in preparing this book, I reread Stoddard's narrative. It was free of the obvious racism common to its age. A skilled writer, with a keen eye for details, he blended history, geography, and religion with a balance unusual for the later nineteenth century. I cannot say that he ignited any special interest in the Middle East for me. It was only one of many regions I would have liked to have seen, including Egypt, where a visitor to Shepherd's Hotel, Cairo, could hire a donkey named Champagne Charley, Abe Lincoln, Prince Bismarck, or Yankee Doodle, and tour the crowded city, the Nile, and the Pyramids. Stoddard ended each lecture with a careful summary of the history and political issues facing a given country. Often, too, he ended a chapter with a few verses of the optimistic poetry of his age, in this case from his fellow New Englander, James Russell Lowell:

> New occasions teach new duties;
>   Time makes ancient good uncouth;
> They must upward still, and onward,
>   Who would keep abreast of Truth:
> Lo, before us gleams her camp-fires!
>   We ourselves must Pilgrims be,
> Launch our Mayflower, and steer boldly
>   Through the desperate winter sea:
> Nor attempt the Future's portal
>   With the Past's blood-rusted key.[6]

This was foreign policy set to the poetry of imperial America, as good a way as any of entering the world of Manifest Destiny, the Monroe Doctrine, and making the world safe for democracy; it was the world in which I grew up.

Muslims in the Movies: "The Thief of Bagdad"

Though we really knew nothing about the Middle East, an ersatz version of it was accessible to young Americans in Oil City in the post–World War II era. Two rival Nobles of the Mystic Shrine bands marched in parades, the musicians decked in red felt fezzes and Zouave-like baggy pants, led by a ramrod-straight drum major who gestured with a curved sword when the white-shoed band should turn smartly off Main Street and march back into the reality of small-town America.

Films were big image builders. Bad Arabs waited to be defeated in the sand-and-scimitar motion pictures shown on Saturday afternoons at the Lyric Theatre. These included reruns of *The Sheik*, *The Thief of Bagdad*, and *Algiers*— "Come with me to the casbah" entered local vocabularies, though none of us knew what it meant. The films were replete with sexual subthemes that I missed: pale, frail English ladies encountering virile Bedouin chiefs were far from my emotional landscape. I remember my Aunt Til dragging me by foot and rattling local bus to see *The Desert Song*. Songs like "One Alone" and "The Desert Song" offered momentary romance and escape from the dreariness of post-Depression America.

The Children's Crusade

Not much was taught about the Crusades in the Oil City school system back then—only that high-minded English knights tightly wrapped in meshed steel were done in by crafty turbaned Muslims who came out of nowhere to capture the Holy Land. It was during a junior high school music class that my first lasting image of the Crusades was formed. Miss Baker, our teacher, had the glint in her eye reserved for introducing a new piece of music as she gave us a new song for spring assembly. "This is called 'Crusader's Hymn,'" she said. "It is the song the little crusaders sang when they went off to fight in the Holy Land." "Stand up straight like little crusaders," she later told us at the assembly, just before the blue velvet auditorium curtains rattled open. We stood at attention and sang:

> Fairest Lord Jesus, Ruler of all nations,
> O Thou of God and man the Son,
> Thee will I cherish, Thee will I honor,
> Thou, my soul's glory, joy, and crown.

Details about the song's origins and the Children's Crusade were spotty. Where did the children come from? What happened to them? We never knew. Sometimes preachers mentioned them in sermons in later years; either they were lost or sold into slavery. The Crusades remained a mystery but the word "Crusade" became a staple in midcentury America's vocabulary. "You are about to embark on the Great Crusade," General Dwight D. Eisenhower told the Allied troops just before the invasion of Normandy on June 6, 1944; *Crusade in Europe* was the title of his best-selling 1948 memoir. Billy Graham traveled around America, filling massive stadiums with his Crusades and his son, Franklin, continued to call them that, long after the word had fallen out of favor. The lines were drawn—good versus evil, Christian versus infidel, fair skinned versus dark skinned—and it would take a long time to disentangle them and move in new directions. Of course I did not know that for Muslims "Crusader" and "Frank" (Franj) were hostile terms until years later, when I was a young diplomat seated in Ouagadougou's open-air Nader cinema. There, I listened to a local audience erupt in cheers during a potboiler Egyptian movie when an Arab warrior shouted, "Take that, Crusader!" as he stabbed a French soldier. Much later, Mehmet Ali Agca, who shot the pope on May 13, 1981, said he was trying to kill "the supreme commander of the Crusades." Clearly, two deeply held, emotionally charged views of history were colliding in music, film, and popular culture, although we did not know it at the time.

A Framework for Looking at a Wider World: Arnold Toynbee

Increasingly interested in a world beyond Venango County, when I learned I was going to college I wanted to find a single book that would provide an introduction to world history. I spent the summer after high school working nights at the local radio station, WKRZ, "the voice of greater Venango County." After the six o'clock news was over and the Pittsburgh Pirates baseball game was switched on, there was a lot of time between station breaks, and I used this time to read history books. The early 1950s was the heyday of Arnold Toynbee's popularity. "This will answer the kinds of questions you have been asking," a kindly high school teacher told me as he recommended Toynbee's work. "Mr. Toynbee has written a history of all civilizations, past and present, and how they all fit together. You ought to read it."

Toynbee examined twenty-six civilizations, sixteen of which were dead, leaving ten survivors. I do not recall reading in detail about Islam or any other particular civilization in his works, only that some were ascending while others were in an advanced state of decline. Never mind that details were spotty, what mattered were the categories Toynbee employed about genius, growth, breakdowns, heroic ages, etcetera. I copied out the examples at night on the radio station's ancient Underwood typewriter, using the red ribbon for important points and the black ribbon for details, then neatly packed the several pages of notes into the trunk I had bought to carry my worldly possessions to Dickinson College in Carlisle, Pennsylvania. But then I only read them once; after I mentioned Toynbee to a thoughtful history professor, John C. Pflam, he said something like, "An interesting but dated figure, why don't you read some specific works on a country or topic instead?" I did not know it at the time, but Toynbee's universe was largely a painted stage setting; someone later compared it to the carefully stitched-together imaginary world of Tolkien's novels. The mid-1950s was dominated both by the cold war and by increasingly expanded global horizons. Arthur Koester explained the inner mind of communism, and Chester Bowles excited a generation of young Americans with his *Ambassador's Report,* an account of his diplomatic adventures in India. The Reverend James Robinson, pastor of Harlem's Church of the Master, and founder of Operation Crossroads Africa, spoke at Dickinson about his travels in Africa, riding by overcrowded buses along perilous local roads to visit isolated schools and finding students interested in promoting international understanding through exchange visits. Others were attracted to Europe and Asia, but I picked Africa, the most unknown of overseas destinations, for further study.

Having run out of money in Carlisle, I transferred to Allegheny College in Meadville, Pennsylvania, in 1954 after finding a job with the local radio station, WMGW, as news editor and nighttime announcer, which included sweeping out the studio and shutting down the transmitter at ten-minute intervals so that its tubes would not break. Foreign travel for students was a rarity in that era, but our student government was asked to nominate someone to be part of a National Student Association delegation to visit South Africa one summer. I was picked and began a total immersion into the study of South African apartheid, history, and culture. Most memorable was reading Alan Paton's novel *Cry, the Beloved Country* and Trevor Huddlestone's account of his time spent as an Anglican priest in crowded Sophiatown, *Naught for Your Comfort.* I reread both works several times in the years ahead. Funding for that trip never materialized, but I was hooked on a career interest in international affairs.

Joining the Foreign Service in 1958: Morocco

In 1958 I joined the Foreign Service and was assigned to Morocco as a first post. I asked a North African desk officer for a good book on Islam; from his desk he removed T. E. Lawrence's *Seven Pillars of Wisdom,* holding it the way Ronald Reagan did refrigerator attachments in his early General Electric television ads and said in the same confident voice, "This is what you need to know about the Arab mind."

Before going overseas there were several weeks of orientation in Washington, where members of our class of junior officer trainees often spent lunch hours in some of the bookshops for which the city was famous. On tables at the stores' fronts were piles of works on international economic development, Barbara Ward on African economics, and Verna Micheles Dean's *The Nature of the Non-Western World*. Dean, who taught political science at the University of Rochester, compared progressive, secular Turkey under Mustafa Kemal Atatürk to Egypt under Colonel Gamal Abdul Nasser, whose impulsive but dramatic politics of seizing British economic assets while courting Soviet bloc support left Western diplomats profoundly upset.

Like other analysts on international politics and economics during the 1950s and 1960s, Dean believed the answer to feudal conditions in many countries would come through large-scale economic development projects. The Industrial Revolution was the great equalizer; soon its lessons would reach the ends of the earth, barren countries would build massive dams and networks of roads, spread the green revolution, and eradicate smallpox, malaria, and other diseases. The Palestinian problem loomed large, but cooperation was still possible between democratic, technologically advanced Israel and its backward, predominantly dictatorial Arab neighbors.

I arrived in Rabat in July 1958, assigned to the embassy public information section, in those days called the United States Information Service (USIS). Morocco, which had attained independence on March 2, 1956, was among the most moderate of Islamic countries. It retained deep ties to France, largely through agricultural and mining interests, and extensive French settlements—the French called Morocco "the California of North Africa," yet no one could doubt the Moroccans' fierce desire for independence or Morocco's support for independence in neighboring Algeria, which since 1830 France had claimed was part of metropolitan France.

Among the students who borrowed films and books from our cultural center were many bright young Algerians, fleeing ruthless French control of their homeland and operating in the friendlier climate of independent Morocco. The embassy film distribution and press section, where I worked on a rotational tour, lent documentary films to schools Algerians ran near the Moroccan-Algerian border, to the consternation of the local French officials. Sometimes I had coffee with young Algerian intellectuals; energetic, articulate, and idealistic, their dream was for their own independent country to have a distinctive place in the world. I thought of them a few years later, as news from Algeria worsened, and a military dictatorship intensified its hold, and people wearing glasses or carrying briefcases or using fountain pens were randomly arrested or killed. Morocco's large resident French community was sharply divided in the 1950s between the *colons*, intransigent local planters, some of whom were second-generation landholders, and a small minority who saw Moroccan independence as both right and inevitable. Tensions were acute; more than two hundred thousand of the five hundred thousand French settlers left Morocco between 1956 and 1960. One Sunday morning, while walking to church, I heard an explosion in the next block. A bomb had been attached to the clutch of a black Citroën sedan by anti-independence French extremists, killing the driver who was a French lawyer and supporter of Moroccan independence, while his wife and children watched from their apartment balcony above the parking lot. The wife screamed, the children panicked, and an ambulance's klaxon wailed; all that remained of the lawyer was his billowing white shirt with wide blue stripes plastered against the car's back window. This was the first violent political death I had witnessed, although I would soon see the aftermath of others in Haiti and Vietnam. Rare in the 1950s, targeted political assassinations became increasingly frequent as instruments of local and international politics in later years.

The main American interest in Morocco at that time was in several strategic air command bases, originally built during World War II. They would serve as launching points should an air attack on the Soviet Union ever take place. Originally the bases had been leased by America from France without Moroccan participation, and as Moroccan-American relations soured only one base remained along with a naval communications center and a Voice of America transmitter site outside of Tangiers.

The week after I arrived in Morocco in July 1958, President Eisenhower sent the Marines into Beirut. Sensitive to the military presence of the United States in the Arab world, Ambassador Charles W. Yost wanted to explain the American position to a widespread Moroccan audience and to immediately translate the president's speech into Arabic and distribute it as a pamphlet to the country's leaders. That was my assignment: to produce a printed pamphlet in Arabic. As the English text came in slowly on the press section's bulky teletype machine, I ripped off sections from a roll of yellow paper and handed them to the embassy's main translator, not knowing he was an Iranian Bahai. To check for accuracy, I asked a second translator to review the text, unaware the new translator was a Palestinian Christian. A flood of corrections was forthcoming in a language I did not know, so I showed the second translator's corrections to the first and, in a positive manner, asked, "What do you think about these edits?" (I had been taught consensus-building teamwork management during a one-day course at the Foreign Service Institute.) Shocked silence was the reply of the first translator. "This is the Arabic of the street, the gutter," was his eventual explosive reply. "The president of a great nation would never speak like this. Mine is the Arabic of the poets, a language a president would speak." To move beyond the impasse, I showed the increasingly edited document to the translation section's only Moroccan employee, who placed both hands in anguish on his forehead and exclaimed, "Whoever translated this is not Moroccan!"

Next, in the depths of the Salé medina, a printer worked all night to produce the pamphlet. To emphasize the importance of the presidential speech, I gave him a cover photo of a stern-faced President Eisenhower at a microphone. On his own, the printer surrounded the grim-faced Eisenhower with a circle of green crescent moons "to bring him good luck." He added a large green hand of fatima, another good luck symbol, to the back cover and proudly arrived at the embassy at dawn with five thousand copies of the pamphlet, smelling of fresh ink sinking through inexpensive paper.

UCLA

From 1962 to 1963 I was assigned to Ouagadougou, Upper Volta (later Burkina Faso), and then to the University of California at Los Angeles for what the Foreign Service called an "academic year." Down the hall from the Africa Studies Center at UCLA in Bunche Hall was the Middle East Center. Both centers were headed by major figures for whom they were eventually named: James S. Coleman, a political scientist who did pioneering work on the independence of Nigeria, and Gustave von Grunebaum, who, after a distinguished career at the University of Chicago, became the first director of UCLA's Middle East Center.

Much of my work in African history, social anthropology, and francophone African literature touched on Islamic themes. Michael G. Smith, whose seminal work was on the Hausa and other peoples of northern Nigeria, was a presence in the anthropology department, and Hasan El-Nouty, a Sorbonne-trained Egyptian, specialized in Arabic literature in translation and in third world authors of francophone expression. We read von Grunebaum's books on medieval and modern Islam, and in his later years, the classical Arabist increasingly incorporated the insights of social anthropology and contemporary literature into his own work. Given to long, cascading sentences with numerous qualifiers, von Grunebaum's writing did not make easy reading. Courtly and charming in personal behavior, von Grunebaum was elusive and spent much of his time abroad, recruiting faculty and students from all over the world in what was the high noon of the geographic area studies programs of the Kennedy era.

I do not recall that Islam was ever a priority issue in any of the embassies where I served in Africa: Morocco (1958–1959), Upper Volta (1961–1963), or Cameroon (1966–1968). No Islamic leaders were on any embassy guest list because of their prominence in that community, few Islamic figures as such were sent to America on study grants, and Islam as a political issue was not a regular reporting requirement. Sometimes a political officer, in describing a legislator or provincial district officer would remark in puzzlement, "He's a Muslim," but nothing more.

The Summing Up: A Personal Statement

Is the glass half full or half empty? Are East–West and Muslim–Christian relations better now, or worse? Destructive forces are not lacking on all sides. According to a Freedom House (NY) report, some Saudi Arabian textbooks teach children that Christians are "swine" and Jews "apes." Exercises ask young children to "fill in the blanks with the appropriate words (Islam, hellfire). Every religion other than _____ is false. Whoever dies outside Islam enters _____." Older children are taught, "It is part of God's wisdom that the struggle between the Muslims and the Jews should continue until the hour of judgment."[7] Friday noon mosque prayers from many Middle Eastern countries repeatedly inveigh against the enemies of Islam, vilify Western leaders, and call for the death of Zionists and for the destruction of Israel.

Conversely, in a broadcast of the CBS News program *60 Minutes* on October 6, 2002, the Baptist preacher Jerry Falwell said, "I think Muhammad was a terrorist. I read enough of the history of his life written by Muslims and non-Muslims [to know] that he was a violent man, a man of war."[8] In his popular television program *The 700 Club*, the Reverend Pat Robertson said, "[Muslims] are crazed fanatics and I want to say it now: I believe it's motivated by demonic power. It is satanic and it's time we recognize what we're dealing with."[9] Falwell and Robertson apologized for the uproar their remarks caused and backtracked and modified their comments but without making any positive overtures to Muslims.

But the wider picture on both sides is more positive than barrages of verbally propelled rockets suggest. A modest growth is recorded in the number of American students learning Arabic, Dari, Farsi, and other languages of the Islamic world. At the local level, many college Middle Eastern or Islamic centers send speakers and media materials to high schools throughout their states and hold informative workshops for high school teachers. Recently I was asked to hold a workshop for church leaders on "Using the Koran for Bible Study." The participants, from several states, said they were there "because this is an important subject and we've got to learn about it." Such efforts are growing.

When I originally gathered material for this book, it appeared that Western images of Islam were universally ill informed and negative, but the reality proved different. In each era, there were landmark voices for a greater understanding of Islam such as the Holy Roman Emperor Frederick II, who, during the early thirteenth century, displayed an informed and reasonably tolerant view of Islam and a curiosity about Arabic science and philosophy; Wolfram von Eschenbach, antiwar poet and author of the important anti-Crusade epic *Parzival*; Montesquieu in his numerous *Persian Letters*; Voltaire, who announced "the time of Araby has come at last"; Edward Gibbon, who wrote favorably of Islam in his *Decline and Fall of the Roman Empire* in 1788, as did Johann Wolfgang von Goethe in *Mahomet* and *West-östlicher Divan*; and Thomas Carlyle in his famous 1840 lecture "The Hero as Prophet." There were also translators of the Koran, like André du Ryer and George Sale, and early teachers of Arabic like Edward Pococke and Antoine Gallard, and publishers of the immensely popular *Arabian Nights*. There were also mission-related figures like Louis Massignon in France, Duncan Black Macdonald in America, and Kenneth Cragg in Great Britain. The twentieth century produced an emerging generation of scholars like W. Montgomery Watt, Albert Hourani, Annemarie Schimmel, and H. A. R. Gibb—the list easily could be doubled.

In short, more accurate information on Islam gradually emerged as did more balanced artistic, political, and religious voices. Progress was never linear and easy to fit on a flowchart; progress was always more episodic, with an individual voice here or there until recent times. But if the forces of mistrust and hatred were present on both sides, so were voices for greater tolerance, understanding, and inclusivity. Historians do not predict the future, but people of faith from the Abrahamic traditions remain steadfast in hope.

I

The Prophet as Antichrist and Arab Lucifer (Early Times to 1600)

This book is neither a traditional political history nor a history of Muslim–Christian relations. Its focus is on the image of Islam prevalent in the West from the Middle Ages to the present; it examines how and why it has changed, as well as the extent to which it has changed.

Such a study is important because the West must deal with Islam as a growing political, social, and religious reality. For some people, a major concept in global politics is the supposed interchangeability of Islam and terrorism, triggered by the tragic events of September 11, 2001, and by the recent war in Iraq and its increasingly negative consequences among Middle Eastern countries. Islamic issues find their way to the forefront as political, military, and economic interests, although we scarcely know what to do about them. And at a local level, the corner shop once run by a Jewish or Korean merchant is now the property of an Urdu-speaking owner who sells the Koran alongside newspapers and doughnuts. Store clerks may converse in Arabic or another Middle Eastern language, and the on-call physician at a southern Maryland hospital may originally be a Farsi speaker. In communities across America the religious skyline now contains mosques, in addition to churches and synagogues, symbols of earlier established religions. The American Muslim community in the early twenty-first century was variously estimated from three to nearly six million people, giving it a solid and rapidly growing place among American religious groups.[1]

Islam in recent times has been called "a very evil religion" and the Prophet Muhammad "a demon-possessed pedophile" by American evangelicals. Don Richardson, a missionary who worked in Muslim countries, wrote in *Secrets of the Koran*, "The Koran's good verses are like food an assassin adds to poison to disguise a deadly taste."[2] Lieutenant General William Boykin, the Pentagon's deputy secretary of defense for intelligence, said of a leading Somalian Muslim warlord whom he visited in a Mogadishu jail in 1993, "I knew that my God was bigger than his. I knew that my God was a real God, and his was an idol." General Boykin, later in charge of the Pentagon's hunt for Osama bin Laden, spoke in uniform to several American church groups and told them Islamic terrorists will only be conquered "if we come at them in the name of Jesus." He also stated that Satan was behind the terrorists because "he wants to destroy us as a Christian army."[3] Despite calls for his removal, General Boykin remained at his intelligence post under then Secretary of Defense Donald Rumsfeld.

The possibilities of excerpting such sensationalist quotes about Islam from political and church leaders are numerous. Many illustrate the same point, that Islam was being selectively presented for a distinct purpose—to rally people against a threatening external enemy, thus increasing the politicians' power or control at home. In short, the worldview we have of Islam has been rarely examined and remains implicit in ongoing games of world politics. Zbigniew Brzezinski reflected this in 1979 when he asked, "What is more important in the history of the world? . . . Some stirred-up Muslims or the liberation of Central Europe and the end of the cold war?" This Carter-era national security advisor clearly reflected long-existing American security policies that had been in place since the mid-1940s. He did not see, nor did many of his political generation consider, the dangers of arming the Taliban, and when asked in 1998 if Islamic fundamentalism was a world menace, replied "Nonsense!" because there was no such thing as global Islam.[4]

No less murky are the arguments of "clash of civilization" proponents who envision hordes of enraged Muslims, angry that Western technology, commerce, and culture have left them behind. This hard edged, black and white picture of Islam, the product of such scholars as Samuel Huntington and Bernard Lewis, has provided the informing vision of Islam for a generation of American military and defense establishment officials. It was Huntington, a hawkish Vietnam-era political scientist, who first popularized this simplistic worldview in an article "The Clash of Civilizations?" in a 1993 issue of *Foreign Affairs*, the Council of Foreign Relations' flagship publication. Huntington, who had little exposure to Islam and the Middle East, presented a global picture of seven or eight major civilizations, of which Islam was one, and concluded that "the domineering source of conflict will be cultural," a global clash between nations and groups that represent different civilizations. He confidently predicted, "The clash of civilizations will dominate global politics. The fault lines between civilizations will be the battle lines of the future."[5] But no satisfactory definition of civilizations was forthcoming from Huntington, who kept tacking data about populations, oil, militancy, and so forth onto a vague and unworkable concept—one that writers like Spengler and Toynbee had tried in their time, and that was discarded by later generations of researchers who looked at the actual interactions among peoples and nations. Huntington's intellectual apparatus resembled the bamboo scaffolding on a Hong Kong high rise. There was no clash of civilizations because there were no civilizations to clash in the sense that proponents of the argument employed. Nations, empires, and smaller ethnic, political, and religious groups of all sizes and orientations clashed. Also, large masses of peoples shared common languages, cultures, and religions, but never achieved the internal political organization or purposefulness that would make them into civilizations capable of clashing with other such massive bodies, except in the fictional settings of *Star Wars* and *Lord of the Rings*.

A historian of the Middle East who taught first in London, then at Princeton University, Bernard Lewis, though holding a similar view of enraged Muslims versus the enlightened, successful West, presented a somewhat more nuanced analysis than Huntington's. The old dualisms were revived. Muslim peasants could exude "a dignity and a courtesy toward others never exceeded and rarely equaled in other civilizations," but make them angry and "this dignity and courtesy toward others can give way to an explosive mixture of rage and hatred" that will allow for kidnapping and assassination, all in the Prophet's name.[6]

The grand lines were clear—as the West advanced economically and institutionally, creating free governments that were the envy of the East, Islamic states remained stagnant. Western wealth passed into Eastern countries to be monopolized by a few wealthy families, and Western governmental institutions, such as presidencies and parliaments, were imported in name only into former colonies, generally resulting in tyrannies. "This is no less than a clash of civilizations," Lewis concluded, "the perhaps irrational but surely historic reaction of an ancient rival against our Judeo-Christian heritage, our secular present, and the worldwide expansion of both." Lewis then qualified his remarks; Islamic governments have imported some Western ideas of governance, such as public elections and written constitutions, Western military dress and weaponry, television, and the symbols of popular culture from Coca-Cola to T-shirts. He ended with a cautionary note: a hard struggle was ahead, one in which the West had few options for action. "Even the attempt might do harm, for these are issues that Muslims must decide among themselves. And in the meantime we must take great care on all sides to avoid the danger of a new era of religious wars, arising from the exacerbation of differences and the revival of ancient prejudices."[7]

The "clash of civilization" argument was hotly contested from the start, not only by the late Edward Said, perhaps its most articulate early opponent, but also by other scholars long at work less dramatically on individual countries or subjects.[8] Said, a Palestinian Christian who became professor of comparative literature at Columbia University, was a well-known essayist on politics and culture. His electrically charged concept of Orientalism was that it represented "a Western style for dominating, restructuring, and having authority over the Orient.... [W]ithout examining Orientalism as a discourse one cannot possibly understand the enormously systematic discipline by which European culture was able to manage—even produce—the Orient politically, sociologically, militarily, ideologically, scientifically, and imaginatively during the post-Enlightenment period."[9] And Said was always in the umpire's chair, deciding who was in or out among writers on Orientalism, who was trumpeting a West that was "rational, developed, humane, superior" and an Orient that was "aberrant, underdeveloped, inferior."[10]

Attempting to sort out the issues in this debate is like walking barefoot through a minefield. As Said's books and essays in the *New York Review of Books* appeared, many people read them with anticipation. Passionately argued, they contained both original insights and problems. Said carpet-bombed opponents, and his use of chronology was, at times, nonexistent. His anger and sense of exile, understandable in the context of his early life as a Palestinian exile, sometimes influenced what he wrote. The historian David Kopf has linked Said's biographical works with Jawaharlal Nehru's *The Discovery of India* and Eldridge Cleaver's *Soul on Ice*—books that describe the experience of being marginalized and humiliated in a dominant culture that also contained deep attractions.[11]

Said wrote with passion and lucidity, but it is hard to trace his arguments to specific historical realities. A British historian of imperialism, John M. MacKenzie, wrote that Said's analysis of imperialism "has a disturbing vagueness about it. It becomes a generalized concept inadequately rooted in the imperial facts, lacking historical dynamic, innocent of imperial theory or of the complexities of different forms of imperialism."[12] In reality, the imperial encounter had been there for centuries and contained reciprocal elements. Its results were evident in cultural borrowings on both sides, and this was the subject "of constant change, instability, heterogeneity, and sheer porousness."[13] Also, as Richard W. Bulliet, a historian of the Middle East, has pointed out, the Orient of the West, as depicted by Said, was not the Orient most Americans knew. Those who were at all familiar with the Orient often learned about it through the charitable, educational, and humanitarian work of American missionaries. Additionally, in the post-World War II period most Americans sided with occupied people, not the colonial powers, in their drive for independence. "They shared the European belief in the superiority of Christian civilization, of course; but they did not think that this, in and of itself, justified conquest and colonial subjection."[14] Said used a handful of selected paintings to advance his argument that Western visual artists were at heart imperialists, but in reality several hundred European and some American artists spent time in the Orient not as imperialists but as painters looking for interesting subject matter that would reflect what they saw and, they hoped, be able to sell back home. Gerald Ackerman, who followed the subject for four decades and wrote numerous books on Orientalist art, said, "Instead of being exploiters of the Muslim world, the Orientalist painters really loved it. They could not simply fly in and out as we did. . . . [T]he trip was long and arduous, and once there the stay was difficult, but only those who found the newness and the strangeness exhilarating would brave it a second time, or many times."[15]

Joined by impassioned spear-bearers on both sides after the main protagonists had spent their shot, the argument showed no sign of abating. Said represented a creative intelligence, able to fashion the argument in a new context, even when its factual details were bent out of shape. Lewis, a painstaking scholar in the Ottoman Turkish archives and lapidarian interpreter of the Arab past, sometimes appeared to be a clumsy analyst of the political present, when he employed a view of the encounter of civilizations like that most famously used by Toynbee, long after historians had abandoned such an analytical framework because of its inadequacies. Lewis based his appraisal of Muslim–Western contact on the question "What went wrong?" (the title of one of his most popular books). But this implies that at another time things were going right, that there was some agreed-upon normative civilization that was the marker by which all others could be judged.

History does not work that way—societies are in constant flux, reflecting change, conflict, progress and decline, brilliant achievement, and horrible crimes committed at national and international levels. Additionally, when emerging Middle Eastern states of the last century were looking at European models of state structures, some of the most readily available examples were the deeply authoritarian states of fascist Spain, Italy, and Germany, and communist Russia—not what Western democratic leaders would recommend as democratic examples.[16]

Finally, not all Muslim interpreters believed they belonged to a culture inferior to the West. Sayyid Qutb, the Egyptian intellectual who lived in the

United States from 1948 to 1950, returned to Egypt convinced Islam was the preferred path to the future. He was later followed by the Ayatollah Khomeini in Iran and numerous other independent Islamic interpreters in countries as diverse as Turkey, India, Pakistan, Malaysia, and Indonesia. The list is long, and the Islamic and Western interpretations of history are diverse, but it remains a distortion, and not a helpful distinction, to reduce the basic elements of the encounter to a vague generalization like a clash of civilizations.

For purposes of this study, it is enough to highlight the difficulty of accurately understanding complex global Islamic ideas and institutions. If they are first filtered through the looking glass of an unreliable analytical instrument and not seen in their fullness, the task becomes more difficult. Provocative and stimulating as they undoubtedly were, both the Huntington/Lewis "clash of civilizations" and Said's Orientalist-as-imperialist arguments had a limited shelf life, despite the strong ripples both left behind.

A wider picture has emerged of contact across the centuries. Richard Fletcher concluded his volume *The Cross and the Crescent* with the observation that Orientalism, as vilified by Edward Said's 1978 book of that title, "did not have to wait upon Napoleon's expedition to Egypt. Its origins may be discerned three centuries earlier." "Moorish clothes were high chic" in late-fifteenth-century Spain, he noted, and visitors to Ottoman Istanbul returned "with whispers of sexual freedoms forbidden in the West, tales of harem and seraglio, of slave markets and eunuchs, of brutal punishments meted out in sumptuous surroundings, to pander to the prurient fantasies of Europeans."[17]

Images of Islam

Internal Islam

There is both an internal Islam and an external Islam that help shape our images about this major world religion. Internal Islam contains the generally unexamined images we have accumulated since childhood—of fearful strangers, curious foreigners, exotic distant countries, and hostile religions whose believers we regard as inferior to us. They represent a deformation of our known values, if not an evil presence. Often we deny that we—rational, educated people—hold such negative beliefs about other faiths and peoples, but they have long existed as "the Islam in peoples' minds." At worst they represent gross prejudices, at best they distort the face-to-face realities of the world in which we live.

The manipulation of fear is an ancient political weapon. From the Middle Ages on, travelers, traders, diplomats and scholars amassed ever more details about the Islamic world. But basic Western images of Islam changed little across these centuries as new information emerged. Why is that so? Probably because every society creates some picture of other more distant people to satisfy its own domestic constituencies. Thus the structures, symbols, and images of strangers are seen through a prism of our own invention for our own purposes. From such a perspective, until recent times Muslims or Jews were not the subjects or objects of truly independent study in the Western world.

There were first of all Muslims portrayed in various settings in response to European fears of invasion, racial assimilation, or commercial and religious competition before and at the time of the Crusades. For most Europeans, Islam arrived with invading armies from the East and remained a threatening force for several centuries. Constantinople had fallen in 1453, Belgrade in 1521, and in 1526 King Louis II of Hungary and Bohemia was killed at the Battle of Mohacs, along with sixteen thousand soldiers, the cream of the Holy Roman Empire's forces. Ottoman troops rolled on to Vienna's gates and were not finally repulsed until 1529. And when the Christian stronghold of Malta was besieged as late as 1565, Canterbury's wardens paid money for parish "books of prayer agaynst ye Turkes."[18]

Behind the carefully crafted negative portrayals of Islam there was generally also a local leader's desire to maintain a unified political and/or religious front. Pope Urban II in 1095 launched the Crusades against Muslims, the infidel occupiers of the Holy Lands, but his unstated purpose was to consolidate political support for the papacy at a time of emergent European nationalism when various monarchs wanted to claim territory of their own free from papal interference.

It is an ancient human strategy to attack the distant enemy in order to consolidate political control at home. Portraying Jews and Muslims as heretics and sexual deviants allowed Europeans in positions of religious and political power to close their ranks. John V. Tolan, in *Saracens: Islam in the Medieval European Imagination,* said such unfavorable images, "provide concrete examples of how one perceived as the other can be pinned down through discourse, made explicable, rendered inert, made useful (or at least harmless) to one's own ideological agenda. . . . They show how the denigration of the other can be used to define one's own intellectual construction of the world."[19]

Several other recent authors, such as Thierry Hentsch, in *Imagining the Middle East,* argue that we are primarily examining our own attitudes about Islam rather than Islam itself, and to an extent that is correct. "The Orient is in our minds. . . . The West is an idea that inhabits us, as surely as does its opposite."[20] Thus we are at once imagining a garden of delights, of temperate climes and handsome courtiers devouring choice fruits in the company of sensual maidens. But soon after comes the contrast, especially in modern times following acts of terrorism, of the "Arab street" as the dimly lit narrow-laned hiding place of terrorists and ideological extremists. The casbah, or native part of the city in films like *Algiers*, was a rabbit warren of passages and lanes Europeans could never penetrate, a mysterious, lawless place, fascinating, but playing by rules different from those of the external world.[21]

"Every ideological movement creates its sacred history," Maxime Rodinson has written, and sacred history is invoked to both explain and control a movement. Its founder's powers increase with the telling, garnished with both wisdom and miracles. Conversely, enemies and their leaders will be exposed for their evil nature and, "in doing so, rendering diabolic what is sacred for the other."[22] Much later, in mid-twentieth-century American history, there was both the reality of a cold war rivalry with the Soviet Union and the systematic distortions of Senator Joseph R. McCarthy that created a state of fear in domestic politics. The creation of a threatening picture of the distant Russian enemy allowed politicians to manipulate the public and potential opponents and rally support at home.[23] A half century later, the imagined threat of a global Islamic jihad provided a similar rallying point.

External Islam

External Islam is more readily understandable through history, political science, anthropology, and the media. It is a world about which increasing demographic, geographic, and linguistic information—the products of virtually every known scholarly domain—become available. We would like to say that as more accurate information emerges, a more balanced picture of Islamic realities and aspirations comes into focus. But that is not always the case.

No single "Islam" ever was known by all Christians and no single transmission line emerged through which an image of Islam was passed from century to century. What gradually crystallized were four somewhat different and at times contradictory models that, with variations, continue to the present. They reoccur in subsequent centuries with costume changes appropriate to the age and can be classified as:

1. the Prophet as Antichrist, heretic, or Satan
2. the Prophet as fallen Christian, corrupted monk, or Arab Lucifer
3. the Prophet as sexual deviant, polygamist, and charlatan
4. the Prophet as wise Easterner, holy person, and dispenser of wisdom

The final image of the Prophet as sage was infrequently employed, and, until recent centuries, appeared only fleetingly. At other times Muhammad was portrayed as a militarily strong, politically cunning but morally flawed ruler. But not a pushover. No one wanted an opponent who would be defeated in Act One, so the Muhammad of much early Western literature was usually a formidable, threatening figure whose flaws gradually led to his undoing.

Historical Roots

Conceptually, the subject matter of this study—the initially negative image of Islam—begins long back in Europe's history, centuries before the Prophet's birth, when fearful images of strangers and the world beyond Europe's home-lands were already in place. Possibly that had been so since earliest times, but clearly such imagery of the Eastern enemy at the gates existed in Greek and Roman times, and was alive in the early Middle Ages. The Greeks had created a self-image in relation to the Asian peoples on their frontiers, such as the invading Persians. It was a contrast between "civilized" and "barbarian," the liberty-loving Greeks confronting warlike Asian despots.

Roman writers also assembled an arsenal of vividly negative images about "the robbers of Arabia" and "the wolves of Arabia" long before the Prophet's birth. In one account, during a battle against the Goths at Adrianople in 378 the Romans had employed Arab mercenaries: "One of them, a man with long hair, naked except for a loin-cloth, uttering hoarse and dismal cries, with drawn dagger rushed into the thick of the Gothic army, and after killing a man, applied his lips to his throat and sucked the blood that poured out."[24] The civilized versus barbarian dualism was thus established by at least the fourth century, reinforced by the continual decline of the once-dominant Western Roman Empire. No clear distinction was yet made among outlying Eastern ethnic, linguistic, and religious groups. Contemporary Christians knew Turks, Moors, Persians, Arabs, and other heretics and infidels, "lesser breeds outside the law," in Kipling's later phrase.

By the time of the Crusades the distant military and religious enemies in the East would be called Ishmaelites, Hagarenes, and Saracens. Ishmaelites and Hagarenes represented the less-favored offspring of the patriarch Abra-ham, male sons by Hagar, an Egyptian slave girl. According to some Christian traditions, Islam emerged through Hagar's first son Ishmael, the wild man and warrior depicted in Genesis 16:12: "He shall be a wild ass of a man, with his hand against everyone, and everyone's hand against him."[25]

The origin of the word "Saracen" is uncertain; by the Christian Middle Ages it had become a sweepingly pejorative term applied to almost all Arabic-speaking populations.[26] "Saracens" was also a play on the Greek word *sarakeonoi*, meaning "easterners." The word "Islam" was unknown in these centuries and did not appear in English until the seventeenth century in works like *Pilgrimage* (1613), an early survey of peoples of the world and their religions by Samuel Purchas (1577?–1626), a chaplain to the archbishop of Canterbury and compiler of early travel accounts.

The Oxford medievalist Richard Southern has described a world where Western writers knew little about Islam. It was "only one of a large number of enemies threatening Christendom from every direction, and they had no interest in distinguishing the primitive idolatries of Northmen, Slavs, and Magyars from the monotheism of Islam, or the Manichean heresy from that of Mahomet. There is no sign that anyone in Northern Europe had ever heard of the name of Mahomet."[27] The image of Islam underwent constant, gradual adaptation, both in response to changes in East–West relations, but even more profoundly in response to the changing ways of thought in Europe itself.[28] An Age of Ignorance, 700–1100, Southern suggested, was characterized by "the ignorance of confined space and the ignorance of triumphant imagination." It was followed by a brief period, 1100–1140, that coincided with the Crusades, when images of Muslims as heretics, apostates, ruthless killers, and sexual predators prevailed.[29] This was also a fertile period in the development of popular imagery in Europe, when mythic histories of Britain and France emerged, as did innumerable popular tales that provided writers in France and England with fanciful material about Muslims.[30]

Islam in the Bible

The Bible was the great anti-Islamic text. Compiled centuries before the Prophet's birth, it made no mention of Muslims, but its apocalyptical passages would soon be used against Islam. They contained graphic descriptions of the "abomination that desolates" foretold in the Prophet Daniel (9:27, 11:31, and 12:11).[31] The temple would be profaned and the wise "shall fall by the sword and flame, and suffer captivity and plunder" (11:33). Matthew later elaborated on Daniel in a central New Testament passage (24:15–31). The desolating presence had now entered the holy place, and people must flee immediately for their lives, followed by great suffering. Further confusion would come from the appearance of false prophets and messiahs cleverly resembling Christ:

> Then if anyone says to you, "Look! Here is the Messiah!" or "There he is!"—do not believe it. For false messiahs and false prophets will appear and produce great signs and omens, to lead astray, if possible even the elect. Take note, I have told you beforehand. So, if they say, "Look! He is in the wilderness," do not go out. If they say, "Look!

He is in the inner rooms," do not believe it. For as the lightning comes from the east and flashes as far as the west, so will be the coming of the Son of Man. Wherever the corpse is, there the vultures will gather. (Matt. 24: 23–28)

In addition to false prophets, there was also the Antichrist, a figure in the Johannine Epistles (1 John 2:18, 4:3). Muhammad, the letters of whose name, by numerological analysis, added up to 666, the sign of the Antichrist, was targeted with that name.

Other biblical accounts added to the evidence against Islam. The great flood of Noah's time was understood as a decisive event in world history. Survivors of this deluge were divided into three distinct groups. Japheth, Noah's favorite son, settled Europe, the Gentile's homeland. Shem, the second son, claimed Asia, the land of the Semites, an inferior people despite having produced Christ and the Hebrew prophets. Ham, the African and servant of the other two, was relegated to last place. This three-pronged distinction provided a rationale for the development of human civilizations. The Bible thus provided divine explanations for humanity's warring races; Adam's Fall, Noah's Flood, and the Tower of Babel all split humankind into contending races and peoples. It was a stretch to apply these and other passages to Islam, but some later biblical commentators linked Islam to various demonic figures in the Apocalypse, Satan, the multi-headed beast, and so on.

A Balance Sheet of Positives and Negatives on Islam

When Islam appeared as a bewildering new political and religious reality, it was easy to give it the inferior status of those who came before from the lands east of Eden. Not all news from the East was negative, though. In the realms of scientific knowledge, particularly medicine, astronomy, mathematics, and in philosophy, Islamic texts were eagerly translated and used by Western scholars.[32] *The Book of Healing and the Canon of Medicine* by the Muslim philosopher Avicenna (ibn Sina) (980–1037) was widely circulated in Europe by the eleventh century as a major medical text. The author incorporated available scientific and religious knowledge across disciplines, and widely revived the works of Greeks like Aristotle. The spread of Arabic influences on Western theology and letters resulted in a dramatic shift in perspectives toward Islam in the half century after 1230, and for a few centuries the accumulated results of Arabic science and philosophy were widely used by the writers in the Christian West.[33]

It was also clear that early Christian writers did not know what to do with Islam. By the early eighth century, Muslim armies occupied parts of Spain,

North Africa, the Arabian Peninsula, Persia, and large parts of northern India. By the 1400s, the Balkans and south-central Europe were subject to Muslim invasions. No one at the time knew this was a turning point in European history; instead Christian writers saw such "Arab" intrusions as God's punishment for their sins, especially sexually related sins. This was the end time toward which the Book of Revelation pointed; the numbers of beasts and their various claws and horns were all linked to fallen historical creatures. Among the early writers, Theodore Abu Qurrah (d. ca. 820), a pupil of John of Damascus, was a rare exception who knew something about the life of Muhammad and the Koran's contents. In *On True Religion* he presented a traditional Christian doctrine of creation and the development of history through Christian eyes, yet he allowed for the political success of its Muslim opponents. Then, using Muslim theological language, he asserted that basic Islamic beliefs were wrong.[34] Later commentators added lurid details about Muhammad's sexual proclivities and numerous wives. He was a magician who could rise in the air, and following his death, according to widespread reports, his tomb levitated from a series of cleverly hidden magnets.

But increasingly, new and difficult-to-explain problems appeared. Many Christians (including those who had been conquered) converted to this expanding Eastern religion, usually to improve their prospects; they found that employment, wives, and wealth would never have been achieved otherwise.[35] There is a touching account of how the French king Louis IX, defeated in 1250 in a crusade in Egypt, encountered a French convert to Islam at the Egyptian court. Jean de Joinville, who accompanied Louis, described the meeting:

> I had drawn the man aside and asked him to tell me his circumstances. He had told me he was born in Provins [about fifty miles north of Paris], and had come to Egypt; he had married an Egyptian and was now a person of great importance. "Don't you realize," I had said to him, "that if you die in this condition you will be damned and go to hell?" He had replied that he knew it, and was moreover certain that no religion was as good as the Christian religion. "But," he had added, "I'm afraid to face the poverty and shame I'd have to suffer if I returned to you. Every day someone or other would say to me: 'Hullo, you rat!' So I prefer to live here rich and at ease than place myself in such a position as I can foresee." I had pointed out to him that on the Day of Judgment, when his sin would be made plain to all, he would have to suffer greater shame than any he spoke of at that moment. I gave him much good Christian advice, but all to little effect. So he had left me, and I never saw him again.[36]

Alarming news was also arriving from the Holy Land, now in the hands of the Muslims who had built an elaborate temple, the Dome of the Rock. Completed in 691, this third holiest place for Muslims was where Muhammad was believed to have begun his night journey to heaven. Islam's main Jerusalem site had also been built on a major biblical location, the portico of Solomon's temple; Muslim–Christian conflict thus became both a religious and a spatial reality.

Some Examples of Early Contact

Several representative moments in the early history of Christian–Islamic contact set the stage for what came later, especially in Spain, 711–1492, Europe during the Crusades, and in Italy under Frederick II, emperor of the Holy Roman-Germanic Empire from 1212 to 1250. Both measured positive interaction and bitter conflict characterized these encounters, as shown in the work of theologians like Isidore of Seville, John of Damascus, Peter the Venerable, and Bede; and creative artists such as Dante, Chaucer, and others.

Muslim–Christian Relations in Spain, 711–1492

From 711, when Islamicized Berbers entered what later became Spain via the Straits of Gibraltar, until 1492 and the conquest of Grenada by the armies of Ferdinand of Aragon and Isabella of Castile, a remarkable Muslim–Jewish–Christian civilization flourished with busy interactive trade and reciprocal cultural contact.[37] In places like Muslim-dominated Grenada in the country's southeast, Christians were adaptable enough to live within a largely Muslim society and learned enough Arabic to transact business. Many adopted Muslim dress and manners, avoided religious conflict, and maintained their own faith and traditions at home. Yet conflict was never far from the surface, and while some Spanish religious writers had grudging respect for Islam as being a monotheistic religion, others saw it as idolatry or heresy.[38] A Spanish bishop (ca. 953) told a visitor from the Rhineland how local Christians survived:

> Consider under what conditions we live. We have been driven to this by our sins, to be subjected to the rule of the pagans. We are forbidden by the Apostle's words to resist civil power. Only one cause of solace is left to us, that in the depths of such a great calamity they do not forbid us to practice our faith. . . . For the time being, then, we keep the following counsel: that provided no harm is done to our

religion, we obey them in all else, and do their commands in all that does not affect our faith.[39]

And despite constant interaction with Muslims, Spanish monks and bishops produced a stream of theological writings whose hostile perspectives toward Islam differed little from what had gone before. How could so many Spanish Christian commentators hold on to such inadequate information when they lived in the midst of an active and generally tolerant Islamic population? Such questions would not occur to most Spanish monks of that era. "If they knew nothing of Islam as a religion, it is because they wished to know nothing," Southern wrote, "They were fleeing from the embrace of Islam: it is not likely that they would turn to Islam to understand what it was they were fleeing from."[40]

The mid-ninth century also produced the Cordovan martyrs' movement, which added further to Muslim–Christian tensions. In a setting where dialogue was not a considered possibility, the only alternatives some Christian zealots understood were conversion or martyrdom. Such sharp-edged encounters that ended badly were an increasing feature of contact between the two faith traditions. A Muslim–Christian theological discussion had gone terribly wrong in Cordova for an aggressive Christian priest, Perfectus. Some Muslims outside a local church had asked him what he thought about Jesus and Muhammad. Jesus was the Son of God, Perfectus answered, and Muhammad was a false prophet possessed of demonic illusions, a sorcerer who led a lascivious lifestyle.[41] Perfectus was summoned before a Cordovan qadi, and was told by the local judge to retract his blasphemies and convert to Islam. In response, the monk turned up the volume on his accusers and received a death sentence. In 851 fifteen other monks were similarly executed; most had sought death by intentionally insulting the Prophet and his teachings in front of Muslim judges. These Cordovan martyrs, who deliberately sought confrontation and death, were a problem for more cautious Spanish bishops, most of whom walked a delicate line in their multicultural dioceses.

More inflammatory than Perfectus were the writings of another martyr, Eulogius, bishop of Toledo (d. 859) who called Muhammad the Antichrist and the dreaded fourth beast in the Apocalypse of Daniel (7:23–27).[42] Eulogius said that dogs devoured Muhammad's rotting corpse, an appropriate end for one "who committed not only his own soul, but those of many, to hell."[43]

What would eventually become Spain (Muslims knew part of it as al-Andalus, or "Land of the Vandals") was a land of contradictions. It was a place of tolerant interaction and sharp religious divisions, a case study in how Muslims, Jews, and Christians initially could live together, but Castilian authorities reneged on earlier agreements that had allowed Muslims to live and practice their faith. Relations in Spain deteriorated to the bitterness characteristic of the Middle East in the early twenty-first century. Starvation, mass murders, seizures of homes and goods, and expulsions from long-settled lands were daily occurrences.

The situation's hopelessness in the 1490s was reflected in the account of a Muslim weaver, working at his loom despite the pleas of his wife and neighbors to leave the small town where they lived:

> "Where do you want us to go? Why should we seek to preserve ourselves? For hunger? For cold steel? Or for persecution? Wife, I tell you that since we have no friend to take pity on our misfortunes and to put them to rights, I prefer to wait for an enemy who covets our goods and who will kill me, so as to be spared seeing the sufferings of my people. I would rather die here by steel [*ferro*] than later in shackles [*ferros*]. For Loja, which once defied the Christians and defended the Muslims, has become the tomb of its defenders and the home of its enemies." Refusing to change his mind, the man remained in his own house till the Christians broke in and killed him.[44]

Even the brutal expulsion from Spain of Jews and Muslims did not satisfy the Spanish Catholic conquerors. Neither Jewish converts (converses) nor Muslims (Moriscos) were ever fully trusted, and in 1483 Pope Sixtus IV appointed a Dominican inquisitor to purge Aragon and Castile of undesirable elements. Possibly seventy thousand to one hundred thousand Sephardic (*Sefard* means Spanish in Hebrew) Jews fled, still others converted to Catholicism to survive. Then in 1502 Isabella ordered all Muslims in the two kingdoms to convert to Christianity. Her husband, Ferdinand, temporarily stood by his coronation oath to protect the religious liberty of his Muslim subjects, representing possibly 30 percent of the population, but soon the Inquisition triumphed and the once-delicate balance of competing but complementary cultures was no more.

Not only in Spain but also in numerous other places around the Mediterranean, Muslims, Jews, and Christians lived in intricate proximity. Mark Mazower wrote about the interaction of the three faith-based communities in Salonica, but his comments could have applied to Spain as well. Interaction, he said, was "a saga of turbulence, upheaval, abandonment and recovery in which chance, not destiny, played the greater role."[45]

Christian–Moorish conflict gained an enduring place in Spanish popular culture, and mock battles between Moors and Christians were features of village festivals then as now. Some concluded with mock battles between elaborately costumed Moorish and Christian soldiers, which ended when an effigy of the Prophet was thrown from a castle wall. In Valencia such village festivals climaxed when a large head of Muhammad, stuffed with fireworks, was exploded while people cheered. The Moros y Cristianos spectacles were even carried by the Spanish conquerors to the New World and presented as demonstrations of victorious Catholic Christianity over pagan opponents.[46] A continuing reminder of contact between Moors and Christians was the prevalence of a black bean and rice dish called "Moros y Christianos."

The Crusaders' Islam: The Twelfth and Thirteenth Centuries

The various Crusades that extended intermittently from 1095 to the 1270s, and subsequent wars that continued until the fifteenth century, allowed Europeans to concentrate on "the enemies of God." The Crusades (the word derives from "cross") represented the most sustained period of interest in Islam in the West until modern times, even if much of the information was distorted then, as it is often skewed now. Pope Urban II (reigned 1088–1099) reportedly told the crusaders in 1095, "Your deeds will be sung down the ages if you rescue your brothers from their danger.... Rid the sanctuary of God of the unbelievers, expel the thieves and lead back the faithful."[47] Urban, a product of the Burgundian monastery at Cluny and the papal court, faced an unenviable task; the papacy claimed absolute temporal and spiritual power over the Latin Church in Europe, but in reality only had a tenuous hold over parts of central Italy. Urban, making the first papal trip out of Italy in half a century, spent much of 1095–1096 visiting parts of France, seeking to restore papal power. When a delegation from the Byzantine church appeared and asked for his help in expelling Muslims from their lands, it gave Urban the excuse he needed to launch a crusade. Such a venture had several attractions: it would rally fractious European nobles to his side, strengthen Rome's presence with the Eastern church, and provide all parties with a sacred cause—liberating the Holy Land from the grip of infidels while opening a fast track to heaven for zealous participants.

No immediate casus belli was on the horizon. Muslims had actually occupied Jerusalem for approximately four hundred years and, despite periodic friction, Muslims and Christians had peacefully coexisted there, much as they had in the Mediterranean basin. Urban launched the First Crusade at an outdoor rally attended by perhaps four hundred people in a field outside Clermont, France, on November 27, 1095. No copy of his sermon survives, and accounts of it were recorded years later by Urban's followers and returning crusaders reflected their postwar perspectives. Urban's strategy was to dehumanize his foes, speaking of "the savagery of the Saracens," a cruel "barbarous people" who slaughtered Christians and destroyed churches. Christian pilgrims, he said, were forced to vomit or void their stomachs and intestinal tracts for any hidden gold or silver, or have their stomachs ripped open.[48]

Urban's appeal was successful, and within a year possibly one hundred thousand Western European men, women, and children made the two-thousand-mile trek eastward, combining religious zeal and barbaric cruelty in equal measure.

One of the crusade's disastrous effects was the constant anti-Islamic propaganda that flowed from Rome. It is not that such negative images of Muslims did not already exist; they were easily available in the writings of earlier Western theologians, and in this Urban invented nothing new. But backed by the power of the papacy and a generation of Europe's leaders who had tasted warfare in the East, the crusaders and the image of demonic Islam they held entered the collective consciousness of Europe, where it stayed to work its destructive effects through subsequent centuries.

What emerged at this time was a more sharply defined image of Islam, but one riddled with errors. Clerics, kings, epic poets and storytellers exercised free rein to spread bizarre tales about the Prophet, his religion, and the Middle East; nearly a millennium later their Western counterparts often draw on similarly incomplete material to express their own root images of Islam.[49] Southern described the setting where Westerners "had some picture of what Islam meant, and who Mahomet was. The picture was brilliantly clear, but its knowledge, and its details were only accidentally true. Its authors luxuriated in the ignorance of triumphant imagination."[50]

Gradually, however, some positive impressions of Islam appeared in the West as overlays to the negative ones. In the twelfth century the archenemy Saladin (1138–1193) was represented as a legendary and often heroic figure. Codes of chivalry were highly developed in Islamic warfare, and Saladin, who could be cruel or generous as circumstances warranted, was presented increasingly in Western literature as the epitome of the chivalrous knight. He supposedly traveled to Europe, and while in Paris was a guest at the French court. The queen of France fell for him, their theological discussions providing a verbal foreplay to their amorous trysts.[51]

Also at this time, Frederick II of Hohenstaufen (1194–1250) displayed both an independent, reasonably tolerant outlook toward Islam and a curiosity about Arabic science and philosophy. An adroit diplomat, Frederick was in contact with several Islamic leaders, including the sultan of Egypt, who sought to engage him in alliances against rivals, as Frederick similarly hoped to use the sultan as an ally. Frederick launched his own crusade in 1229, but never attempted a military conquest and settlement in the Holy Land. Instead, he negotiated a ten-year truce with local Muslim rulers and an agreement to restore the largely abandoned city of Jerusalem and other towns to Christian hands, while allowing Muslims to worship at the Dome of the Rock. Married to Yolanda, daughter of the King of Jerusalem, he adroitly played Muslim rivals against one another, and visited Muslim and Christian holy sites as their self-proclaimed protector. But his cleverness did not work as planned; both sides suspected Frederick, and when he left the fortress bastion of Acre in May 1229 the inhabitants pelted him with dung and animal innards.[52]

Frederick was also emperor of the Holy Romano-Germanic Empire from 1212 to 1250, and king of Sicily, whose territorial boundaries were only fifty miles from Rome in places. His domains thus included a sizable part of southern Italy, where he sponsored a garrison of Muslim mercenaries, skilled archers, and crossbowmen. Small, widely scattered communities of active Muslim traders, farmers, and craftspeople existed throughout southern Italy, Spain, and elsewhere along the extensive Mediterranean coast, largely interacting peacefully and in accommodating ways with their Christian counterparts. Legal documents were often written in Latin, Greek, and Arabic. Muslim raiders, sometimes operating from garrison towns, seized Christian ships and raided freely for slaves. Muslim officials, however, were expected to become Christians; a backslider was burned at the stake, and following Frederick's death a pogrom was launched against the Muslims, whose numbers steadily declined as members quickly moved elsewhere.[53] Frederick always had an uneasy relationship with the Vatican, whose temporal powers he sought to contain. The aging Pope Gregory IX (reigned 1227–1249) excommunicated Frederick in 1239, although they later made up.[54] The pope called the emperor the "Antichrist," and Frederick hurled the same accusation at Gregory's successor.[55]

On May 18, 1291, the Mamluk sultan of Egypt seized Acre, greatest of the crusader fortresses in Syria. The supposedly impregnable castle with its thick stone walls had fallen to the "perfidious Muslims." Sacred vessels became dinnerware at the sultan's tables, and holy books became collectors' curios in local markets. Accounts of the Crusades predictably described the Holy Land's desecration by Muslims, and with the fall of Acre, papal resolve to reclaim the holy places was renewed. In contemporary writings, the Holy Land was a revered but indistinct landscape where nameless, faceless infidels appeared (much like enemies in a videogame in our present world), and were as promptly destroyed. One account had an idol of "Machomet" confronting a crucifix, which miraculously bled. In another, Muslims on Jerusalem's walls held crucifixes on which they inflicted lashes and insults recalling Christ's Passion. The Europeans' vengeance was swift. Accounts spoke of Crusaders riding about with Muslim blood up to their knees or splashed on their horses' reins.[56]

In the pluralistic present, ecumenical relations are the norm. The archbishop of Canterbury visits Cairo's venerable al-Azhar University, and an imam reads the Koran in Arabic at Washington National Cathedral, followed by a Jewish leader who recites the Hebrew scriptures. Such contact is now usual, but it was rare for most of human history. Ecumenism was not an option for medieval Christians, and mixed emotions of rivalry and contempt existed on both sides, "tinged or tempered at times with feelings of doubt, inferiority, curiosity, or admiration," Tolan has written.[57] When a Turkish siege threatened Malta in 1565, one English diocese prayed regularly "to repress the rage and violence of Infidels," adding, "if they should prevail against the isle of Malta, it is uncertain what further peril might follow to the rest of Christendom." Following the Turks' defeat, the archbishop of Canterbury ordered thrice-weekly prayers across the land against "that wicked monster and damned soul Mahumet" and "our sworn and most deadly enemies the Turks, Infidels, and Miscreants."[58]

The Defeat of Constantinople, May 29, 1453, and Its Aftermath

Major military victories or defeats leave their marks on history, and their subsequent meaning, for both victors and vanquished, is constantly reworked in the public mind. World Wars I and II are obvious recent examples, but the Turkish victory of Constantinople on May 29, 1453, was another such event, sending shock waves across Christian Europe.

The ancient rivalry of Latin and Greek Christendom, Rome versus Constantinople, was now overlaid with an even sharper Christian–Muslim divide, but one with less clear geographical boundaries. The Byzantine emperor was replaced by an equally powerful Turkish conqueror who soon exercised political, military, and commercial control in much of the Mediterranean and its surrounding lands.

Christians responded to the loss of Constantinople by employing the worldview and imagery of their time. A modern analyst would credit Mehmed II's victory to superior armaments, numbers, and strategy, but this was not an option for the Christian chroniclers of that time. For them, defeat came because of their sinfulness or that of their leaders, or because of a lack of faith by European Christians.[59] Accounts of the fall of Constantinople were filled with details of sexual violations and the destruction of sacred objects. Central to these accounts were lurid descriptions of the desecration of Byzantium's central church, the Hagia Sophia, where the only Christian symbol retained was a wooden statue of the Virgin Mary, used as a chopping block by Muslim executioners. Women were raped, the chronicles continued, and men were beheaded and their bowels were ripped open. Strong, handsome young men were led off into slavery and forcibly converted to Islam.[60] Lurid details multiplied.

The fall of Constantinople soon became a theme for traveling entertainers and popular ballad writers who were looking for materials to hold audiences in market squares and churchyards. In one such work, the *Lamento di Constantinopoli*, both pope and emperor were blamed for the loss of the Holy Land and Constantinople, and with it the massacre of over two hundred thousand persons. The thirty-nine-stanza lament ended with an appeal for repentance and a renewed effort to return Constantinople to Christian hands.[61]

Christian rulers employed the cultural resources available to them to propagandize their anti-Turkish sentiment, in the hope of stirring up another crusade. A year after the fall of Constantinople, Philip the Good, Duke of Burgundy from 1419 to 1467, organized an elaborate civic-religious pageant as a rallying cry against Ottoman advances in Europe and as a fundraiser for an anti-Turkish crusade.

His means was an elaborate Feast of the Pheasant held in Lille on February 17, 1454. The best artists and artisans available were drafted for the day-long spectacle. It began with a crowd pleasing jousting competition. Next, important guests were led to an elaborate banquet that featured themed displays set on tables, including a replica of a small church with musicians inside, and a pie that contained twenty-eight playing musicians.

All this led to the duke's table, in front of which a high and a low pillar were placed. On the high pillar stood a thinly veiled woman with Greek symbols on her diaphanous robe, representing Constantinople. Her golden hair fell down loosely, and from her right breast slowly flowed a stream of spiced wine to refresh guests. A live lion representing the Turkish menace was chained to the low pillar. And, should anyone miss the point, a placard stood in front of the lion: "Ne touchié à ma dame" (Do not touch my lady).

Next came a procession of jugglers, falconers, and musicians, led by a turbaned giant who entered the banquet hall with a battleaxe in one hand, leading an elephant with the other. On the elephant's back a wooden tower was set; inside it was a sad-faced woman of high birth dressed in mourning, representing the church. Halting before the duke, she delivered a dolorous lament about the losses the church had suffered from the infidels. Finally, a richly decorated cooked pheasant was placed before Philip by members of the Order of the Golden Fleece. It was customary to swear oaths on the bodies of noble birds, and Philip stood, looked knowingly at the church's representative on the elephant's back, and swore "to resist the damnable menace of the Grand Turk and the Infidels" in individual combat if necessary. Princes attending the banquet rivaled one another in displays of florid anti-Turkish rhetoric, but nothing came of it.[62]

The full imaginative resources of papal pageantry were called on by Pius II (reigned 1458–1464) during Holy Week, 1462, with the hope of launching a new crusade against the Turks. But European states of the mid-fifteenth century were feuding with one another, and there was little enthusiasm for a new military expedition to the Levant.

Pius began his drive with a lavish religious spectacle, the centerpiece of which was the embalmed head of St. Andrew, one of the original apostles. The relic had been rescued from Constantinople and brought to Rome in 1462. As a way of assuring roadside crowds, Pius granted a plenary remission of sins to all who gathered to witness its passage. A high platform was built in a meadow outside Rome at the start of the final ceremony during Holy Week. There the pope kissed the sacred relic and lifted it for the throng of palm-branch worshipers to see; the valley echoed with a sung *Te Deum* while red-robed cardinals processed forth to venerate the relic. The Pope prayed that if God "is angry with our sins, which are many, His anger may be transformed to the imperious Turks and the barbarian nations who dishonor Christ the Lord."[63] Next the relic was solemnly carried to the high altar of St. Peter's with even more elaborate ceremony.

Bizarre as they might appear to modern viewers, these civic and religious spectacles, typical of their times, reflected a more knowledgeable impression of Islam than had been held in the West prior to the Crusades. More was now known about the geography of the Levant and the political, military, and social structures of local societies. The Ottoman invasions of Europe and their impact aside, European rulers also by now knew of Islamic advances in science and medicine, and gradually an isolated few commentaries acknowledged some merit to the Prophet's teachings. Reviled in most places, but admired in others, Islam was becoming a more complicated reality in the West.

Emerging Accounts of Islam

Building on images inherited from antiquity, like those discussed above, numerous Western writers of the early and late Middle Ages contributed to the unfolding picture of Islam. Several representative figures follow, such as the early anthologist Isidore of Seville, Arabic-speaking John of Damascus, and Bede, who never left Northumbria but fashioned a comprehensive vision of human society. Other such figures were Peter the Venerable, who gathered information about Islam to more efficiently convert Muslims; the activist Franciscan and Dominican missionaries; Thomas Aquinas, who had only a marginal interest in Islam; and the enigmatic missionary figure, Raymon Llull. These were followed, at the end of an age, by Martin Luther, to whom Turks and popes were equally objects of scorn.

Bishop Isidore of Seville (ca. 560–636), a contemporary of Muhammad, provides a convenient point to examine early European attitudes toward Islam. Drawing on manuscripts in Arabic and Latin, Isidore tried to assemble all the world's knowledge in encyclopedic form that would explain the divine order of creation, the composition of human societies, and their histories, leading logically to the present age in Spain. While still managing an active diocese, Isidore also compiled a history of the world, a dictionary, and a widely circulated book of *Etymologies*. Not an original thinker, Isidore was a steady cataloguer of the work of others. It is not for nothing that the Roman Catholic Church in 1999 designated Isidore the patron saint of the Internet and computer users.

Isidore wrote at a time when Islam expanded about him, but he never knew it as a separate reality. Most likely he thought little about it. Like other Christian scholars of this time, Isidore wrote of a divine hand in history, which guided it through a series of mathematically determined ages fitting a harmonious scheme. By the sixth age, the era of the apostles Peter and Paul, heretics began spreading messages closely resembling traditional Christian beliefs. Islam represented such a heresy. His was an elaborate construction of sacred history, and at its borders intruding forces could be shoehorned into established categories that included pagans, heretics, and the Antichrist. And in succeeding centuries Isidore's works were cited as proof texts of how history worked. This was not an age when Christian authors attempted to understand Islam on its own terms, on the basis of its own sacred texts. No one thought to move beyond the Christian worldview of the plan of salvation; anything outside it was error or heresy, to be corrected by conversion or the sword.[64]

Arabic-speaking John of Damascus (675–749) was another important early writer to whom Islam was a Christian heresy. An Orthodox Byzantine Christian in a cosmopolitan Islamic city, John worked for many years, like his father did, in a significant post in the caliph's administration. Christian critics complained that John was too "Saracen-minded" or "inclined to Muhamedenism."[65] He became a monk and in midlife left Damascus for Palestine, where he composed his *Fount of Knowledge*; in this he described a hundred heresies facing the church, the last of which was Islam. John lived at a crossroads of Islamic–Christian contact, and his brief, unpolished arguments foreshadowed those of later critics of Islam. A theologian who wrote for Christians, not Muslims, John considered Islam not a new religion but a Christian heresy, the religion of idolaters among whom a false prophet, Mamed, arose. A corrupted Arian monk had exposed Mamed to Christian beliefs, but claimed God had given him unique revelations in the Koran. John produced an accurate early summary of Muslim beliefs; he did not try to totally refute them, but specifically challenged the Prophet's rejection of Christ's divinity and the Crucifixion. John's *Disputation between a Saracen and a Christian* followed a much-employed catechismal form: a participant asked a simple question and was quickly over-whelmed by a convincing response. Tolan wrote, "John's dozen pages repres-ent . . . the defense of a beleaguered Christian community struggling for sur-vival at the center of an expanding, confident Muslim empire."[66]

Far to Europe's north, the great English chronicler of the Middle Ages, the Venerable Bede (ca. 673–735), wrote voluminously about contemporary events from the confines of his Northumbrian monastery at Jarrow. Bede was the first Anglo-Saxon to describe Muslims; he called them "shiftless, hateful, and aggressive."[67] In his *Ecclesiastical History*, Bede mentioned the Saracens, but only in a cameo appearance along with a string of Irish and Roman monks and bishops and other events:

> In the year of our Lord 729, two comets appeared around the sun, striking terror into all who saw them. One comet rose early and preceded the sun, while the other followed the setting sun at evening, seeming to portend awful calamity to east and west alike. Or else, since one comet was the precursor of day and the other of night, they indicated than mankind was menaced by evils at both times. . . . At this time, a swarm of Saracens ravaged Gaul with horrible slaugh-ter; but after a brief interval in that country they paid the penalty of their wickedness.[68]

Bede's few comments on Muslims were interlarded with others on unrelated subjects. A product of his times, he was informed by a sweeping, religiously grounded view of history that could only see Muslims as heretics or infidels. The Islamic invasions of Anatolia and of Christian lands in Sicily, Spain, and Italy triggered a few alarm bells for Bede, but in general the growing spread of Islam was not a subject of interest to even this most inquisitive mind of Latin Europe.[69]

Later Catholic Views of Islam

Several centuries after Isidore of Seville, John of Damascus, and Bede, Peter the Venerable (ca. 1094–1156), abbot of the great Burgundian monastery at Cluny, wanted to reap the harvest of Arabic scientific and religious documents to better refute the religious arguments of Muslims. Peter differed from his Catholic coreligionists by favoring persuasion rather than threats toward non-Christians. Peter had the Koran translated into Latin in 1143 by Robert of Ketton, an English monk who knew Arabic and who was persuaded by Peter "with entreaty and a high fee" to help defeat "the vile heresy of Mahomet."[70] Ketton, with access to a large collection of Arabic manuscripts in Toledo, was best known for introducing several Arabic mathematical inventions into Europe, including algebra (from an Arabic word meaning reduction of an equation).[71] Peter's marginal manuscript notes expressed his views of the Koran in words like "stupidity," "insanity," "superstition," and "lying."[72]

For Peter, the Prophet was an illiterate Arab schemer and epileptic whose rise to power was tied to cunning, murder, and warfare, and whose religious statements were a façade for seizing political power. Additionally, Peter believed Sergius, a heretical monk, and some Jews colluded with Muhammad to create this new heresy. Peter's *Liber contra sectam sive haeresim Saracenorum* was an early attempt at constructing a systematic refutation of Islam. His manner of argument was heavy-handed; he told Muslims that if they believed the Koran they must regard the Bible equally as a work of divine revelation. Then, in a bait-and-switch move, he wrote that God had not revealed the Koran and Muhammad was not a prophet. Peter initially presented his material in a charitable manner, convinced that a loving perspective informed his arguments. Muslims should not be dealt with "as our people often do, by arms, but by words; not by force, but by reason; not in hatred, but in love." But, despite fleeting attempts at kindness, his tediously repetitive arguments locked on to obvious Muslim errors and heresies as Peter saw them. Peter was a solitary figure; his work was not translated into Arabic, and few later polemicists and scholars ever used the rich collection of manuscripts and translations he assembled at Toledo.

Like the stubborn Cordovan martyrs before them, a wave of thirteenth-century Franciscans, unsuccessful at converting Muslims, deliberately sought a martyr's crown, sometimes speeding the process by publicly denouncing the Prophet or the Koran in front of Muslim leaders. The Franciscans exemplified the church's missionary zeal. Francis (1182–1229), their founder, set out for the Holy Land in 1212 intent on martyrdom, but was shipwrecked instead. A later trip to Morocco was aborted after an illness, and finally in 1219 Francis joined the Fifth Crusade in Egypt, where he tried to convert the sultan, who attempted instead to woo him with expensive gifts. A variety of Muslim rulers offered the Franciscans inducements, but the monks refused and were tortured and killed. Franciscan preachers made no effort to shape their message for Muslim audiences, and there was no formula for regrouping and moving on once the message was rejected. Converts were rarely forthcoming, and the martyrs remained zealous for holy deaths, which they believed affirmed their love of God and place in heaven. "To expose oneself to death for Christ, and to delight in the agony of death is an act of perfect love," wrote Bonaventure, minister general of the Franciscans from 1257 to 1274.[73]

An exception to the general Franciscan approach was the work of an isolated English brother, Roger Bacon (ca. 1214–ca. 1294), who set out to construct a non-Biblical science of religion, gathering such fragments of contemporary knowledge as he could, including the work of astrologers and mathematicians. In Bacon's world there were six religions, all in various states of evolution— Saracens, Tartars, pagans, idolaters, Jews, and Christians, each influenced by a different planet.[74] An ardent opponent of the church's approach and that of his fellow monks to missionary work, the contentious Bacon was sentenced to a Franciscan prison for his efforts. He opposed the Crusades—wars did not win converts, he argued. Missionaries should learn foreign languages and study other religions, all the better to assert the superiority of Christianity. Bacon remained a footnote to the debates of his time; his influence was minimal and, despite his study of Arabic manuscripts, few later commentators ever turned to his writings.

The scholarly Dominicans tried a somewhat different approach. Some members learned Arabic and Hebrew; studied the Bible, Koran, and Talmud; and wrote detailed refutations of Islam and Judaism. Still others preached (with modest success) to the captive subjects of Christian rulers. The Dominicans produced a *Pugio fidei* (Dagger of Faith) handbook full of arguments against Jews, but no such work against Islam. The Catalan Dominican Ramon Martí (d. 1285) carefully studied the Koran and alluded to its compatibility with Christianity, such as its references to Jesus and the Virgin Mary, but there was no mistaking his purpose—to put down the false beliefs of Islam and its sexually debauched founder, Muhammad.[75]

Thomas Aquinas (ca. 1225–1274) was the Dominicans' heavy artillery in most theological questions; he totally opposed Islam as a religion while drawing on Jewish and Islamic writers in his own philosophical writings. For Aquinas, writing in the *Summa contra Gentiles*, Muhammad was not a comprehensive religious thinker, and issued only enough uncomplicated doctrinal statements to attract an average person. He cleverly mixed his teachings with folk fables and produced no miracles. His personal life style "gave free rein to carnal pleasures," and his followers were "brutal men and desert wanderers" ignorant of religion.[76] Thomas said, "Those who believed in him from the outset were not wise men practiced in things divine and human, but beastlike men who dwelt in the wilds, utterly ignorant of all divine teaching; and it was by a multitude of such men and the force of arms that he compelled others to submit to the law."[77]

Aquinas wrote from Naples, a southern Italian center long exposed to Islamic trade and intellectual influences, and drew on non-Christian sources in his work, including the Jewish philosopher Moses Maimonides (1135–1204) and the eleventh-century Persian Muslim physician-philosopher Ibn Sina, known to Europeans as Avicenna. He also was aware of the Cordovan Muslim philosopher Ibn Rushd [Averroës] (1126–1198), who wrote extensively about Aristotle. Aquinas never dealt directly with the Islamic philosophy of the latter two writers, but saw the value of their methodological frameworks, which he employed—especially in presenting arguments for the oneness of God, the doctrinal construct that opened his *Summa Theologiae*.[78]

Raymon Llull (1232–1315), an enigmatic fourteenth-century Catalan, was sharply critical of both Franciscans and Dominicans, and documented their failures in colorful language. It was Llull who, at a Ecumenical Council in 1311, suggested a bold proposal to create schools for the study of Oriental languages, history, and beliefs in several cities such as Paris, Oxford, Bologna, and Salamanca. Find common ground with Christendom's enemies he argued, then set a trap that will lead them step-by-step to Christian truth. Once the dialogue was established, Llull believed, coercion was a perfectly acceptable next step. Llull was a knight, mystic, and poet, and was probably the most knowledgeable missionary figure of his times about Islam. His more than two hundred works included several in Arabic, but his methods proved no more effective than others, and in old age he reverted to railing against pagans and the Koran's "absurdities." His final salvo was to call for a sweeping land and sea embargo of all Muslim lands, followed by carefully planned raids that included Arabic-speaking missionaries. These Christian forces would make seized Saracens read translations of key Christian texts, including Llull's works, and convert, after which they would return as missionaries to their own lands.[79] But the Crusades were over, and his plan had no takers. On his third preaching trip to Tunisia in 1315, Llull was stoned to death.

Gradually, though, more information about Islam emerged, some of it from long-distance traders who, with little fanfare, made their way from ports such as Venice by boat, then by caravan. Maps of the East became available, as did the location of rivers, seas, and cities, and the sources of spices and other desirable commodities. Agricultural practices and local industries in Muslim lands were described by returning traders, and with them information on customs, such as hospitality for strangers, respect for the elderly, and the sequestering of women. Serious studies of Islam appeared at this time, including the first history of the Arabs written in the West, the thirteenth-century *Historia*

Arabum by Rodrigo Ximénez, archbishop of Toledo.[80] The *Chronique Universelle* of Godfrey of Viterbo, secretary to the German emperors, contained an early life of the Prophet. Fragmentary as they were, these works represented the faint emergence of fuller information on Islam.

Protestant Views

Toward the end of this period, as Protestants faced off against Catholics, antagonists added Islam to their arsenal of verbal arrows to fire at one another, and though Protestants used such weapons more readily against Catholics, Catholics also turned them against Protestants. Martin Luther (1483–1546) was the leading Protestant theologian for whom the Turks and the pope were equally odious. The pope was the Antichrist, and the Catholic canonical texts "our Korans"; and for Luther, "The Pope is the Spirit of the Antichrist and the Turk the body of the Antichrist."[81] Elsewhere Luther said, "Turk is Turk, devil is devil, you can be sure of that."[82] J. S. Bach's Cantata 18, "Gleichwie der Regen und Schnee von Himmel fällt" (Just as the Showers and Snow from Heaven Fall) adds as a brief choral passage Luther's stern lines, "And from the Turk's and the pope's cruel murder and blasphemies, rage, and fury, protect us as a father."[83]

While religious commentators on Islam are numerous during this period, no less interesting are the reports of pragmatic Venetian traders for whom the Mediterranean was a roadway for a widening circle of commerce.[84] Marco Polo, the most famous of such authors, said little about religion and politics in the lands he visited, but much about the availability of fabrics and spices. Venice was the catalyst for East–West contact during much of this time, beginning in 828 when two Italian merchants spirited the relics of the martyred St. Mark the Evangelist from Alexandria to Venice. Venetian envoys and merchants lived in or frequently visited cities of the Islamic Near East, whose merchants and political leaders in turn spent time in the island republic. Fabrics accounted for perhaps half of Venice's imports from the East during much of this period; the rest included spices, precious metals, grains, foodstuffs, and pharmaceutical ingredients.

Venice thrived on its Eastern trade, and its artists and artisans made constant use of Eastern themes until the mid-sixteenth century, by which time the major trade routes had moved elsewhere than the Mediterranean and the Ottoman military push toward Vienna resulted in growing Turkish unpopularity in Europe. In 1479 Gentile Bellini (1429–1507), one of Venice's most renowned artists, was sent to Istanbul, where he spent two years painting several portraits of Mehmet II, the Ottoman emperor.[85] Islamic themes were depicted by numerous other artists as well. Some employed turbaned figures as Eastern royalty in paintings of *The Adoration of the Magi* or as cruel killers in *The Arrest and Trial of St. Mark* or *The Stoning of St. Stephen.*[86] Other representations showed the Virgin Mary wearing elaborate, imported gold brocade fabrics.[87] Similar fabrics were worn by doges and rich merchants, and it was common to make liturgical vestments out of imported brocade, some with Arabic inscriptions woven into the fabric, others with symmetrical geometric designs.[88]

Both the pragmatism and difficulties of long-distance trade were reflected in this letter from a world-weary Venetian merchant living in Aleppo in 1556:

> We must abandon this country, where in truth we are mistreated. They take our goods and want to pay for them in their own way; worse still, they say they never received the money, which is what the pasha did even though he devoured 500 sequins, but he said he gave them to the Jew who served as our interpreter and who is now dead. Of business very little is done, neither for cash nor barter, there is no silk, and even though spices here cost little there aren't any. You can find walnuts, cloves, mace, and ginger in good quantities and at decent prices, but the sellers stubbornly insist on 15%, may God be their guide! I must tell you that the caravan from Mecca arrived at Damascus, very poor compared to previous years, when it brought few spices that we could buy; but this year is even worse because the camels died during the outward journey for lack of water and during their return due to cold: furthermore many pilgrims on their way to Mecca died for the same reasons.[89]

Luther's fear-inducing comments were written in the aftermath of recent warfare. Constantinople had fallen to the Turks on May 29, 1453, and a day later the Hagia Sophia, one of Christendom's great churches, became a mosque. Most of the lands south of the Danube came under Ottoman control, as did parts of the Mediterranean. The Turks routed the Hungarian army in the Battle of Mohács in 1526, and by 1529 Ottoman armies were camped at Vienna's gates. Luther was familiar with several Latin texts about Islam, and in 1529 wrote two inflammatory anti-Turkish tracts himself.[90] If Turks attacked Christians, he reasoned, Christians were free to respond in kind. A Christian "should not worry that in killing a Turk he might spill innocent blood.... Rather, they must be certain that they are killing an enemy of God and a blasphemer of Christ, who, according to the Book of Daniel, has been condemned to hell-fire."[91] Like others of his time, Luther invoked imagery from the Book of

Türkischer Krieger mit österreichischen Bauern.
Holzschnitt von Hans Guldenmundt aus der Zeit der ersten
Belagerung Wiens durch die Türken.

The Battle of Vienna. By late September 1529, a large army of Ottoman
soldiers had surrounded Vienna, capital of the Holy Roman Empire. This
period illustration shows a triumphant Turk on horseback, with a child im-
paled on his spear, leading a chained European couple into captivity. Even
after their 1683 defeat at Vienna, the Turks continued to provide the image
of the threatening outsider. Bach's Cantata No. 18 contains the lines "And
from the Turk's and the Pope's cruel murder and blasphemies, rage, and
fury, protect us as a father." (Mary Evans Picture Library)

Daniel to seal his arguments. The Turk was "the last and the most severe wrath
of the devil against Christ," after which the fire and sulphur foretold in the Book
of Revelation (20:8) would destroy them.[92]

If the East had the "black devil" of the Turks to deal with, the West had
the pope, a "subtle, beautiful, hypocritical devil who sits within Christianity."
"The coarse and filthy Muhammad takes all women and therefore has no wife.
The chaste pope does not take any wife and yet has all women."[93] Muslims had
some admirable features; they did not drink wine, ate and dressed moderately,
were not ostentatious in living, and were respectful of their emperors. Islam's
greatest flaw was its religious teaching, Luther concluded, for it borrowed from
the Bible while denying the Trinity, Incarnation, and Christ's crucifixion. Luther wanted the Koran translated into German so that "everyone might see what

a rotten, infamous book it is." In short, Luther did what others had done before him—he found enemies of Christ in the Bible and, if they were not specifically named in that book, he added the words "pope" or "Turks" wherever he found a possibility. And in turn Roman Catholics fired back. William Rainolds, an English Catholic exiled to the Continent, published a late-sixteenth-century polemic called *Calvino-Turcismus* that said of Calvin and Islam, "Both seek to destroy the Christian faith, both deny the divinity of Christ, not only is the pseudo-Gospel of Calvin no better than the Qur'an of Muhammad, but in many respects it is wickeder and more repulsive."[94]

The Turks were the subjects of over six hundred books, pamphlets, broadsides, and ballads between 1520 and 1545, including this Catholic bromide: "The Turk tears down churches and destroys monasteries—so does Luther, the Turk turns convents into horse stables and makes cannon out of church bells—so does Luther. The Turk abuses and treats lasciviously all female persons, both secular and spiritual. Luther is just as bad for he entices monks and nuns out of their monasteries into false marriages."[95]

An additional major Protestant work against Catholicism and Islam came from John Foxe (1516–1587), an English cleric who spent several years in European Calvinistic enclaves and compiled detailed, polemical volumes that chronicled Roman Catholic persecutions of Protestants and dissenters within their own ranks. In volume 4, the author consciously took a hundred-page "History of the Turks" digression to present a similar indictment against Islam, fanning the fires of sixteenth-century anti-Muslim sentiment. Foxe began and ended his account by equating papal and Muslim excesses. Additionally, the Turks were responsible for "rising and cruel persecution of the saints of God." Subsequent paragraphs on Islamic history, rulers, and beliefs were studded with an assembly line of invectives about "wicked proceedings," "cruel tyranny," "bloody victories," and "horrible murders." Foxe's theological undergirdings were conventional for their times. Drawing mainly on New Testament sources, especially the Book of Revelation, Foxe mined the Bible for detailed imagery, equating its dreaded beast with Muhammad. Turks could only prosper, Foxe argued, because Christians were sinful, corrupt in their doctrine, and divided by internal conflict. Finally, a good, convincing battle against the Satanic Turks would be an excellent way for Christians to better learn of the Lord Jesus and his holy life and teachings.

The author ended his "History of the Turks" with a lengthy prayer against the Turks. An excerpt reads:

O eternal Lord God! Father of our Lord Jesus Christ; Creator and disposer of all things; just, gracious, and wise only; in the name and reverence of thy Son Jesus, we prostate ourselves, desiring thine Omnipotent Majesty to look down upon these afflicted times of thy poor creatures and servants; relieve thy church, increase our faith, and confound our enemies. . . . Miserably we have walked hitherto, like sons, not of Sarah, but of Hagar, and therefore these Turkish Hagarenes have risen up against us. . . . We have plowed and tilled, but without thy heifer; and therefore this untidy ground of ours bringeth forth so many weeds. We do fish apace and that all night, but because we fish not on the right side of the boat, in our fishing we never catch a fin. . . . O Lord God of hosts, grant to the church strength and victory against the malicious fury of these Turks, Saracens, Tartarians, against Gog and Magog, and all the malignant rabble of Antichrist, enemies to thy Son Jesus, our Lord and Savior. Prevent their devices, overthrow their power, and dissolve their kingdom, that the kingdom of thy Son so long oppressed, may recover and flourish over all; and that they who wretchedly be fallen from thee, may happily be reduced again into the fold of thy salvation, through Jesus Christ, our only Mediator and most merciful Advocate. Amen.[96]

Positive Signs in France

The seeds of several positive strains of interpretation of Islam were also planted during this time. Relatively free of the doctrinal fretwork characteristic of his predecessors, Michel de Montaigne (1533–1592) made numerous references to Turkish history and customs in his widely circulated *Essais* (1580). Montaigne, a tolerant, skeptical Catholic, several times attacked superstition in religion, but did not single out Islam. Turkish soldiers were better disciplined than unruly French troops, he believed, and the sultan's direct military leadership was responsible for their success. The sultan habitually murdered potential rivals, and Montaigne cited this example of cruelty to condemn capital punishment in both Turkey and France. The Amorous Turk, so prevalent elsewhere, did not interest Montaigne, who was one of a gradually growing number of authors who explored human nature in a wider-than-European context. His comments were as accurate as the sources from which he drew them, and he contributed to the relatively new way Islam was presented in the West.[97]

In France, Guillaume Postel (1510–1581) learned Greek, Hebrew, and Arabic, and made several trips to the Orient, including one with a French diplomatic mission to Istanbul in 1536, from which he returned with a collection of

The Roman Catholic Church was one of the early translators of the Bible into Arabic. This illustration of the beheading of John the Baptist from the Gospel of Mark (6:25–26) is from a 1591 version of *The Medicean Arabic Gospels*, printed in Rome; it contains both Arabic and Latin texts and numerous woodcut illustrations, some depicting heathens in Turkish dress. Through the Arabic-Latin Bible the church hoped to unite Eastern and Roman Catholic Christians, and expected missionaries to use Arabic Bibles in winning converts in the Middle East and North Africa. (The Scheide Library at Princeton University)

Arabic scientific manuscripts. In 1539 Postel was named to the chair of Arabic in what would become the Collège de France. The first book in Arabic movable type appeared in 1514, and by 1591 the Medici Press turned out four thousand copies of the first four Gospels in Arabic. Eventually this Vatican-controlled press was moved from Rome to Florence; later Napoleon ordered it moved to Paris to print propaganda edicts for his Egyptian expedition.

Literary Works

Western literary works of the Middle Ages depicted Islam in a manner that differed little from what the theologians wrote, except they were more attuned to popular audiences. Such works both provided lively entertainment and re-inforced an uncomplicated doctrinal lesson—heretics and idolaters come to a bad end, not so faithful Christians.[98] Carnival entertainers and puppet shows required a readily identifiable enemy or comic characters, and turbaned sultans provided ample material. Muslims became straw dummies for generations of writers steeped in the Catholic culture of the Crusades, who turned out pred-icable characters that fought first, then converted, or remained as highly visible comic subjects. Arabic contributions to science and mathematics aside, it would not be until the seventeenth century and an age of exploration, a time of more broadened scientific inquiry and a more complex humanistic portrayal of life that this picture would change as increasingly accurate information about Is-lam made its way into Europe. What follows are the representations of Islam in several early European literary works such as the French *Chanson de Roland*, the Bavarian *Parzival*, several popular English sources including *Pier's Plowman* and *The Canterbury Tales*, and Dante's *The Divine Comedy*, the most compre-hensive portrayal of Islam of any literary work of this time, and one as negative in content as the others.

The Crusades had worked their way into European popular culture by the late Middle Ages, providing writers of epic poetry with rich subject matter—beleaguered knights, cunning Moors, pitched battles, treachery, and final ven-geance on the enemy. Cruel potentates dressed in rich silks and living in jewel-bedecked palaces sent scimitar-wielding champions into battle, and always, despite the intensity of battle, the Christian won, by either killing or converting the Saracen. Writers and entertainers wanted to tell stories that would attract listeners, the more fanciful the account the better. "The Crusades created a huge market for a comprehensive, integral, entertaining and satisfying image of the enemy's ideology," Rodinson has written, adding "the general public demanded an image be presented that would show the abhorrent side of Islam by depicting it in the crudest fashion possible so as to satisfy the literary taste for the marvelous so noticeable in all the works of the period."[99]

The *Chanson de Roland* (ca. 1095) was an early example of a genre of mo-rality tale that extended for several centuries. The Christlike Frankish knight Roland was aided by the Angel Gabriel in defeating pagan Muslims, whose statue of their god Muhammad was thrown into a ditch where pigs and dogs destroyed it. Roland laid down his life for his cause early in the drama, and after a prolonged battle, victory went to the Frankish hero-king, Charlemagne. This good-against-evil canticle became a skillfully employed propaganda piece during the Crusades. In reality, in 788 a Basque army had caught the rear of Charlemagne's unprotected forces and massacred his army. The Franks had invaded Spain not as a crusade but at the request of one of the country's Muslim rulers, Sulayman ibn al-Arabi, who sought an alliance with the Europeans to defeat a rival emir, and sweetened the offer with the promise of Saragosa as a fiefdom had they won.

Elsewhere, Muslims appeared in popular drama as carnival characters and the Prophet as a villain. In such works Saracens were depicted as pagans who worshiped Mahumet, Apollin, and Tervagant, the moon goddess. Tervagant was often portrayed as a shrewish, overbearing Muslim comic character, providing ready laughs, and pagan Muslims were stock characters in the York and Chester mystery plays as well.

What gradually emerged by the later thirteenth century were prospects of a less hostile relationship with Muslims voiced by writers like Wolfram von Eschenbach (1170–1220?), a Bavarian Minnesinger, in *Parzival* (ca. 1210), a long, convoluted story that drew on earlier Grail legends and later became the inspiration for Richard Wagner's opera by the same name.[100] *Parzival* opened in Baghdad, where the hero's father, the knight Gahmuret, served at the caliph's court and married Belakane, a black heathen queen, whom he impregnated, then abandoned during her pregnancy. The child of this mixed union became King Feirefiz, who was born with spotted black-and-white skin. Eventually he appeared as a mysterious knight in Europe in search of his father and, without knowing it, battled his half-brother Parzival in mortal combat; this was an often-employed literary form for the Christian–Muslim confrontation. Parzival's sword broke and his death was imminent, but suddenly his unknown opponent and half-brother stopped the fight. Feirefiz next fell in love with the beautiful Grail-bearer Repanse de Schoye, married her, converted to Christianity, and returned to his Eastern homeland as a bearer of the Christian message. Their son was Prester [Presbyter] John, who became the legendary just ruler of a mysterious kingdom hidden somewhere in distant Muslim lands.

In *Willehalm*, a later long epic poem by the same author, Willehalm and his wife Gyburc, another beautiful convert from Islam, took issue with popular European views of the Crusades. It portrayed terrible suffering on both sides in a war that was partially triggered by Gyburc's renouncing her Muslim faith and leaving her family to become a Christian. Her plea for tolerance and humanity transcended religious differences and represented a remarkable early statement at variance with the unequivocal anti-Muslim language of the Crusades.

For all the conflict and confrontation in these tales, the outcome was never in question. The stage was set for the Christian to win, and the defeated Muslim to convert. The religions were not equal in combat, nor were the warriors. As for the women, "The heathen brides are not really heathen at all: they cannot wait to marry a Christian and become baptized," Todd Kontje has written, adding that such works "are clearly more about salvation than sex: the hero wins his bride for Christianity and forgoes the pleasures of the bedroom for his eternal reward."[101]

Wolfram's underlying message in *Parzival* and *Willehalm*, written in the shadow of the Crusades, represented new departures; Muslims should not be unilaterally persecuted, war was vicious, and although Christianity would win, it should win in an atmosphere of tolerance.[102] G. Ronald Murphy sees the two great epics as a poet's protest "against the whole notion of religious crusade and in particular against Christian-Muslim enmity." It was a sign of sickness to fight wars over the site of Christ's grave, when the real presence of Christ came not from a particular geographic location but in the living bread of the altar, an antiwar sentiment that would go against the grain for more militant kings and popes.[103]

Muslims as warlike or comic figures were sometimes employed by authors of the English Middle Ages. As Catholic–Protestant polemics heated up, Protestants equated Muslims with Catholics and Muhammad with the pope. Islam was clearly the enemy, as in "The Man of Law's Tale" in *The Canterbury Tales* by Geoffrey Chaucer (ca. 1343–1400). Chaucer was expertly conversant with Arabic science, then making its way into England, and with astronomy and astrology; in 1391 he began a treatise on the astrolabe that displayed knowledge of Arabic sources, possibly gained during his travels to Spain. He also knew as much about Islamic beliefs as anyone of his time. All the ingredients of a star-crossed Muslim–Christian encounter were employed in "The Man of Law's Tale." A Syrian sultan learned from rich international Muslim traders of a beautiful Roman Christian princess, Constance, whom he desired to marry. Her father consented, but only if the sultan would convert to Christianity. In many stories, the exchange might have ended there, but for the sultan the agonizing choice presented no problem—he feigned conversion to gain a wife and a lucrative trading relationship. Then the trouble started. Constance, kind and virtuous, was increasingly distraught during her time in Syria, where the sultan's angry mother, whose bloody plots rivaled those of a later Lady Macbeth, ordered her son murdered for apostasy. She told her followers:

> You all know that my son
> Is now upon the point of giving up
> The holy hallowed laws of our Koran,
> Given by God's apostle, Mahomet.
> But I make one vow to almighty God—

> Sooner the life shall be torn from my breast
> Than from my heart the faith of Mahomet![104]

The sultan was hacked to pieces at a banquet, together with the Christians who accompanied him and the members of his court who had converted. Constance was placed in a small rudderless boat to travel the seas in exile until she reached Britain three years later. Chaucer deftly made the Muslim–Christian encounter a negative one. His Syria was an uncivilized, barbarous place, peopled by treacherous, deceitful rulers who belonged to a false religion. In contrast, Rome represented the world's true center, a place of law, right religion, and virtuous people. Even the elements conspired in the agonizing encounter; Constance's eastward movement reversed the westward flow of history and progress, and represented a regression to paganism. Chaucer added Arabic astrological imagery to confirm that the journey was ill fated from the start (2.299–305).

In part 2 of "The Man of Law's Tale," a parallel set of events faced Constance, but this time she succeeded in Britain. Her marriage to a weak but well-situated King Alla successfully produced a male offspring who would become a Christian ruler of the nations. Each event in Constance's new life paralleled one in the old, and each Christian success highlighted a further weakness of Islam.[105]

Piers Plowman by William Langland (1330–1386?) was another popular work using Islamic imagery, but its themes were more distinctly religious in nature. Here Muhammad was the heretic and magician who trained a white dove to peck corn from his ear; people saw the bird as God's messenger, but it was all trickery. Langland also repeated a stock story about Muhammad—that he was once a Roman cardinal, a successful preacher to the Saracens, whom he converted in large numbers. The other cardinals promised Muhammad he would be the next pope, but they elected someone else instead, so the angry Muhammad left to found his own heretical religion.[106]

In the *Faerie Queene* (ca. 1599) by Edmund Spenser (1552–1599), the Red Cross Knight, Christ's representative, confronted Duessa, his female opponent who rode a many-headed purple beast and defeated the Whore of Babylon (the Church of Rome). Duessa, the woman whom the Red Cross Knight would slay in the final battle, wore a "Persian mitre" and was "clad in scarlot red." Spencer had little interest in Islam; his message was about religious issues close to home, even when the imagery spoke of a distant religion and people.[107] In this case his attack was on an opposing element of English society, and Spencer portrayed Catholics as a barbarous, heretical people.

Christopher Marlowe's two *Tamburlaine* plays (1587–1588) also perpetrated the hostile image of Muslims among English viewers. Marlowe could have drawn on the nearly one hundred versions of the Tamburlaine story circulating in England. Tamburlaine, a Scythian brigand-shepherd turned sadistic conqueror of India, Syria, and Persia, converted to Islam, and by the play's end became a Christian and ordered Babylon destroyed and "the Turkish Alcaron and all the heaps of superstitious books" to be burned. Of Mahomet he said:

> Thou art not worthy to be worshipped
> That suffers flames of fire to burn the writ
> Wherein the sum of thy religion rests...
> Well soldiers, Mahomet remains in hell.[108]

In *The Divine Comedy* (1306–1321), Dante Alighieri (1265–1321) awarded Saladin a higher place in the underworld than Muhammad. Whereas the Prophet was to spend eternity in a place of endless torment, Islam's most illustrious military figure was consigned to a higher place in Limbo along with non-Christians of the past, such as Socrates and Plato. Muhammad was relegated to the dreaded Eighth Circle, a place reserved for sowers of scandal and schismatics. Dante, like many Catholic religious figures of his time, believed Islam was a Christian schism, not a separate religion. The Prophet was repeatedly wounded, and when his wounds healed, a blow from Satan's sword reopened them. He was "ripped right from his chin to where we fart: his bowels hung between his legs, one saw his vitals and the miserable sack that makes of what we swallow excrement" (*Inferno* 38: 24–27).[109] Dante was familiar with Muslim literary sources; there was considerable knowledge of Arabic writing in his time and it is highly possible that Dante, consummate literary artist that he was, knew the work of Arabic-language mystics and storytellers and incorporated some of their ideas in his narratives. One such source might have been *The Book of the Ladder*, a prose work in Arabic that recalled Muhammad's journey to the other world, told as a first-person narrative, like the *Divine Comedy*.[110]

Dante wrote at a time when the mentality of the Crusades was very much alive in Europe. The great fortress of Acre had fallen in 1291, and with it the neighboring Frankish possessions of Tyre, Sidon, and Beruit, among others.[111] The *Divine Comedy* drew on the growing number of pilgrim narratives and travelers' accounts coming into Europe, but parted company with them in a significant way. Instead of the siege mentality of us against them that informed most such religious commentaries, Dante's subject matter was broader than the Crusades and Islam; it was about the moral failures of emerging

European society, widespread clerical corruption in the Catholic church, and papal arrogance.

By the early sixteenth century, the intellectual weapons forged in earlier centuries had become the tools monks and bards employed to describe this strange, intrusive force that threatened Europe.[112] A sameness pervades this output; it was not intended to produce new, accurate information about Islam, only to provide a more informed means to attack it. And the attacks were similar to those used against Jews, heretics, Tartars, and pagans—most indistinguishable from one another. Behind this effort was a primarily domestic intent, the desire of European popes and kings to keep local populations religiously and politically in place.

The steady presence of Islam, especially in the Mediterranean and in the Balkans during these centuries, posed a conundrum for Western Christians. Muslim numbers expanded, and infidel armies struck deep into Europe and held vast sections of the Mediterranean and Middle East—including the Holy Land. Philosophically and scientifically, Islam contributed to enriching European life. Yet religiously, it remained a subject of constant attacks as heresy, a schism, and a deformed version of Christianity. Still, it remained a thriving presence, disputing Christianity on its central doctrines and offering a clear but demanding morality and prayer life to its adherents.

Across the centuries, there were subtle changes in the contours of Western imagery about Islam. By the early sixteenth century, several Western leaders, including those in commerce, statecraft, and religion, seemed aware of an expanding world whose geography, peoples, beliefs, and commercial possibilities were vastly different from those of earlier times. Soon there would emerge suggestions that Islam might be an understandable religion separate from Christianity, that its founder might not be totally depraved, and that the response to it should be something other than total warfare. Like it or not, Islam was here to stay.

2

"The Time of Araby Has Come at Last" (1600–1800)

From 1600 to 1800 a certain unity existed in the West that affected Europe's image of Islam. The Ottoman Empire gradually receded in military importance, and Islam ceased to be a direct threat to continental Europe. The Turks lost the important eastern Mediterranean naval battle of Lepanto in 1571, and finally withdrew from the gates of Vienna in 1683, after a two-month siege and the military intervention of the Polish king, Jan Sobieski, and his large army. To celebrate the victory, Viennese bakers turned out small curved rolls shaped like the Ottoman crescent moon, which became known across Europe as "croissants." The Ottoman forces further retreated, and by 1774, when the Treaty of Kutchuk-Kainarji ended the Russo-Turkish war, they were a spent military force in most of Europe. Military confrontation turned into a diplomatic chess game, an attempt to balance shifting Ottoman-European alliances—a deft game at which the Turks were adroit players. Parts of the Balkan Peninsula remained under Ottoman control, but "Turk bells" no longer sounded the alarm in German villages, and Ottoman Turks were no longer fire-breathing enemies inducing fear in southern and central Europe. Turkish fearfulness and excesses moved from the battlefield to the popular imagination, where they remained lodged for centuries, recalled in tavern curses and children's stories. European parents told their children to behave or the "Black Moor" would carry them off, and even in the early twentieth century Sicilian mothers repeated ancient tales of Turkish invaders who repeatedly raided the island in large numbers, stealing goods, raping women, and carting off children.[1]

Ancient trade routes through Muslim lands ceased to be the main long-distance commercial arteries between Asia and Europe, as European countries launched larger ships with better sails and improved navigational instruments, aided by newer world maps that replaced the fragmentary ones of the East used until then by Europe's voyagers. Expanding European commercial empires thus gradually opened up the globe and provided broader conceptual horizons on Islam at a time when reports by traders, diplomats, and missionaries filtered back to European capitals. Meanwhile, the Catholic religion had lost much of its political hold in a changing Europe, where the Holy Roman Empire gave way to new nation-states and emerging Protestantism.

A subtle shift in spiritual geography took place in these centuries, matching the changing political landscape. Western interest in the Middle East lost much of its earlier religious hostility. A handful of isolated translators of Arabic manuscripts in scattered continental and European universities produced works in European languages, many of them isolated documents from a long-distant past. Philosophes and creative writers continued to fashion an Islam for their own purposes, inventing "Persians" to provide a convenient way of suggesting reforms in France, for instance, while avoiding the heavy hand of censors. And among playwrights and musicians, Islam was the frequently employed exotic setting for tragedy or comedy.

Despite the gradual increase in new information about Islam and the Orient, European perspectives remained filtered through the prism of local needs and interests. Thierry Hentsch has written, "The Orient was, in the hands of those who wielded it, an optical instrument: a lens, a mirror for examining oneself at a distance from other angles.... And, necessarily, an object: "the Orient itself never questioned the west; never called it into question; it merely reflected or filtered those questions which Europe asked of itself."[2] The French scientist and religious writer Blaise Pascal (1623–1662) had little tolerance for Islam; his Muhammad was the opposite of Christ—Muhammad was a killer and trickster who kept his people in ignorance and was "sans authorité ... il est ridicule" (without authority ... he is ridiculous).[3]

The comparative study of religions would soon become the academic interest of a handful of scholars, along with the comparative study of societies. When the natural philosopher Robert Boyle (1627–1691) urged people to look seriously at the content of Judaism and Islam, he reflected a new critical spirit. Most participants understandably employed a Christian perspective, but still the comparative study of other religions was launched.

A spirit of skeptical inquiry also emerged at this time, reflecting a general tolerance of other religions and a growing curiosity about Islam. Pierre Bayle (1647–1706), at different times either a Protestant or a Catholic, was a leading voice for such tolerance. A state would be strengthened by extending tolerance to all religions within its borders, Bayle believed. "If each religion adopted the spirit of tolerance I recommend, there would be the same concord in a state with ten religions as in a city in which different artisans and craftsmen mutually support one another"; he included Jews, Muslims, atheists, and other religious minorities.[4] Bayle's *Dictionnaire historique et critique* (1697) was a popular work in its time and also influenced writers as different as Voltaire and John Locke. Barthélemy d'Herbelot's encyclopedic *Bibliothèque orientale* (1697) became a source of information on Islam in France, as did Simon Ockley's *History of the Saracens* (1718), an early English attempt at Arab history with minimal doctrinal subthemes.

Writings on Islam during these centuries were clearly contradictory and reflected the fragmented views Europeans held on the subject.[5] The old stereotypes were repeated by most writers, alongside newer observations that found some favorable things in Islam, such as in Henri de Boulainvillier's *La vie de Mahomet*, translated into English in 1757, and Edward Gibbon's *Decline and Fall of the Roman Empire* (1788).

The emergence of new nation-states among the monarchies of France and England caused political theorists to view Islam with the curiosity of early political reformers, suggesting new ideas for governance in Europe under the guise of reporting on the habits of Turks, Persians, or Moors, as has been said, while avoiding the scrutiny of censors. Meanwhile, as religion diminished in importance, and science and political ideas emerged as new ways of looking at human society, Islam's image changed accordingly from being the Devil's handiwork to a complex subject worthy of study in its own right.

But change in attitudes toward Islam came slowly. The Ottoman Empire remained the "great terror of the world" in the widely circulated *The General Histoire of the Turkes* (1603) by Richard Knolle (ca. 1540–1610). A fear-inducing chronicle, it was filled with accounts of atrocities, rape, pillage, and torture. Prisoners were buried waist-deep in the earth and were the targets of Muslim bowmen. Knolle, like earlier Western writers, called Islam the work of Satan and Muhammad a false prophet. But—here is the difference—Knolle also acknowledged Turkish determination, courage, and frugality. His twelve-hundred-page work, written over twelve years, was a harbinger of other accounts that gradually found positive information to share about Muslims, until then considered mortal enemies.[6]

An early illustration (1623) of a Turkish sultan, Murad IV (1612–1640), from Richard Knolle's widely disseminated *The Generall Histoire of the Turkes*. The youthful Murad assumed the Ottoman throne in 1623, had his Grand Vizer beheaded, three brothers killed, and numerous political and military opponents strangled or slaughtered. (Harvey S. Firestone Library, Princeton University, Rare Books and Special Collections)

Gradually, Islamic forms of government began to figure in the works of political theorists, usually representing the despotic model of how societies were organized. This was evident in the work of Niccolò Machiavelli (1469–1527), whose *The Prince* (1513), written in Italian rather than Latin, was a modern humanistic analysis of political society. Machiavelli separated the study of politics from theology and described how political societies actually functioned. In *The Prince* all power was held by the Prince as a "praetorian" source of control over all his subjects. Machiavelli also included brief analytical comments about Turkish authoritarian government among other types of government modeled in chapters 4 and 19. Machiavelli called the Turks "a cruel enemy," and they appeared rarely in his writings. "The whole monarchy of the Turk is governed by one ruler; the others are his servants; dividing his kingdom into sanjaks, he sends them various administrators and charges and varies these as he likes."[7] The Ottoman sultan's power derived from his hold over the army; thus it was necessary for a Turkish leader to please the army rather than the people. Machiavelli gave few details about Turkish politics, and his brief remarks about the sultan could have applied to numerous other authoritarian leaders as well.

No less important a political theorist was the French writer Jean Bodin (1530–1596), remembered chiefly as one of the first modern voices for state sovereignty. Bodin wrote of the Ottoman sultan, whom he regarded as successor to the Roman emperor, "His military might rivals that of all the other princes combined . . . he has conquered Christian kingdoms and the Byzantine empire and has even laid waste the German provinces."[8] Bodin in his *Six Books of the Commonwealth* compiled a systematic universal legal compendium drawn mainly from Roman law, but he acknowledged the contributions of Persians, Greeks, Turks, North Africans, Egyptians, and others. At the same time, he laid out the rudiments of looking at history not as a branch of religion but rather as a humanistic discipline in its own right. Bodin's pathbreaking attempts provided the foundations for a generation of later jurists and historians. Bodin's political writings included strong elements of climate theory; he claimed that mountainous northern nations were naturally more democratic than southern ones, whose people were more attracted to theocratic absolutism because of their more contemplative natures. France, both by nature and geography, had a special capacity for governance, he believed.[9]

Islam in France

Since 1535, the French had sent ambassadors to Constantinople to the palace of the Sublime Porte (French for "high, or exalted, gate"), and French writers showed an insatiable curiosity about life at the sultan's palace. All of the traditional ingredients constituting the Orient were there—wise rulers, proverb-spouting elders, amorous exploits, tales of the seraglio, and brutal tyrants and their powerful armies. Such works provided French audiences with an elaborate and contradictory picture of Middle Eastern life and customs.

French travelers such as Jean Baptiste Tavernier and Jean de Thévenot also wrote detailed observations about Islam, far more favorable than what had appeared until then. These works recognized that what had been lumped together as Saracens were numerous peoples, including Turks, Persians, Arabs, Egyptians, and Moors. Geographic boundaries were blurred, but such accounts provided increasingly rich detail about geography and life in various places. These early travel works recycled long-circulating mythic material, and the old examples of Muhammad's shortcomings were revisited. But once the dross was screened out, a considerable body of accurate information on Islam and the people of the Middle East emerged. This early travel literature was not purposely "exotic"; that came later when writers such as Montesquieu and composers such as Mozart consciously crafted their images of Persians and Turks for specific audiences.

Increasingly, French travel writers were complimentary toward the Muslim lands they visited. The French writer Henri Comte de Boulainvilliers (1658–1722) in his *La vie de Mahomet* (English translation 1757) has sometimes been cited as writing the first friendly study of the Prophet to appear in Europe. Anticlerical in outlook, de Boulainvilliers rejected the prevalent Christian view that Islam lacked rationality and coherence and that Muhammad was a "coarse and barbarous imposter."[10] Corruption and hardness of heart were everywhere, he said, but "it cannot be unreasonable to set before men's eyes some amiable examples of the contrary virtues; nor ought it be taken amiss if we desire such Christians to learn integrity, temperance, benevolence, and liberality from the Saracens, Turks, and Mahometans."[11] Muhammad, in de Boulainvilliers's account, had a nimble political mind and preached a creditable religion, albeit one less advanced than Christianity.[12] It was the tendency of eighteenth-century writers to fashion a Prophet that fit their own school of philosophical or religious thought, and for de Boulainvilliers Muhammad could have fit comfortably into a Parisian philosophe's salon.

In the early seventeenth century, Cardinal Richelieu (1585–1642) was the architect of French overseas policies, but his éminence grise, Père Joseph, deserves scrutiny in his own right for his lengthy *Turciade* (1617–1625), a turgid statement of French foreign policy in 4,637 lines of ponderous verse. In the *Turciade*, Christ, distressed that the Holy Land was ruled by Muslims, invoked heaven's saints and angels to march with Europe's armies in a new crusade. There were problems, though; France had active alliances with the Ottoman Empire and was engaged in warfare with its Christian Spanish neighbor. There remained the question of how Christian France, daughter of the church, could enter into an active alliance with the Turks. Père Joseph provided an easy answer: the Turks were less of a threat to France than was the perfidious neighboring Spanish. Critics who with "diabolical malice" objected to the arrangement should realize that all Christians gained from the French-Turkish alliance, which was commercially advantageous to France.

Moreover, he said, Christians were allowed to practice their religion freely in Turkey, and although the Ottoman Empire occupied the Christian holy places, pilgrims were allowed to visit them each year. As further justification, the monk-politician cited fifteen different alliances of potentially irreconcilable warring parties in the Old Testament. In short, close relations with the

Turks were imposed on France by circumstances; before it could take any action against an enemy, France's own security must be assured. Prolonged wars with Spain and other European powers prevented the realization of Père Joseph's ambitious project, and he reportedly died with a copy of Godefroy de Bouillon's exploits in the Holy Land in his hands.[13] He died hoping for the day when Europe's Christian princes would "chaser de l'Europe et de l'Asie cet enemy public de la Religion" (chase from Europe and Asia that public enemy of religion).[14]

The French literary work containing the most extensive comments about Turkey in the seventeenth century was the four-volume novel *Ibrahim ou l'illustre Bassa* (1641) by Madelaine de Scudéry (1607–1701). The novel, on which her author-brother George may have collaborated, was a Turkish-Christian cliff-hanger. Ibrahim, a Christian prince, was named a pasha at the court of Sultan Soliman in Constantinople. Ibrahim hoped to marry Isabelle Grimaldi, like him from Monaco. The sultan became passionately attracted to Isabelle, causing Ibrahim's swift downfall at court. At one point Ibrahim refused to wear a turban and carry a scimitar, but at the sultan's insistence, he feigned converting to Islam. The long work ended surprisingly: the sultan renounced his love for Isabelle and pardoned Ibrahim.

Several subplots mixed love, lust, self-sacrifice, cruelty, and the exotic local color of the sultan's palace. And when the plot faltered, as it did periodically, the author resorted to elaborate descriptions of ceremonies, the palace, and the seraglio. French readers who had never left home read of a sultan's procession: he was preceded by fifty trumpeters, two thousand mounted archers in satin vests, and six thousand janissaries, each armed with sword and musket. Camels, elephants, slaves, and a chariot carrying captured Persian flags followed. Next, Sultan Soliman arrived, resplendent in elaborate jewel-bedecked cloak and turban, riding a horse whose harness was covered with emeralds and rubies. Meanwhile, frenzied dervishes danced, and the extravaganza ended with a mock battle between Persians and Turks, which the latter won handily.[15] The book helped establish an image for French readers of a Turkish world of color and cruelty, pageantry and intrigue, on which other writers would build.

Most students who have taken a Western Civilization course will have encountered two other seminal French works, *Lettres persanes* (1721) and *L'Esprit des lois* (1748) by Charles Louis de Secondat, Baron de Montesquieu (1689–1755). The wise, entertaining Easterners of the *Lettres persanes* could never find their way through the streets of Tehran, but they accurately represented the author's voice in suggesting much-sought reforms for eighteenth-century France in the period after Louis XIV's death. The over one hundred and fifty *Persian Letters* described the imaginary voyage of two Persians, Usbek and

Rica, from Paris to Isphahan (their names are actually Turkish).[16] Filled with brilliant satire and wry observations, the letters were a thinly disguised criticism of France's despotic monarchy and the Roman Catholic Church's rigidity. Shah-Sephi was equated with Louis XV, vizars were cabinet ministers, and fakirs and imams were Catholic clergy in Oriental dress.[17] When Usbek, writing from "Paris, the 26th of the moon of Gemmadi I, 1715" observed that in Persia:

> It is all very well to say that the toleration of several creeds in a state is contrary to the interests of the sovereign. Though all the sects in the world were gathered under his dominion, it would not do him any harm; for there is not a single one of them in which the duties of obedience and submission are not ordained and preached. I acknowledge that history is full of religious wars; but it is an indisputable fact that these wars have not been produced by the multiplicity of religions, but rather by the intolerance of the dominant creed.[18]

In *L'Esprit des lois,* the jurist described three sorts of governments: republics, monarchies, and despotic regimes. Turkey was the model of the latter. Montesquieu also subscribed to the then-popular idea that political behavior is influenced by climate and environment, which helped explain Persia's despotic government.

Writing in the same period as Montesquieu, Voltaire (1694–1778) had the same purpose as Montesquieu in his scattered writings about Islam: to advocate reforms in France, for which Islam provided window dressing.[19] With a pen dipped in acid, Voltaire constructed a deeply duplicitous character in his early play *Fanatisme, ou Mahomet le prophète* (1739–1741), a work that was Islamic in name only. The idea was novel—a classic French tragedy about a major world figure only beginning to be known in France. The play was produced in Paris in 1742, but Catholic critics sought to have it banned. The work was a statement against fanaticism, and Roman Catholic critics quickly saw that if "Christianity" was substituted for "Islam" it could be read as an anti-Catholic polemic.[20] Already in trouble with the royal censors, Voltaire withdrew it, and the play was not presented again until 1751.

Voltaire's Muhammad had political ambitions to create a vast Arabic nation under his control. In one scene, the Prophet surveyed world history. Persia was in a weakened state, India in slavery, Egypt in disorder. Now was the time to lead the Arab world to victory. "Sur ces debris du monde élevons l'Arabie" (II.v) (On the debris of the world let us elevate Arabia). Subplots of intrigue, incest, and murder allowed the play to conform to dramatic models of the time, but with only partial success.

Hypocrisy was the trademark of Voltaire's Muhammad. The "merchant of camels," one of Voltaire's preferred phrases, produced an "unintelligible book which affronts common sense at every page" and he was remembered as a brutal warrior, skilled at whipping up fanaticism among his followers.[21] Toward the play's end Muhammad, in Caesar-like language, summarized his message of world conquest, while giving religion and government to a backward, warring people:

> See who Mahomet is. We are alone; now listen:
> I am ambitious; all men are, we cannot doubt;
> But never has a king, a pontiff, a chieftain or a citizen,
> Conceived a project as great as mine. . . .
> The time of Araby has come at last.
> This generous people, too long known,
> Has let its glory be entombed within its deserts;
> Now the days marked out for victory are at hand. . . .
> Do not reproach me with deceiving my native land;
> I am destroying its weakness and its idolatry.
> Beneath one king, beneath one God,
> I come to reunite it,
> And to make it renowned it must be made to serve.[22]

Later commentary on Islam by Voltaire was somewhat more tolerant, as in his *Essai sur l'histoire générale et sur les moeurs et l'esprit des nations* (ca. 1756). The Prophet remained a driven fanatic, but Islam as a religious system demonstrated a tolerance and adaptability missing in its earlier years. Voltaire had carefully calculated praise for Muhammad—his eloquence, air of authority, and knowledge of his people. He compared Koranic passages of soaring literary and spiritual beauty with those containing contradictions and absurdities, and concluded that Muhammad was an imposter.[23]

The mercurial Voltaire presented no consistent picture of Islam, and the contradictions and shifts in his outlook are difficult to reconcile. Muhammad was both an impressive leader and a self-deceived zealot. In *Candide*, Voltaire's valedictory (1759), various Islamic figures made cameo appearances, including a licentious imam and a wise old Turk who, aided by his children, cultivated a twenty-acre plot near Constantinople and kept himself from the three great evils—idleness, vice, and want. Candide and companions, their travels and adventures over now, settled nearby where they worked the soil and snacked on preserved fruits and pistachio nuts. "Let us cultivate our garden," Candide's final injunction, can be read as an invitation to religious tolerance. Such comments as Voltaire made about Islam, despite their negative aspects, by mid-eighteenth century represented a considerable advance over what had gone before.

Translations of the Koran and a More Detailed Study of Islam

It was during this time that a more detailed study of Islam began in earnest, primarily through the study of languages. In England, in 1632 a chair of Arabic language was created at Cambridge University by a London cloth merchant, Thomas Adams. In 1636 William Laud (1573–1645), at that time chancellor of Oxford, established the Laudian Chair of Arabic. He was also busily adding manuscripts and coins to his growing collection, although he never visited the Orient and knew none of its languages. "If you do light upon any manuscripts, forget me not," he wrote an overseas correspondent.[24] When Laud became archbishop of Canterbury he secured a royal letter requiring every ship of the Levant Company to bring him one manuscript in Arabic or Persian (not including the Koran, which was by then well represented in his collection). Laud's Oxford benefactions included more than six hundred manuscripts, several cabinets of Oriental coins, a press with Arabic and Greek letters, an Arabic astrolabe, and funding for the chair of Arabic.

One of the earliest English Arabists was William Bedwell (1562–1632) whose career reflected many of the problems his isolated counterparts faced elsewhere in Europe: access to few manuscripts, dictionaries, and linguistic informants, and few opportunities to publish. Widespread prejudice against Islam and Arabic existed as well. Bedwell studied Semitic languages, with a special interest in Arabic, at Cambridge in the 1580s, even though it was not formally taught. He gained the support of Lancelot Andrewes, then a fellow of Pembroke Hall, who both included Arabic among the many languages he knew and promoted its study as a way of learning more about the early church. Andrewes, later bishop of Chichester, Ely, and Winchester, found Bedwell various clerical positions, where the latter pursued his multiple interests in mathematics, logic, and languages. Bedwell made one trip abroad, to Holland in 1612. Leiden was one of Europe's few centers of Arabic studies, and Bedwell spent time with its university's Arabic manuscript collection; he also found a Dutch commercial publisher with one of the two sets of Arabic type fonts in Europe, and a printer who knew how to use them. The other type set was in Rome, used by the Vatican to publish parts of the Bible for missionaries to distribute in the Middle East.

Bedwell admired the beauty and structure of the Arabic language, but abhorred Islam as a religion. His viewpoint was evident in the subtitle of his translation of a Christian Arabic manuscript called *Mohammedis Imposturae* (1615), which Bedwell called "A Discovery of the manifold forgeries, false-hoods, and horrible impieties of the blasphemous seducer Mohammed: with a demonstration of the insufficiencies of his law, contained in the cursed Alkoran."[25]

Bedwell published little in his lifetime, and is remembered mainly as the teacher of Edward Pococke. Much of his life was spent meticulously preparing a nine-volume Arabic dictionary that never appeared in print during his lifetime, and by the time of his death was obsolete. Bedwell's student Edward Pococke (1604–1690), on the other hand, became the first occupant of the Laudian chair in 1636, although he wrote and translated little, and during his later life con-centrated on the study of Hebrew and commentaries on the Minor Prophets.[26]

Pococke probably learned Arabic as a student of Matthias Pasor, an Ori-entalist from Heidelberg who lectured at Oxford, as well as William Bedwell. Pococke prepared translations of four epistles from the Syriac New Testament, and in 1630 became chaplain to the Levant Company in Aleppo, where he lived for five and one-half years, learning Arabic, Hebrew, Syriac, and Ethiopic, while collecting manuscripts and making friends with local Muslim leaders. From 1637 to 1641 Pococke lived in Constantinople, where he was chaplain to the English ambassador, and continued his language studies and manuscript col-lecting. In 1650 he published *Specimen historiae Arabum*, the first Oxford book printed in the new Arabic type fonts Laud had acquired. It represented a compilation of such impressions of Islamic history and religion as Pococke could assemble. The author also published a translation of an Anglican cate-chism in 1671 and a shortened version of the Book of Common Prayer in 1674.

At that time medical students were nominally required to study Arabic because of the Arabic contribution to science. But few pupils attended Po-cocke's courses over the fifty years he lectured at Oxford, and he struggled to keep the study of Arabic alive. After his death, the Bodleian Library acquired his manuscript collection of 420 works in Arabic, Hebrew, and other languages.

Pococke treated Arabic as a dead language and Islam as ancient history, but he also translated a life of the Prophet from Arabic into English.[27] He wrote poetry in Arabic, and urged Oxford University Press to publish works in that language. Pococke's work was "limited in both its scope and its impact," P. M. Holt has noted. "His publications consisted of the text and translation of two late Christian Arabic chronicles, and the erudite notes, not confined to history, but ranging over the whole field of Arab antiquities and Muslim religion, which he appended to his *Specimen historiae Arabum*."[28]

By the time of Pococke's death, Arabic studies had been established in Leiden, Rome, the Vatican, and elsewhere. Collections of documents in Arabic and Persian were gathered in Oxford and Cambridge, and the number of language students grew modestly. Several dictionaries and grammars also appeared in Europe and England, and in 1680 a massive Turkish dictionary was published in Austria.[29]

The Koran, meanwhile, had been inadequately translated from French into English in 1649 by Alexander Ross (1592–1654), whose style was described as "uncouth and his tone . . . harsh and uncompromising."[30] A. J. Arberry said it was "as hostile in intention as it was incompetent in execution."[31] Ross's work was based on a version by André du Ryer, a French diplomat-linguist. Du Ryer (ca. 1580–ca. 1672) lived in Egypt as a vice consul and in Constantinople as interpreter and secretary to the French ambassador (1630–1634). Fluent in Turkish, Arabic, and Farsi, he later became the French ambassador to the sultan and compiled an early Turkish grammar in 1630. He completed a translation of the Koran in 1647 that was soon translated into English, Dutch, German, and Russian. Reflecting the conventional Catholicism of his time, he described the Koran's meaning as being "as ridiculous as the text." Both the poetry and the division of the original into chapters were ignored, and du Ryer employed Christian religious language and ecclesiastical style to translate Islamic concepts. Ritual ablutions became "washing away of sins," and so on.[32]

Ross's commentary followed in the same vein. He said the purpose of his translation was to allow the "sweet evangelical manna" of Christianity to contest Islam's "poysonable quails."[33] His translation appeared just as Oliver Cromwell came to power, and the wisdom of publishing such a controversial work in revolutionary times sparked lively debate. Ross wrote a preface to the Koran attacking the Puritans, whom he said were already heretics—so how could publishing the Koran corrupt them further? Then he added lurid stories about Muhammad, including a report that Muhammad wore a turban because of a misshapen head. Despite the flaws in Ross's work, a new translation would not come for eighty-five years.

This translation was to be by George Sale (ca. 1697–1736), a layman and London solicitor, whose avocation was the study of Arabic, which he probably learned from Syrian Christians living in London.[34] A corrector of Arabic texts for the Society for the Promotion of Christian Knowledge (SPCK), he helped produce an Arabic translation of the New Testament and his own translation of the Koran in 1734. His version lasted until the Rodwell translation of 1861, and was reproduced and in wide circulation as late as 1984. Sale's footnotes contained comments from a 1698 Latin translation of the Koran. These notes, along with his English translation of much of the Arabic original, were popular

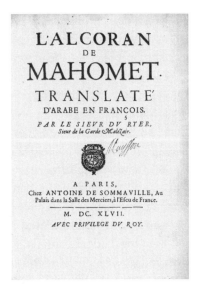

L'ALCORAN
DE
MAHOMET.
TRANSLATE'
D'ARABE EN FRANCOIS.
PAR LE SIEVR DV RYER,
Sieur de la Garde Malezair.

A PARIS,
Chez ANTOINE DE SOMMAVILLE, Au
Palais dans la Salle des Merciers, à l'Efcu de France.

M. DC. XLVII.
AVEC PRIVILEGE DV ROY.

André du Ryer's *L'Alcoran* (1647) represents the first complete translation of the Koran from Arabic into a modern European language. The French diplomat-linguist also published a Turkish grammar. Du Ryer (ca. 1580– ca. 1672) hoped his new translation of the Islamic holy book would aid Roman Catholic missionaries in converting Muslims. (Harvey S. Firestone Library, Princeton University, Rare Books and Special Collections)

with readers, although Sale's declared intention was to "expose the imposture" of Muhammad and refute Islam's idolatry and superstition.[35] Edward Gibbon later said Sale was "half a Musulman" for having said that "for however criminal so ever Mohammad may have been in imposing a false religion on mankind, the praises due his real virtues ought not to be denied him."[36] Elsewhere Sale called Muhammad "a man of at least tolerable morals, and not such a monster of wickedness as he is usually represented."[37] Holt concluded, "His work was of great importance. His freedom from religious prejudice (in which respect he compares favorably with many of his nineteenth- and twentieth-century successors)...marks an enormous advance on the hodgepodge of (earlier) 'authorities.' "[38]

English Religious Writings on Islam

For most of the seventeenth century, English Protestants invoked the Bible's apocalyptical passages against not only Muslims but Catholics as well. The

"Little Horn" of the Book of Daniel and the dreaded "Beast" of the Book of Revelation were variously directed at Prophet or pope. Polemical preachers built stock caricatures of the Prophet as a "poysoned serpente" or "cruell wolfe" and Muslims as a "troop of locusts" and "a brood of vipers."[39] Generations of British and Scottish Protestant preachers drew on Martin Luther's 1529 injunction, "May our dear Lord Jesus Christ, help and come down from heaven with the Last Judgment, and smite both Turk and pope on earth."[40] Catholics fired back in similar language with comparable intensity.

But the complicated mix of seventeenth-century religious thought was not black and white. Some writers tried to make common cause with the often-vilified churches of the East, urging them to rebel and overthrow their Muslim rulers. Others, handy at number symbolism, believed that the Jews would defeat the Romans in 1650, then the Turks in 1695 (the dates were calculated from the Bible). Protestants and Jews would then form an alliance against pope and sultan, for which the Jews would be rewarded with a return to Palestine, after which they would convert to Christianity. Such English expectations were chimerical. Jews had been badly persecuted by Christians, and the likelihood of their jumping at the opportunity for a military alliance with their oppressors was nil. The English promoters of revolt, often called Restorationists, laced their political arguments with biblical quotations and they believed they had found a leader in Sabbatai Sevi (1626–1676), Jewish leader of a messianic cult. He would complete the conquest in the favorable year 1666, the number of the Prophet Muhammad as Antichrist (666) as calculated from the Book of Revelation. But Sevi, faced with the prospect of a quick execution by the sultan's guards, converted to Islam and became Mehmet Efendi, an honorary doorkeeper to the sultan. His followers denounced him, or said he was merely trying to understand Islam, or had gone to heaven. In any case, the British hope of uniting Muslims, Jews, and Christians in one empire was a spectacular failure. British divines regrouped in its aftermath. The great coming together would have to await Christ's return to earth in the final days. Meanwhile, Jews and Muslims remained as outcasts.

Among writers on religion, attacks on Islam remained intense during most of the seventeenth century. Isaac Barrow, a preacher whose vituperative comments were considered authentic because he had spent a year in Constantinople, wrote a widely circulated sermon (ca. 1670), "Of the Impiety and Imposture of Paganism and Mahometanism." In contrast, John Bunyan, another anti-establishment figure, demonstrated tolerance toward Islam: "And could I think that so many ten thousands, in so many countries and kingdoms should be without the knowledge of the right way to heaven . . . and that we only, who live in a corner of the earth, should alone be blessed therewith."[41]

Among early-eighteenth-century writers on Islam was Simon Ockley (1679–1720), a Cambridge cleric with a gift for languages who studied both Hebrew and Arabic. Ockley became Sir Thomas Adam Professor of Arabic at Cambridge and, drawing on the rich collection of Arabic manuscripts in Oxford's Bodleian Library, published *The Conquest of Syria, Persia, and Aegypt by the Saracens* (1708), an *Account of South-West Barbary* (1713), and his monumental *The History of the Saracens* (1718). This two-volume work was the first effort at a comprehensive history of the Arabs in English. Although Ockley wrote of "Mahomet, the great Impostor," the book's emphasis represented a subtle shift from the unrelieved polemics of his contemporary, Humphrey Prideaux (whom we examine next), and was a work whose emphasis was more on history than ecclesiastical controversy.[42] Arberry said of it, "for sheer readability, the *History of the Saracens* has never in its kind been excelled; it is at once a pioneering work, and a classic."[43]

Ockley had spent over a year in a debtor's prison and always had difficulty in making ends meet; he wrote at a time when the study of Arabic was barely established in England. Socially awkward, his energies were concentrated on a large family and poor parish. His influence was limited to the small circle of academics engaged in Oriental studies, although later Gibbon credited him as the person who "first opened my eyes; and I was led from one book to another, till I ranged around the whole circle of Oriental history."[44]

These early scholars, most of them linguists and translators, laid the foundations for what became an increasingly informed understanding of Islam, although none claimed to be historians and few were interested in Islam as a political or military presence. Nevertheless, they provided skeletal information about the life of the Prophet and the Koran, which polemicists eagerly used against both Islam and religious opponents in Europe.[45] Bernard Lewis and P. M. Holt have written, "As late as the eighteenth century...it is still impossible to draw a hard and fast line between the controversialist and the scholar."[46]

The "controversialists" were, indeed, going strong at the turn of the eighteenth century. This time it was the Unitarians, small in numbers, who were involved in debate against the much larger, established Church of England. The basic Unitarian position was that Muhammad was a reformer, not an apostate, and the Koran reflected a monotheistic view of God compatible with true Christianity while refuting the distorted doctrine of the Trinity. The Anglican counterargument was to link Unitarians with Islam and then seek to discredit the latter. Unitarians were "scouts amongst us for Mahomet" and could not be called Christian, and were "far greater enemies to Christianity than the Mahometans."[47]

Humphrey Prideaux (1648–1724) took up Anglicanism's defense in his *The True Nature of Imposture Fully Displayed in the Life of Mahomet* (1697). Prideaux was dean of Norwich Cathedral and had studied Hebrew at Oxford, but had no interest in original scholarship. He said the Koran was the work of two heretical Christians writing in Medina, and the Prophet, to disguise his epileptic fits, feigned visions of the Angel Gabriel. Prideaux laid bare the errors of Islam as he saw them, then linked them to Unitarians and Deists. Nevertheless, despite its shortcomings, Prideaux's *Life of Mahomet* represented an advance over earlier such works and added a framework of chronological facts to the legends it repeated.[48]

In contrast to Prideaux, a more positive view of Islam had earlier appeared in *An account of the rise and progress of Mahometanism with the life of Mahomet and a vindication of him and his religion from the calumnies of the Christians* by Henry Stubbe (1632–1676). This work did not appear in print form, however, until 1911, when a group of Turkish and Indian Muslims were responsible for its London publication.

Stubbe, keeper of Oxford's Bodleian Library, said Muhammad was "a great law-giver" and "the wisest legislator that ever was"—comments that may have cost him his job. Stubbe went further, praising Muslims for their religious devotion and military skills, and suggesting that Islamic polygamy was no less shocking than the marriage customs of the biblical patriarchs. He also argued that both the Muslim and biblical interpretations of heaven were allegorical and symbolic.[49]

Stubbe's position was eclectic; he basically held that the early church was heavily influenced by Jews who became Christians and who never believed in the divinity of Christ, the Trinity, or a church hierarchy. Comparing the Bible and Koran, Stubbe wrote, "I have often reflected upon the exceptions made by the Christians against the Alkoran, and find them to be no other than what may be urged with the same strength against our Bible."[50] Neither Prideaux nor Stubbe was directly interested in Islam; both used it as ammunition in the religious conflicts of their time. Prideaux was alarmed by the rise of Deism and Unitarianism in England, whereas Stubbe's favorable comments about Islam laid the ground for positive support for the emerging Quaker movement.[51]

Meanwhile, John Milton had joined the anti-establishment fray, calling the established church "Turkish tyranny," and in 1659 he enjoined the largely Presbyterian Long Parliament against forcible conversions, a practice, he said, like that of the Turks. On the other side, Milton said that Muslim governance provided a desirable model for royalists who wanted a strongly centralized, unchallenged monarchy, and wished to eliminate sedition.[52]

Charles Wesley (1707–1788), a prodigious writer of hymns, reflected a widespread negative Christian attitude hostile to Islam:

> The smoke of the infernal cave,
>   Which half the Christian world o'erspread
> Despise, Thou heavenly Light, and save
>   The souls by that Imposter led,
> That Arab-thief, as Satan bold
>   Who quite destroy'd thy Asian fold.[53]

No eighteenth-century European figure held a more omniscient perspective as a historian than Edward Gibbon (1737–1794), for whom Islam had several positive attributes, and who as a child had been infatuated with the *Arabian Nights*.[54] Gibbon's *Decline and Fall of the Roman Empire* (1788) and Thomas Carlyle's much later (1840) lecture on the Prophet Muhammad as a hero are the two major works in English before the twentieth century to present Islam in a comparatively favorable light, along with other major religious figures and movements. Gibbon's Arabs and their Prophet were set in the wider context of the rise and fall of the Greek and Roman empires, and of other conflicts in the Mediterranean world. The over two hundred pages of chapters 50–52 of his magnum opus were a carefully drawn panorama of Arabic geography, history, and religion.[55]

Gibbon was aware of the main Latin-, French-, and English-language sources available for Islam in his time, and dismissed the grossest myths then in circulation, such as that the Prophet's tomb was suspended by magnets. Gibbon's Muhammad was a good, unexceptional man during his years in Mecca, but once he accepted the role of prophet and political leader after the hijrah to Medina, he became an ambitious politician given to fraud, fanaticism, and cruelty. The pivotal chapters on Islam contained an accessible biography of Muhammad, memorable for portraying the complexity of the Prophet's religious growth and evolving political role, and for the relative balance of Gibbon's perspective, despite some obvious blind spots; he insisted, for example, that Islam was free of dogma, schism, and conflict.[56] Even though it was both cautionary and negative in places about Muhammad, it was still the most advanced historical commentary on Islam in its time:

> According to the tradition of his companions, Mohammed was distinguished by the beauty of his person, an outward gift which is seldom despised, except by those to whom it has been refused. Before he spoke, the orator engaged on his side the affections of a public or

private audience. They applauded his commanding presence, his majestic aspect, his piercing eyes, his gracious smile, his flowing beard, his countenance that painted every sensation of the soul, and his gestures that enforced each expression of the tongue.... His memory was capacious and retentive; his wit easy and social; his imagination sublime; his judgment clear, rapid, and decisive. He possessed the courage both of thought and action; and, although his designs might expand with his success, the first idea which he entertained of his divine mission bears the stamp of an original and superior genius.[57]

Despite these admirable aspects, Gibbon's Muhammad preached a religion "compounded of an eternal truth and a necessary fiction, that there is only one God and Mohammed is the apostle of God."[58] The Koran's arguments were "most powerfully addressed to a devout Arabian, whose mind is attuned to faith and rapture; whose ear is delighted by the music of sounds; and whose ignorance is incapable of comparing the productions of human genius." Still, for Gibbon, Islam was more compatible with reason and less superstitious than much of the Christianity he had experienced.

Gibbon also warned Europeans to be cautious; a new menace might arise to replace Islam, whose restive members "had languished in poverty and contempt, till Mahomet breathed into those savage bodies the soul of enthusiasm."[59] Gibbon, whose views on Islam and the Prophet remained strongly influential until modern times, told his audiences that had Christians not defeated Muslims at the Battle of Tours (732), perhaps "the Koran now would be taught in the schools of Oxford, and her pupils might demonstrate to a circumcised people the sanctity and truth of the revelation of Mahomet."[60] Such fear of Islam, often translated into ridicule, remained a constant in Western thought.

Representative of an emerging, ambivalent view of Islam was Joseph White (ca. 1746–1814), who studied Arabic, Syriac, and Persian at Wadham College, Oxford, where he was named to the Laudian Chair of Arabic in 1774. He is best remembered for his 1784 Bampton lectures on Islam and Christianity, which Gibbon acknowledged in his own writings on Islam. White saw Islam's rise as a direct result of a divided Christendom, caused by Rome's doctrinal excesses. Islam for him arose "like smoke out of the bottomless pit, suddenly overshadowing the Eastern world, and involved its wretched inhabitants in darkness and in error." Muhammad was a political-military genius, talented, possessed of a great mind, skilled at overcoming adversity, yet driven by lust and greed. White warned people in other continents, "And while we declare to the savage of America the joys and glories of everlasting life, let us lead also the disciples of Brama and the followers of Mahomet, from the error of their ways into the glorious light of the gospel of peace."[61]

White, like many writers on religion in the late eighteenth century, reflected the era's intransigence. Many were like the parson in Fielding's *Tom Jones,* who said, "When I mention religion, I mean the Christian religion, and not only the Christian religion but the Protestant religion." Given the tenor of the times, if Anglicans yielded no ground to Catholics, and Methodists and Unitarians conceded nothing to Catholics and Anglicans, who could be expected to find much favorable in Islam?

English Popular Views of the Middle East

Meanwhile, popular interest in the East grew; coffee, silks, and spices flowed steadily into the hands and homes of Europeans who could afford them; and writers slowly but steadily showed interest in the curiosities of an overseas world. Emblematic of the newly emerging interest in life abroad were the letters of Lady Mary Wortley Montagu (1689–1762), who accompanied her husband, the British ambassador to Istanbul from 1716 to 1718. The ambassador's wife spent considerable time with the wives of local Turkish leaders and, in writing about such encounters, produced a body of descriptive literature on customs and religion of unusual quality and interest. An accomplished figure in London literary life, and friend and later enemy of the acerbic writer Alexander Pope, she had suffered a smallpox attack in December 1715 and later became active in promoting the controversial use of smallpox vaccination in England on the basis of its clear success in Turkey, which she described in her letters. Much of her life was spent with her dull husband, a plodding Whig parliamentarian who resembled a figure from a Restoration comedy. Her husband had used his connections to obtain a five-year appointment as British ambassador to the Sublime Porte, but was inept at diplomacy, and the appointment was soon withdrawn. He returned to England and political obscurity.

Most of the *Embassy Letters* were published in 1763, a year after their author's death; they had been rewritten from memory and notes after her return to England. Gibbon and Voltaire, among others, praised them. A Deist herself, Lady Mary's perceptive observations represent an early and important attempt by a woman author in the study of comparative religion; as Jane Shaw has observed, she was "a woman who was engaging with other religions in their context," a rarity in Enlightenment England.[62]

Lady Mary Wortley Montagu (1689–1762) is pictured here (on the left) in Turkish dress. The wife of the British ambassador to the Sublime Porte, she visited frequently with leading women in Istanbul. The "Sublime Porte" (High Gate) was named after the large gate leading to the sultan's reception area for foreign ambassadors. Lady Mary's *Embassy Letters* (1763) were an important source of information to English audiences about daily life in mid-eighteenth-century Turkey. (Mary Evans Picture Library)

Several of the letters were to the Abbé Conti, an Italian Roman Catholic priest, philosopher, and poet whom Lady Mary had known in London, and these discussed her views on Islam. Aspects of the religion were favorable, she wrote; a high local official "assured me, that . . . I should be very well pleased with reading the Alcoran which . . . is the purest morality, delivered in the very best language. I have since heard impartial Christians speak of it in the same manner."[63] She also commented on the place of women in Islam, saying essentially that women had souls, preferred marriage to single status, and would have a separate place in Paradise. As for the Prophet, he was courteous toward women: "He was too much a gentleman, and loved the fair sex too well, to use them so barbarously."[64] Her letters reinforced a late-eighteenth-century image of Islam in Turkey as promoting a religious system that was comprehensible in its own right. She concluded:

> Muhammadanism is divided into as many sects as Christianity, and the first institution as much neglected and obscured by interpretations. I cannot here forbear reflecting on the natural inclination of mankind to make mysteries and novelties. The Zeidi, Kadari, Jabari, etc. put me in mind of the Catholic, Lutheran, Calvinist, etc., and are equally zealous against one another. But the most prevailing opinion, if you search into the secret of the effendis, is plain Deism, but this is kept from the people, who are amused with a thousand different notions according to the different interests of their preachers.[65]

In another letter she described visiting the Selimiye Mosque in Adrianople, dressed in Turkish garb, and was shown about by a mosque attendant. The mosque's magnificence was "infinitely beyond any church in Germany or England." Lady Mary showed greater familiarity with Islam than most contemporaries, and her writings lacked the heavy judgmentalism common to many other writers. Given her position, she had little contact with lower classes, but had unusual access to the women of the sultan's precincts, and her meticulous recording of her contacts with them offered a rare entrée into aspects of eighteenth-century Turkish life.

Growing trade with the Middle East also resulted in the spread of coffee to England and to the gradual emergence of a coffee culture there and on the continent. By the late seventeenth century, coffeehouses were numerous in London. Waiters dressed in robes and turbans, and "Turks Heads" appeared above doors.[66] During the Crusades, an actual enemy's head from the Orient might have been brought back as a souvenir in a soldier's kit, and sometimes was used for target practice, but by now the Turk had been captured by an artist as either a menacing or comic figure, such as remain visible in modern European coffee ads.[67]

Starkly contradictory claims emerged about coffee, the "Mahometan berry." It was said to help in the "drying of rheumes, and flegmatick coughes and distillations, and the opening of obstructions, and provocation of urin."[68] Also, coffee made "erections more vigorous, the ejaculation more full," adding "a spiritual ecstasy to the sperm," rendering it "more firm and suitable to the gusto of the womb."[69] J. S. Bach wrote a "Coffee Cantata" (1732–1734) in which a soloist laments that if she is unable to drink three bowls of coffee daily, she will shrivel up "like a piece of roast goat." Opponents argued that coffee contained secret contents that risked causing the drinker to "turn Turk" and also

Increased trade between Europe and the Arabian Peninsula meant that the use of coffee, tea, and spices spread throughout Europe. Coffeehouses became popular in eighteenth-century England. Waiters wore turbans and "Turks Heads" appeared above coffeehouse doors. "The Mahometan berry," was believed to have medicinal properties and stimulate sexual desire. A singer in Bach's "Coffee Cantata" (1732–1734) required three bowels of coffee a day or she would shrivel up like "a piece of roast goat." (Getty Images/Hulton Archive Image)

become sexual eunuchs. Additionally, those who drank the "ugly Turkish Enchantress" could become dark, swarthy, and Moorish; in short, this was an addictive satanic brew designed to destroy Christians.[70] One writer said,

> 'Tis, methinks, faint defying
>   Old-Nick and his Works;
> To be fond of a Berry,
>   Which comes from the Turks.

The Barbary Pirates

As Mediterranean maritime commerce increased, North African navies or pirates captured great numbers of English and other European sailors. By the seventeenth century, such pirate raids on European shipping were commonplace, most of them originating from the North African ports of Tunis, Algiers, and Salé, the non-European ports that the English ships would first encounter on entering the Mediterranean.[71] Algiers was the largest city and consumer of slaves in North Africa until seized by the French in 1830. So numerous were the Christian slaves that one account said that you could "swap a Christian for an onion."[72] Possibly a million to a million and a quarter Christians were taken as slaves by the Barbary pirates between 1530 and 1780.[73] This means that for two centuries, the Barbary raiders seized almost as many European slaves as were taken from West Africa to the Americas.

Probably the most intensive sustained raids were on the long, unprotected Spanish and Italian coasts, and historians have speculated that the Barbary pirate menace in the Mediterranean, which Italians called "the sea of fear," was responsible for the demise of Italian maritime expeditions in the post-Columbus era.[74] Barbary corsairs, in addition to conducting carefully planned maritime operations with large numbers of ships, also allowed a steady number of individual coastal raiders to pursue targets of opportunity—a European fishing boat that had wandered too far out to sea, some villagers working in a seaside garden, a harvest left unguarded next to an estuary. In 1617, a Turkish pirate ship was captured in the Thames estuary; others preyed as far north as Ireland and Iceland, raiding coastal communities for crops and plunder—and for men, women, and children, who were taken as slaves.[75]

A seventeenth-century English captive, Francis Knight, called the Algerian pirates "the scourge of Christendom."[76] Some of the captured sailors were sold into slavery, others were kept as galley slaves, and still others converted to Islam and established families and trades in North Africa. But if thousands of Britons remained in Muslim lands and some converted to Islam, hundreds also returned to England, either ransomed or freely released. One result of their large number was that it became less easy for English villagers to condemn Muslims outright, especially if someone from your own village had converted to Islam and then returned home. One such person was Joseph Pitts, an English sailor captured by Algerian pirates, who was forced to convert under torture, made a pilgrimage to Mecca, and then returned to England. He candidly said that living and working conditions were better in Algiers than in England, and much was admirable about Muslim devotional life.[77]

The high number of English sailors seized in naval battles who converted to Islam inspired a literature about such "renegades." The question was—how should those who returned be treated? Although villagers were happy to see neighbors and kinsmen return, the returnees represented a problem for the church. Clerics had little sympathy for the hardships of captivity and the hard choices of conversion or death faced by these people, who were often regarded as traitors to their country and supporters of a satanic religion. Three sermons that discuss the return of the "renegade" survive from the 1620s and 1630s. Clergy wanted to make sure returnees denounced their apostasy, but no litmus test existed to determine the religious state of such people. One preacher urged clandestine checks to see if the men in question had actually been circumcised. Some sermons elaborated on the horrors facing the damned; preachers would not accept returnees' arguments that although they had professed Islam publicly, in their hearts they remained Christians. Archbishop Laud, not remembered for his pastoral compassion, devised a three-Sunday ceremony of repentance. It began with the offender standing outside the church during the entire service, "in a penitent fashion in a white sheet with a white wand in his hand, his head uncovered, his countenance dejected, not taking particular notice of any person that passeth him by; and when people come in and go out of the church, let him upon his knees humbly crave their prayers and acknowledge his offense in this form: 'Good Christians, remember in your prayers a poor, wretched apostate or renegado.' "[78] The conversion to Islam was branded as a "heinous and horrible sin," and after being reminded of it for three successive Sundays, the penitent was forgiven but told once more of "that woeful condition whereinto you had cast yourself" that has "dishonored and provoked Him by this your shameful revolt from Him."[79] In the eyes of the established church, favorable consideration of Islam would await more modern times.

English Drama and Literature

If Muslims were no longer actually falling on Europe's battlefields, they were being repeatedly defeated and converting to Christianity onstage. Turks or Moors as fearful or comic characters and menacing Barbary pirates became staples on the English stage. One critic counted at least forty-five mid-sixteenth-century English plays that featured Moors, and by the end of the eighteenth century at least fifty Turkish-themed operatic works circulated in Italy.[80] The popular theatrical impression of Islam in these years contained many ingredients carried over from earlier times: "Turkish" ignorance, cruelty, and sexual drive. Such themes found their way into representations of Turks and Moors on the London stage, as in Thomas Heywood's *The Fair Maid of the West* (1604–1610), where Clem, the Englishman, was castrated and became chief eunuch to a North African king; or Philip Massinger's *The Renegado* (1624) where the English eunuch became a personal slave to the Muslim queen.[81]

The Christian who "turn'd Turke" was the subject of *A Christian Turn'd Turke* (1612), a play by Robert Daborne (ca. 1580–1628) about John Ward, a poor Plymouth sailor who became a rich, daring pirate hero of popular ballads, and who lived comfortably in Tunis in "a fair palace, beautified with rich marble and alabaster stones," after converting to Islam in 1610. Ward, sometimes called Captain Wardiyya or Issouf Reis, commanded a Barbary corsair fleet that attacked European shipping. The highlight of Daborne's play was Ward's conversion ceremony, which opened with a procession of flag carriers and Muslim believers:

> After them [came] Ward on an Asse, in his Christian habite, bareheaded. The two Knights, with low reuerence [reverence], ascend, whisper the Muffty in the eare, draw their swords, and pull him off the Asse. He layd on his belly, the Tables (by two inferior priests) offered him, he lifts his hand up, subscribes, is brought to his seat by the Muffty, who puts on his Turban and Roab, girds his sword … offers him a cup of wine by the hands of a Christian: Hee spurnes at him, and throws away the Cuppe, is mounted on an Asse.[82]

The play ended with Ward, who actually died of old age, committing suicide and being torn to pieces, his remains tossed into the sea.[83]

In another such play, Thomas Kyd's *The Tragedye of Solyman and Perseda* (1588), an English sailor named Basilisco converted to Islam for the love of a woman and a better paying job. This required him to undergo circumcision, vividly described as "they lopt a cololp of my tenderest member."[84] Accounts of circumcision and castration could always hold an audience's attention in an otherwise dull play.

Suspect Islamic characters existed as well in Shakespeare's work; in *Othello, the Moor* (1622) Iago called Othello "the old black ram" (I.1.92) or "the lascivious Moor" (I.1.135). When the shifty Iago said, "These Moors are changeable in their wills" (I.3.352–353), he reflected a sentiment held not only in the play but in society as well. The once-confident Moorish general, military commander of the Venetian-Moorish army against the Turks, became increasingly jealous, murdered his white wife, Desdemona, then killed himself.[85] And in *The Merchant of Venice* (1600), the prince of Morocco, an exotic figure and unsuccessful suitor for Portia, was described as being "in the shadowed livery of the burnished sun" (II.1.515).

In addition to such Moorish characters, Shakespeare employed a few other topical references to Islamic lands, which reflected curiosity about the magical, sexual, cruel, and exotic; in *The Tempest* (1610), Prospero's magical island was set in the Mediterranean somewhere between Tunis and Naples, and when Caliban's mother Sycorax was banished, it was to Algiers. In *Henry V* (1599), part of Henry's marriage proposal to Katherine of France is a union destined to produce a son "that shall go to Constantinople and take the Turk by the beard" (VI.2.223–225).

Othello the Moor strangles Desdemona in Shakespeare's ca. 1603 tragedy. In this photograph, popular American singer-actor Paul Robeson chokes actress Uta Hagen in the 1940s Broadway production of *Othello*. A Moor in Shakespeare's England could be either a Berber or a sub-Saharan African. Human jealousy, rather than race, provided the play's main theme, but Iago, the villain, called Othello, prince and military leader, "the old black ram" and a "blackamoor." (Getty Images/Photo by Herbert Gehr/Time-Life Pictures)

But Shakespeare's use of Islamic imagery was limited and uninformed. He made few references to Barbary, and his plays contained neither mosques nor minarets, or references to the Koran, or any discussion of Islamic beliefs. A few generally negative references to Turks appeared in places, like the expression "turn Turk" or references to "out-paramour the Turk" (*Lear*, III.4.94) such as would appeal to popular audiences in Elizabethan times, but Islamic themes never ignited the interest of England's greatest dramatist.[86]

The Thousand and One Nights

Of growing popularity through succeeding centuries were *The Thousand and One Nights*, sometimes called the *Arabian Nights*, colorful and suspenseful Oriental tales that enjoyed a lasting vogue among European readers. Almost void of religious content, some were adventure stories or bawdy yarns, others were philosophical or moral tales, and still others were boldly drawn satires. The work contributed to but did not cause the growing interest in the Orient. The tales influenced many Western writers in modern times for their content and technique, but it is difficult to make a case for their religiosity. Interlarded in the *Arabian Nights* were two dozen or so pious stories that could have come from many folk cultures, and a few short Islamic-specific accounts like "The Muslim Hero and the Christian Maid" (she converted to Islam) and "The Prior Who Became a Muslim" (and brought forty monks with him). The tales were in turn bawdy, misogynous, virtuous, heroic, adventurous, and comic, often displaying the "fun-under-the-turban" school of lowlife humor. Joseph Schacht has written, "Islam was no longer seen as the land of the Antichrist but essentially that of an exotic, picturesque civilization, existing in a fabulous atmosphere peopled by good or evil, wayward genies—all this for the delight of an audience that had already shown so much taste for European fairy tales."[87]

The works circulated in translation from 1704 to 1717 from the French version of Antoine Galland (1646–1715), and hastily translated sections soon appeared in English, but it was not until 1778 that a complete translation was published in English. Galland was part of a French mission to the Ottoman Turkish sultan in 1670 and studied Turkish, Greek, Arabic, and Persian during a five-year residency in Istanbul, while amassing a collection of manuscripts, including an incomplete Arabic manuscript of the *Arabian Nights* from Syria. Some of the tales were traceable to India, many were of Persian origin, and others came from Baghdad and Cairo. Most of the stories were long circulated and common to both Islamic and Mediterranean cultures.

Galland, who spent nearly twenty years abroad, became professor of Arabic at the Collège Royal in 1709. He published Barthélémy d'Herbelot's encyclopedic *Bibliothèque orientale* (1697) and a translation of the Koran (1710). He also translated the *Mille et une nuits* into French, completing some stories, and adding others of his invention. The author toned down violent and picaresque scenes and eliminated obscene passages in the tales; a century later Richard Burton put the sexually explicit material back in and added some of his own.

By the late eighteenth century, various English and French versions circulated, adding or subtracting material at publishers' whims, while other versions of the *Arabian Nights* appeared in major world languages. One estimate is that almost seven hundred romances written in an Oriental manner were published in eighteenth-century France.[88] Less skilled authors rushed into print quickly written Chinese, Tartar, and other tales. The *Arabian Nights* description of popular tales of clever fishermen, scolding wives, comic sultans, and crafty, beautiful women retained the interest of audiences, and the *Arabian Nights*,

The mediaeval Persian epic *The Arabian Nights* or *The Thousand and One Nights* went through multiple translations and editions in many world languages, beginning in the eighteenth century. There is little about Islamic religion in the work, but these suspenseful tales, adventure stories, and magical fables with their giants, genies, and magic lamps earned an enduring place in Western culture. (Mary Evans Picture Library)

with their world of a lush, jewel-clad Orient, toe-curled shoes, and curved scimitars, became bedtime reading for children, and a doorway to the Orient for travelers, missionaries, and colonial officials.

The *Nights* had an amazing influence, introducing a whole school of pseudo-Oriental writing in several countries. Joseph Addison published several such tales in the *Spectator* (1711), and Oliver Goldsmith wrote Montesquieu-type letters in *The Citizen of the World* (1760). Later, the influence of the technique or content of the *Nights* could be traced to writers as diverse as Sir Walter Scott, Jane Austen, and Charles Dickens. In music, Rimsky-Korsakov's *Scheherazade* (1888) and Puccini's *Turandot* (1920–1926) drew on the *Nights* for subject matter. And in the twentieth century, the Broadway musical *Kismet* (1953), the Douglas Fairbanks *Sinbad* films, and Walt Disney's top-grossing film *Aladdin*

(1992) were follow-ons. Parenthetically, neither the *Aladdin* tale nor the popular *Ali Baba and the Forty Thieves* was part of the original *Nights*.[89]

Islam in Spanish and German Literature

Islam was a topic not only in French and English political, religious, and cultural writings but also was the focus of a major seventeenth-century Spanish writer, Miguel de Cervantes, and of leading German writers such as the dramatist Gotthold Lessing and the poet Johann Wolfgang von Goethe. As such, Islam in Spanish and German literature resembled the Islam of English authors, an exotic subject laced with combats which the Europeans always won.

Miguel de Cervantes (1547–1616) spent five years as a captive in Algiers, and several chapters in *Don Quixote,* the first part of which was published in 1605, contained substantial Moorish material. The second section, published in 1615, came after Jews and Muslims had been expelled from once-tolerant Spain, giving poignancy to the book that supposedly was written by a Moorish author.[90]

The Algiers Cervantes knew was a bustling international city dependent on piracy for its livelihood. Several thousand captive slaves lived there, some in miserable conditions, but often no more so than if they had been on English ships or in English jails. Others "took the turban," joined flourishing corsair bands, and were rewarded with wives and attractive homes. In *Don Quixote,* a Christian dressed in Moorish clothes and recently released from captivity appeared at an inn and was identified as a Spanish officer seized in battle by "Uchiali, the king of Algiers." The officer and his veiled female companion then told their story (chapters 39–41). The captive captain, Ruy Pérez de Viedma, was ransomed by Zoraida, a beautiful Moorish maiden, who had fallen in love with him, developed a deep devotion to the Virgin Mary, and wanted to convert to Christianity. The couple and some other Christians escaped by boat from Algiers, but were seized by French privateers, who took everything but their clothes. Eventually the couple made their way to Spain, where the captain was reunited with his family; Zoraida became a Christian and the captain's future wife.

The story's leading Moorish character was Zoraida's stately father, a wealthy, generous elderly gentleman who was surprised during his siesta by the escaping Zoraida and her lover, and then kidnapped by them. Hajji Murad was later released by his abductors, and he denounced his treacherous daughter. "Infamous, misguided girl," he said to her, "where in your blindness and madness are you going in the hands of these dogs, our natural enemies? Cursed be the hour when I begot you! Cursed the luxury and indulgence in which I reared you!" Then Hajji Murad called on Muhammad to pray to Allah with a series of maledictions to destroy his daughter and her lover.[91] Like so many Christian–Muslim conversion encounters, it was a well-told tale, full of intrigue and suspense, but the outcome was never in doubt—the Muslim converted.

Cervantes wrote at the fault line between two ages; an older time of tolerance and chivalry had yielded to a newer, more violent age. Jews and Moors were gone now from Spain, brutally expelled by the Spanish Catholic rulers or forcibly converted to Christianity, despite a guarantee of religious tolerance promulgated in 1492 by Ferdinand and Isabella. The novel's multiple layers reflected the complex levels of Spain's religious life. First there was the anonymous translator of the Arabic book, a Muslim record, hidden now in a blatantly Christian setting. Then there was Don Quixote, mad at times, clairvoyant at others, seeking to give meaning and hope to the madness around him, which included the destruction of the country's Muslim past.

What Germans thought of Islam in the seventeenth and eighteenth centuries was conditioned by the reality that there was not one but several Germanies, and the Thirty Years' War (1618–1648) had wreaked devastation. For Germans the "East" mostly meant neighboring states like Poland and other Central European countries. Additionally, the Catholic–Protestant conflict loomed large, and in Germany Protestant hostility was equally strong against Turkey and Rome. Few German travelers visited the Orient; they never approached the numbers sent from France or England.

Also, by the late eighteenth century German scholars were constructing a mythology that Germans were descendants of an "Aryan," not a Semitic, race that originated in the mountains of northern India. Sanskrit, an Indian language, was taught at the University of Bonn in 1818, other chairs were established elsewhere, and a productive school of German Indology was in place by the mid-nineteenth century. Arguments of a linguistic affinity between German and Sanskrit provided support for a concept of racial superiority.[92] A number of German writers established comparable racial theories. Immanuel Kant (1724–1804) believed that humanity was divided into four races. Johann Gottfried Herder (1744–1803) argued that history was in constant, organic flow, from which specific cultures rose and fell, and if humanity's childhood originated in the Orient, its maturity was realized in Europe's north, where a "new man" had been born to lead the world.[93]

The most elaborate statement of the notion that all civilizations lead to Europe was contained in *Lectures on the Philosophy of World History* by Georg Wilhelm Friedrich Hegel (1770–1831), which surveyed the histories of China,

India, Persia, Greece, Rome, and Christian Europe. The state was the place where freedom was realized for Hegel, and although each "world-historical peoples" was unique, the dead societies of East Asia, India, and Persia had nothing to contribute to the record of later history. Oriental states failed to make it past the starting gates; in his *Introduction to the Philosophy of History* the author wrote, "The Orientals do not know that the spirit or man as such are free in themselves. And because they do not know this, they are not themselves free. They only know that One is free; but for this very reason, such freedom is mere arbitrariness, savagery, and brutal passion, or a milder and tamer version of this which is itself only an accident of nature, and equally arbitrary. This One is therefore merely a despot, not a free man and a human being."[94] For Hegel, "the great journey of the spirit" began in Asia, but the road led steadily to Germany. He was not sure where to fit Islam. In addition to a few allusions here and there, Islam ended up with three pages in the *Philosophy of History*, in a section on the Germanic world (chapter 2, part 4). Acknowledging early Islamic contributions to science, philosophy, and poetry, Hegel was not negative in his appraisal of the Muslim world but he was a philosopher, not a historian, and his system was long under construction before he encountered Islam, about which he had only spotty information. Hegel's Muslims were contradiction-ridden fanatics and enthusiasts, indifferent to the social fabric around them, capable of both generosity and valor, but producing, according to his own image, a civilization built on sand.[95]

In the previous generation, Gotthold Lessing (1729–1781) had challenged many of the racial, religious, and literary ideas prevalent in the eighteenth century in his play *Nathan the Wise* (1779), an early work about religious tolerance that drew on Muslim, Jewish, and Christian themes. Nathan was modeled on a Jewish intellectual, Moses Mendelssohn, a close friend of Lessing's. The play was set in Jerusalem about 1187 during the Crusades, where a Christian monk gave Nathan, a wealthy Jewish merchant an infant girl, Rachel (Recha), to raise. Nathan, whose own wife and seven sons had been killed by the Knights of the Cross, raised the child to be virtuous without following any particular religion. A young German Templar knight, who was in Jerusalem as a crusader, saved Rachel from death in a fire. Although the knight was initially contemptuous of the Jewish Nathan, he fell in love with Nathan's daughter. The plot thickened when the young knight learned that Rachel was born a Christian. He appealed to the pompous patriarch of Jerusalem, who would have nothing to do with him. Then he asked for help from Saladin, the benign sultan and "Reformer of the World," who agreed to unite the lovers. Next it was discovered that Rachel and the knight were really sister and brother, and their father was the sultan's brother.

A pivotal scene was an encounter between Nathan and Saladin (Act 3, Scene 7) where the Islamic ruler asked Nathan to say which religion he has found most acceptable. The question was an obvious trap; if Nathan answered Judaism, the Muslim ruler would be offended; if he said Islam, he might be required to convert. At this point Nathan employed the Story of the Three Rings, which Lessing borrowed from Boccaccio's *Decameron*.[96] In the story, a wise man living in the East owned a magic ring, which he promised individually to each of his three sons. As he neared death, the owner had a jeweler make two duplicate rings, so that each son received one. After the father's death the sons quarreled over who owned the real ring, and thus all rings lost their power. But when each son believed his ring to be true and aspired "To emulate his father's unbeguiled, unprejudiced affection" (III.7.135–136) the magic power of each ring would be manifest to all.

Misunderstanding and reconciliation were the play's themes, and Lessing had Saladin, the leading Islamic ruler, plead for tolerance and compassion in language rare in that or any other day. He said to the templar:

> Would you remain with me? Here at my side?—
> As Christian, Musselman, all one! In cloak
> Of white, in Moslem robe; in turban, or
> In Christian cowl; just as you will. All one!
> I never have required the selfsame bark
> To grow on every tree. (IV.4.30–35)

Johann Wolfgang von Goethe (1749–1832) had a long fascination with Islam, although he never traveled south of Italy.[97] He had read the poetry of the Persian mystic Mohammad Hafiz and the Koran, and translated Voltaire's *Mahomet* into German. Books of the time portrayed Muhammad as an imposter, but Goethe instead planned a bold "flawed genius" drama, *Mahomet* (1773), that he never completed. A fragment from it remains, *Mahomet's Song* (1774), originally sung in praise of Muhammad's success by Ali, the Prophet's cousin and son-in-law, and Fatima, his daughter. It contained no references to Islam and was a symbolic poem typical of the period built around the progress of an Alpine-like brook from the mountains through winding hills and flowering meadows to the sea where the Prophet (never mentioned by name) like Atlas, carried his family and followers "in boisterous joy to the heart of their welcoming creator."[98] There are hints that had Goethe finished the work, Mahomet might have emerged as a character comparable to Faust or Prometheus, an amoral *Kraftmensch*, in Todd Kontje's view, "a powerful force of nature who swept up his followers like a mighty river and carries them to the sea."[99]

Goethe explained the proposed play's design: *Mahomet* would open with the Prophet singing a hymn alone in the desert under the stars. His admiration for the moon and sun was expressed, and the vast cosmic scene was called God's handiwork. The Prophet then converted to Islam, followed by his family and friends. In later acts Muhammad defeated his enemies but increasingly engaged in cunning to achieve his goals. Goethe's basic approach mirrored that of Voltaire and Gibbon: Muhammad as the flawed genius and spiritual leader who became increasingly worldly in his ambitions.[100]

Over forty years later, at age sixty-five, Goethe resumed his interest in the Orient, drawing on the resources available in early-nineteenth-century Germany. He briefly studied Oriental languages, admired the calligraphy of a fragment of an Arabic manuscript, periodically wore his "prophet's mantle" (a white robe and turban), smoked opium, and was fascinated by the sound of praying by Muslim members of a Russian regiment stationed in Weimar. Memorable among his later poetry was the *West-östlicher Divan* (1819), a set of love lyrics in twelve short books inspired by a beautiful younger woman to whom the aged Goethe was attracted. The word "divan" originally meant a collection of poems in an Oriental language, or possibly a three-walled meeting room in an Oriental palace, with the fourth side open to a garden. The poem's subtitles suggested their content—the timeless, temperate setting of love: the Singer, Hafiz (the Persian poet admired by Goethe), Love, Contemplation, Sadness, Proverbs, Timour, Suleika (named for the Austrian dancer with whom Goethe was infatuated), Wine-house, Parables, Persians, and Paradise.[101]

Despite their Oriental imagery, the poems were clearly about Goethe's inner journey in their quest for idyllic landscapes, sensual young maidens, and a steady supply of quality wine and almonds. A work of German Romanticism, *Divan* also provided Goethe a literary respite from war-torn Napoleonic Europe, and Oriental subject matter for a successive generation of younger poets such as Freimund Rückert (1788–1866), who became a professor of Oriental languages, translated works from Arabic, Persian, and Chinese, and wrote imitations of Middle Eastern verse, some of which were set to music by Schumann and Mahler.[102]

Muslims in Classical Music and Theater

In no forum was the Muslim image more vividly and sharply depicted in Europe than in the music and theater of the seventeenth and eighteenth centuries. Muslim–Christian encounters took the form of carefully staged crusader combat in several lengthy musical works. Christians always won, but usually after bloody fighting and sometimes with brief but generous encounters with Muslim opponents. One such story was *Combattimento di Tancredi e Clorinda* (1624) by Claudio Monteverdi (1567–1643), a one-act opera-oratorio. Its plot was extracted from *Jerusalem Liberated, the Love of Tancredi and Clorinda* by Torquato Tasso (1544–1595), a long epic poem set in 1095 and the beginning of the Crusades. The plot was simple: outside the walls of Jerusalem the Norman crusader, Tancredi, encountered a mysterious, veiled adversary, whom he defeated in mortal combat, only to discover the enemy was the Muslim woman he loved, Clorinda, who asked to be baptized before dying.[103]

Bajazet by Antonio Vivaldi (1678–1741) was one of the most representative musical dramas on the "tragic Turk" theme, a reworking of the Bajazet-Tamerlane story. (There were several spellings of the protagonist's name.) In Vivaldi's version (1735), the Ottoman sultan Bajazet was defeated by the Tartar emperor Tamerlane. A complicated love story followed in which both Tamerlane and a Greek prince, Andronico, fell in love with Bajazet's beautiful daughter, Asteria. Toward the drama's end Tamerlane ordered that Asteria, who tried to poison him, be ravaged by a mob of slaves in the presence of her father. The distraught Bajazet committed suicide, but Tamerlane, horrified by the way things turned out, pardoned Asteria and Andronico.[104]

In the seventeenth century, Molière's comedie-ballet *Le Bourgeois Gentilhomme* (1670) had used Turkish-type costumes, characters, dances, and phrases drawn from the patois of Arabic, French, Italian, and Spanish spoken in Mediterranean port towns. In a climactic final act M. Jourdain, the bourgeois gentleman, was dressed in a Turkish costume and was invested as a "Mamamouchi" in the Turkish court by a Mufti wearing a crown of candles in his turban, and accompanied by dervishes, musicians, and flag bearers. Turkish interludes were staples in ballets and operas, and several Ottoman sultans became opera characters, including Mohammed I and Suleiman I. Jean-Baptiste Lully (1632–1687) wrote a *Marche pour la cérémonie des Turcs* as part of Molière's *Le Bourgeois Gentilhomme*. Haydn's *Military* symphony, Mozart's *Rondo alla Turca* and *Die Entführung aus dem Serail*, and Beethoven's Turkish march in *The Ruins of Athens* are among the best-known examples of Turkish themes making their way into mainstream European music, but lesser musicians wrote distinctly identifiable Turkish marches as well for what was often called a "batterie turque." The music suggested the very popular janissary bands that played in European towns.

Mozart made widespread use of Oriental motifs in his operas. Selim, the pasha in *Die Entführung aus dem Serail* (1782), was a wise, restrained monarch. Osmin, the colorfully costumed comic harem guard, telegraphed his intent to audiences through exaggerated gestures and was identified with distinctive music. Elsewhere, in *Die Zauberflöte* (1791), Monostatos, the lecherous Moor, was a contrast to Sarastro, the wise Egyptian high priest, and in *Cosi Fan Tutti* (1790) the two European officers who want to test their lovers' fidelity disguise themselves as Albanians with turbans and Oriental garb.

One of the best-known such works was *Les Indes galantes* (1735) by Jean-Philippe Rameau (1683–1764), which played for over three hundred performances following its opening. More a tableau than an opera, the work assembled Turkish generals, Incas from Peru, a Persian fête, Amazons, and North American natives. In Act I, Osman, the Turkish general, helped Emile, a European woman seized in a naval battle, find her lost love, Valère, who was taken as a slave by Osman. The magnanimous Osman freed the couple:

> Go to your boats,
> My orders have been given . . .
> Go, live happily . . .
> Remember Osman.[105]

Valère expressed the couple's gratitude: "Was there ever a more generous heart?" he asked of Osman, "Worthy of our praise, he would not hear it. . . . He has the right to claim the most perfect happiness." The lustful Turk was now replaced by the compassionate Ottoman ruler, still absolutist but now stoic and wise. Tolerance and understanding were considerably advanced in such works beyond where they had been a few centuries earlier.[106]

Two roads were now open, the exotic and the more dispassionate examination of the East. The exotic East was by now solidly established as an imaginary realm, a mental setting to be drawn on as needed as a place of escape, a theme that would become important during the nineteenth century, when distinctive escapist art, literature, and music came into its own. But there was also a second, different Orient emerging, a place with real geographical features, archeological ruins, growing commerce with Europe, and a religion and cultures worth study on their own.

3

The Prophet as Hero and Wise Easterner (1800–1900)

He was by now a hero, founder of a major world religion that was also a political force to be reckoned with; yet for many Westerners Muhammad remained morally deficient, as did the religion he espoused. Nevertheless, the image of Islam in the West underwent several dramatic changes in the nineteenth century, more than in any previous hundred years' span. New positives were added, old negatives were reinforced. A steady influx of new information made its way to Europe from scientists accompanying Napoleon's Egyptian expedition, and from French, British, and German travelers, archeologists, and linguists; and later in the century, American missionaries and popular writers like Mark Twain and Washington Irving. Except for the missionaries, many of the writers were indifferent to religion. The Suez Canal's opening in November 1869 and the growth of steamship travel resulted in heightened European and American interest in the Orient. Additionally, Thomas Cook's Eastern Tours attracted an outpouring of five thousand British and American middle-class tourists to Palestine between 1869 and 1882.[1]

Thus the centuries-old measuring filters by which Islam was held to the light and found to be a false religion increasingly lost their impact. They were still used, but to them were added the works of a generation of new writers who found more favorable aspects of Islam to write about. On balance, the old negatives about Islam remained, but to them were added a wealth of new information, more detailed and tolerant in perspective, plus a steady outpouring of new details about languages, cultures, and societies than had ever been previously available.

Napoleon and the French in the Nineteenth Century

Napoleon Bonaparte (1769–1821) was the first modern European military leader to make a concerted study of the religion, customs, and characteristics of the country he set out to conquer. He listened intently as scholars from the al-Azhar expounded the Koran, and presided over Egyptian religious festivals. At times Napoleon, temporary conqueror of Egypt, wore native dress over his French general's uniform and printed his military decrees in Arabic on a press seized from the Vatican. Pragmatically religious when he wanted to be, he called himself a Muslim while in Egypt, a Catholic in France, and a freethinker at the Institute in Paris. Megalomaniac that he was, Napoleon believed he could forcibly amalgamate East and West. It didn't work, but the encounter left lessons for future generations on how the military might interact with conquered peoples. Long after Napoleon was defeated on the battlefield, the seeds of his cultural-scientific interests bore fruit in Egypt. Almost two centuries later, Egyptian authors and scholars wrote in both Arabic and French, and an Egyptian, Boutros-Boutros Ghali, former secretary general of the United Nations, headed the world association of francophone countries from a Paris office.

On May 19, 1798, *L'Orient*, flagship of Napoleon's fleet, set sail for Egypt from Toulon harbor. "Europe is a molehill," Napoleon was famously quoted as saying, "We must go to the Orient; all glory has always been acquired there." Possibly he said this, or something like it; Napoleon was a skilled propagandist and maintained an enduring fascination with the East, but his was an Orient that existed largely in his mind. The twenty-nine-year-old general, whose admitted role model was the Eastern conqueror Alexander the Great, said, "I saw myself founding a religion, marching into Asia, riding an elephant, a turban on my head and in my hand the new Koran that I would have composed to suit my needs."[2] French irrigation methods would make the desert blossom like a rose, a Suez Canal would connect Egypt with Arabia and India, and immigrants from Europe's far corners and the Mediterranean would simultaneously flock to Egypt and make it a prosperous colony.

But militarily, Napoleon's campaign fared disastrously; fewer than half of the thirty-four thousand troops accompanying him returned to France three years later. Planning was harebrained; his troops were ordered on desert marches without water, and dysentery and bubonic plague were the army's constant companions. Napoleon's troops were not adequate in numbers to control the country, did not speak Arabic, and had no clear mission.

The French general set sail for Egypt with a team of Arabic translators, natural scientists, engineers, and archaeologists—a loosely organized Commission on the Sciences and the Arts of the Army of the Orient, the first such nonmilitary expert auxiliary to be part of a colonizing army. Several artists were among their ranks, and from this assemblage a school of modern Egyptology was born. The 167 experts spent three years preparing detailed observations, leaving lasting results in linguistics, archaeology, and cartography.

Napoleon arrived in Alexandria on July 2, 1798, and distributed a carefully written proclamation in Arabic, Turkish, and French. Opening with the traditional Koranic salutation, "In the Name of God, the compassionate, the merciful," it castigated the foreign beys who ruled Egypt. Napoleon assured Egyptians, "I respect His Prophet Muhammed and the Admirable Koran." France was the true friend "of the Ottoman sultan (may God perpetrate his rule)." A propaganda tract against the ruling Mamelukes, the Ottoman military leaders that controlled Egypt, the proclamation recalled the country's former greatness, and promised to restore it under French rule. "Happy, thrice happy are those Egyptians who side with us. They shall prosper in fortune and rank." Sheiks, kadis, and imams would continue in their posts, and all Egyptians were ordered to shout, "May God preserve the glory of the French army."[3] Napoleon insisted sheiks wear a tricolored cockade as a badge, which they did in his presence, then removed it on leaving.

Alexandria's inhabitants were ordered to add tricolor cockades to their usual headgear, and ranking religious and civil dignitaries were presented with the red, white, and blue sashes of French mayors (one leading Cairo religious leader threw the new French symbol on the ground). In an act of visible gastronomic excess, an Alexandrian sheik invited General Jean-Baptiste Kléber, the French governor, for dinner and served him a plate of red, white, and blue cooked rice.[4]

Napoleon went native at times, presiding over the annual ceremony flooding the Nile and the Prophet's birthday celebration, at times wearing a local caftan, and joining the sheiks in prostrating himself for prayers. Napoleon knew the value of religion as a rallying force in nation building and declared his intention "to establish a uniform government, based on the principles of the Koran, which alone are true and capable of bringing happiness to men."[5]

Napoleon's forays into Islamic religion never convinced anybody but himself. The al-Azhar sheiks shrewdly said, if he was so interested in Islam, why didn't he convert? Napoleon thought about it and replied that he and the French soldiers were circumcised and drank wine, both prohibited in Islamic tradition, so they could not become Muslims. Not to be deterred, the religious leaders said neither objection represented a final impediment; a person could still drink wine and be a believer, though in a sinful condition that would prohibit access to paradise. Napoleon, turned theologian for a moment, said it would make no sense to join a new religion and already be condemned to hell.[6]

The French leader's attitude toward Islam reflected the major problem nineteenth-century Europeans faced in dealing as conquerors of subject peoples. Power was in the hands of those who held the sword, and implicitly or explicitly their religion was likewise presented as superior to that of the conquered people.

Few writers were as politically influential in early Napoleonic France as Constantin François de Chassebouef, who wrote as Volney. His *Le Voyage en Syrie et en Egypte* (1787) became a Baedecker's guide to many in the emperor's expedition. The twenty-five-year-old author spent over two years in these countries but rarely left the comforts of large cities. He interviewed Europeans settled in Egypt and Syria, and distributed a carefully prepared questionnaire covering over a hundred categories about the political and physical setting of both areas. The book was attractive to the French military because of its detailed observations about local life in the two countries.

Although a product of its times in its support of French positions, Volney's writings also contained striking anticolonial passages that might have been written much later. He urged the French to take care of their homeland first: "It is in our homes, and not beyond the seas, that our Egypt and Antilles are to be found. What need have we of foreign land when one sixth of our own land remains untilled. We should well look to improve our fortunes and not to expand them: we should know how to derive benefit from those riches which are in our hands and not practice, beneath foreign skies, a wisdom which we do not utilize at home."[7] Volney hoped France would restore Egypt to a present worthy of its glorious past; in contrast, the Ottoman Empire's political and religious despotism had been responsible for its present decline. Still, he was no flag-waving imperialist; in language that could have emerged from the recent Iraq war, Volney wrote: "These men must be governed, and we do not know their language, nor their manners and customs; misunderstandings will arise which will cause trouble and disorder at every turn. The character of the two nations, opposite in every way, will be reciprocally antipathetic."[8]

In this work, and in his later *Les Ruines; ou, Méditations sur les révolutions des empires* (1791), Volney commented on the political state of several countries; his basic viewpoint was that if France was going to colonize, let it do so with

Le general Bonaparte et son état-major en Égypte (General Bonaparte and His General Staff in Egypt) (1867). Napoleon's Egyptian expedition of 1798–1801 opened the way for French artists and writers to focus on Egypt and other Middle Eastern subject matter. Jean-Léon Gérôme portrays a dejected French emperor returning to Egypt, and soon to France, after his army's resounding defeat by Turkish troops, the British navy, and disease at the coastal seaport fortress of Acre in 1799. (From Gerald M. Ackerman, *La vie et l'oeuvre de Jean-Léon Gérôme* [Paris: ACR, 1986])

accurate information, aware of the considerable risks in such a venture. It was a stark picture Volney painted of countries living in the ruins and on memories of their past, ruled by despotic governments. Harems and sunsets did not interest him, nor did he have any grand political scheme he hoped to trace out in the sands. Muslims were basically good people, he believed, but were kept down by a despotic Prophet who sought not to enlighten but to reign through his "wretched" book, the Koran. Volney found Islam's sacred scriptures deficient in providing a framework for governance. Its legal provisions "are so contradictory that the doctors are still engaged in dispute in an effort to resolve them. All the rest is naught but a tissue of vague phrases empty of meaning."[9]

Following Napoleon's adventure, Oriental studies became established in France. "The patriarch of Orientalists" was how colleagues described Silvestre de Sacy (1758–1838), a gifted linguist who functioned with equal skill in several Semitic and Romance languages. De Sacy singlehandedly secured the place of Oriental studies in the France of his time, through parliamentary contacts, ties with international colleagues—especially in England and Germany—and sup-port of a generation of students, some of whom became officers with French missions in Egypt and Algeria.[10] In 1795 de Sacy was named to the chair of Arabic in the newly founded Ecole des Langues Orientales; two years later he became professor of Persian at the Collège de France, and in 1815 he was named rector of the University of Paris. Equally productive as an academic adminis-trator and scholar for over fifty years, he became conservator of Oriental man-uscripts at the royal library in 1832. A *Grammaire arabe* (1810) and several collections of Arabic documents annotated and translated into French were among his multiple publications, as was *L'Exposé de la Religion des Druses* (1838) and the publications of the Société Asiatique, which he helped found in 1822. Though an active Catholic, de Sacy had no demonstrable religious agenda in his work, and he pioneered a new approach to language learning and scholarship in translating and teaching a range of languages until then little known in France.

French Orientalist Literature

Gustave Flaubert (1821–1880) was almost twenty-eight when he set out on an extended tour of Egypt from November 1849 to July 1850 with Maxime du Camp, a photographer-journalist friend.[11] The burning desert sun and old ruins were symbols Flaubert reworked frequently in novels like *Salammbô* (1862), set in Carthage. But in his letters from Egypt, mostly to his mother and to Louis Bouilhert, a friend back in Normandy, Flaubert poured out a series of postcard-sized literary impressions that would have little lasting interest if they had not come from the author of *Madame Bovary* (1857).

Flaubert's eye was for the bizarre. A frequent visitor to male and female brothels, his account of time spent in Egypt was filled with lurid sexual en-counters (described in the letters to Bouilhert, not to his mother) and of the grotesque, as in an account of idle time spent shooting stray dogs in a Cairo dump, or in the description of a dishonest baker sentenced to have his ears nailed to the door of his shop and to hang for several hours with his feet off the ground. Snake charmers, tour guides, and street musicians all made cameo appearances, but almost nothing of beauty or serious reflection was contained in the *Letters*.

In his *Voyage en Orient* (1844), another literary figure, Gérard de Nerval (1808–1855), recounted an 1843 trip to Egypt, Lebanon, Syria, and Istanbul. What passed for a seven-hundred-page novel was largely the author's quest for self-discovery with the Orient as a background. Nerval's Oriental imagery came largely from libraries, and he skillfully absorbed the lore of storytellers and books, patching materials together in an entertaining collage that oth-erwise had little to do with the countries he visited.[12]

It would be anachronistic to judge such authors by later standards about the image of Islam they presented. Products of their times, they wrote in a different setting for different purposes, primarily to extend their own personal or national horizons, for which a fantasy construct of the Orient proved useful.

The French writer who most consistently portrayed the exotic in countries France occupied was Julien Viaud (1850–1923), whose pen name was Pierre Loti. Neither historic Islam nor its spiritual content interested Loti, for whom Islamic countries provided little more than local color for romantic adventures. Born in Rochefort on the Atlantic Ocean of old Protestant stock, Loti was not demonstrably religious himself. A career naval officer at an early age, he seemed to turn out a novel per port of assignment—including Turkey, *Aziyadé* (1879); Tahiti, *Le Mariage de Loti* (1880); Senegal, *Le Roman d'un Saphi* (1881); and Japan, *Madame Crysanthème* (1887)—until his retirement in 1910. The ingredients were generally the same: a lush setting filled the with sights, sounds, and smells of a distant non-European country, plus a passionate, ill-fated romance between two people of different races and classes, and a drawn-out tragic ending where race, class, and circumstances conspired against the fated couple. Audiences clamored for more, and Loti, with his unerring gift for colorful narration, serialized much of his work in popular magazines, and eventually produced thirty-nine published volumes that sold millions of copies.

Aziyadé was his work most clearly placed in an Islamic setting. In it, Loti, thinly disguised as an English naval officer, spent a year in Salonica and Istanbul, enraptured by Aziyadé, a beautiful former slave and a wife of a local Turkish merchant. Loti and Aziyadé knew the impediments of their continuing relationship, which ended badly. Aziyadé died brokenhearted after never hearing from her departed European lover. (Her stubborn maid, determined to end the romance, burned both his incoming and her outgoing letters.) Later a distraught Loti returned to visit Aziyadé's grave, joined the Turkish army under the name of Arif-Ussam, and was killed in battle.

What was the picture of Islam Loti presented in his immensely popular works? It was essentially an exotic setting that differed little from Loti's colorfully decorated personal museum room back home in Rochefort. A photograph remains of the author, dressed in flowing Oriental robes and carrying a sword, flanked by elaborate wall hangings, ostrich eggs, piles of embroidered pillows, layers of Oriental rugs, silver mosque lamps, and large brass candlesticks, under a meticulously carved cedarwood ceiling.[13] For Loti and many artists of the Romantic era, Islam became a stage setting for creative fantasies they devised in their own minds about the newly emerging world beyond Europe's borders.

Pierre Loti was the pen name of the French writer Julian Viaud (1850–1923), whose fictional works about overseas life appears in thirty-nine volumes that sold millions of copies. Loti, of French Protestant ancestry, often appeared in native dress, as in this setting of an opulently furnished room he constructed in his family home in Rochefort in the west of France. (From Lesley Blanch, *Pierre Loti* [New York: Tauris Parke, 2004])

The Racial Profiling of Islam

By the late nineteenth century, biology, anthropology, and other sciences had combined in the hands of some practitioners to produce a relative ranking of world civilizations along racial lines. Islam did not fare well in such categorizations. Typical of early racial profiling was the work of two French scholars, Ernest Renan and Gustave Le Bon.

Originally a student for the priesthood, Renan (1823–1892) abandoned theology for the study of biblical languages, philosophy, and history. A gifted linguist and student of ancient texts, his *Vie de Jésus* (1863) was popular in France for decades, and his eight-volume *Histoire des origines du Christianisme* (1888–1890), and five-volume *l'Histoire du peuple d'Israel* (1887–1893) were early attempts to place key religions in their social-historical setting. For Renan, Jesus was divine because he reflected the divine goodness latent in humanity. As for Islam, Renan saw it as a spent force in history.

On a superior-inferior scale, Christianity was the leading religion, the product of the higher Aryan race. Islam, of contrasting lower Semitic origin, inhibited progress, represented an "iron circle" around the heads of believers, and kept them from understanding modern science or philosophy. Additionally, Renan believed that the scientific or philosophical contributions to civilization credited to Islam really originated with other civilizations. Arabic civilization's great gifts to the world were monotheism and the Arabic language, but otherwise it was despotic, and lacked poetic imagination, mythology, or theology. "La langue, rien que la langue," Renan wrote, "En tuant la science, il s'est tué lui-même, et s'est condamné dans le monde à une complete infériorité" (Language, nothing but language. Killing science, they killed themselves and condemned themselves to a place of inferiority in the world).[14]

And while the two great civilizations, Aryan and Semitic, coexisted for a while, the Semitic people declined rapidly once they had passed on the gift of monotheism to the rising Aryan race. Writing in 1883, Renan said, "who has been in the East or in Africa will have been struck by the hidebound spirit of the true believer, by this kind of iron circle which surrounds his head, rendering him absolutely closed to science, incapable of learning anything or of opening himself to a new idea."[15] Elected to the French Academy in 1878, Renan was named director of the Collège de France in 1883, where he was also professor of Hebrew. But all was not smooth sailing. French Catholics constantly attacked Renan for his controversial views about the origins of Christianity, and the pope called him a blasphemer. Such "racial theory is so old-fashioned now that it is difficult to understand the force of its impact," Albert Hourani wrote in 1980, adding, "But Renan was by no means alone in thinking in this way. Gobineau in his book on the inequality of human races put forward a similar thesis."[16]

Joseph Arthur Comte de Gobineau (1816–1882) claimed Nordic Viking ancestry and served as a French diplomat in Persia; in his *Essai sur l'inégalité des races humaines* (1853–1855), he wrote that different races had different levels of mental abilities, and if a superior race mixed with an inferior one, the former would perish.[17] Humanity was divided into three races, the Negroid (black), Caucasoid (white), and Mongoloid (yellow). At the pinnacle of this grouping were the white Aryans, supposedly derived from an ancient Indo-European culture. Arabs and Jews were members of an inferior race, because the Semetic peoples were a mixture of various racial elements. Gobineau's friend and sometime racial theorist, Richard Wagner, had a different theoretical approach, opining that the decline of a race was attributable not to miscegenation but to eating red meat.

Renan's and Gobineau's immediate intellectual successor was Gustave Le Bon (1841–1931), a social psychologist and physician who visited North Africa and Asia, and who wrote extensively about national traits and race. Either a dilettante or a genius, depending on the viewpoint of his detractors or admirers, Le Bon cobbled together a theory of history based on racial characteristics; these in turn determined the political and cultural levels of civilizations.[18] Le Bon believed that a vibrant Arab civilization existed, but not an Islamic one. Born among the Arabs, Muhammad provided a unifying religion that shaped the Arab culture around him, and later much of the world. But it contained destructive contradictions, which explained to Le Bon why the once-flourishing Arab civilization died precipitously in the early modern period. Unrelenting militancy, valuable in early times of expansion, tore apart later Muslim states as they turned on one another. The law, once a unifying force, became a deadening agent of stagnation. Competent leaders and state builders became sluggish despots in later generations.

Le Bon concluded his lengthy *La civilisation des Arabes* (1884) with a section on the "grandeur and decadence of the Arabs." Arabs were prisoners of their fate; their character would not allow them to develop further, nor could they make the next step to become Europeans, for that went against their basic characteristics. "Few races elevated themselves so high, but few races descended lower. None presents a more striking example of the influence of factors present in the birth of empires, their grandeur, and their decadence," Le Bon concluded.[19]

Evolving race theory was as elaborate as it was inaccurate. Works like J. J. Virey's *Histoire naturelle du genre humain* (1802), which employed phrenology, the measurement of skulls and brain size as an index of mental capacity, consigned Turks, Persians, and Egyptians to secondary status, followed by the "Arab hordes." The French naturalist Bory de Saint-Vincent (1780–1846) created fifteen categories of superior and lesser racial types in his *L'Homme. Essai zoologique sur le genre humain* (1827). Arabs ranked next after Europeans and "Japetic" races that displayed bilious and sanguine temperaments, which resulted in their being miserly and given to brigandage.[20]

Orientalism in French Art

Paintings of the period differed in an important way from the travel literature of writers who might have taken the same ships from England to Egypt. Whereas writers might attack Islam as a heathen religion and Muslims as living in unsanitary conditions, European painters were more interested in depicting pious believers at prayer in the impressive sacred space of vast, elaborately decorated mosques, and invariably the streets and sites were brushed clean. The art historian Gerald Ackerman has written, "For most of them this was an act of homage to a world they visually loved, even if they were ignorant of many aspects of its social reality."[21] Such artists were responding to new availabilities of easy steamship travel to the Middle East, and with it a corresponding development of a tourist infrastructure of hotels, maps, guides, and guidebooks.

Artists both responded to and helped create markets for Middle Eastern and North African watercolors and paintings; advances in printing and the reproduction of illustrations in books and magazines multiplied the market for such art, as did the burgeoning Bible and Sunday school publication industry. "This 'voyage to the East' industry is still well and robust," Ackerman has written.[22] What is especially interesting when the panoply of Orientalist art is considered in its full sweep is how little it fit the categories Edward Said railed against. Of course there were works distinctly imperialistic in perspective and execution, but more than three hundred European painters, both professionals and amateurs, had made their way to the Middle East by the later nineteenth century. Most went about the traditional work of artists, painting landscapes, buildings, people, and animals, trying to tell a story through color and composition, and hoping to sell the result on their return home.

Several French painters presented their subject matter with mystical reverence that differed little from how they might portray traditional Catholicism.[23] This was true of the numerous works of Jean-Léon Gérôme (1824–1904) of mosques and Muslims at prayer in hushed, seemingly timeless settings; and in the contemplative figures of the Austrian artist Ludwig Deutsch (1855–1935), who lived in France but who made several extended visits to Egypt.

Some French Catholics saw at least surface parallels between Christian and Muslim piety; there were similarities between the dark, cool, religious hush of mosque and cathedral. Catholic Revivalists during the 1870s sought a return to the nostalgic certainties of a medieval past, and paintings of pious Arabs at prayer fit favorably into such a setting. Henri de Castries, an ex-colonial officer in Algeria, wrote of seeing Muslim troops at prayer, "that simple concept of divinity took on a meaning in my soul beyond anything theology or metaphysics had taught me."[24] The French writer Théophile Gautier also wrote of the "dignity and even the chastity which exists between a Muslim and his wives," which contrasted with the image of Muslim indolence and sexual permissiveness evoked by other writers.[25]

But there were artists whose subject and style were very much in line with the writings of Orientalist novelists. Baron Jean-Antoine Gros (1771–1835) was what later generations would call a combat artist. He never visited the Middle East but turned out massive propaganda canvasses that helped define the

Napoleonic era: *Le Combat de Nazareth* (The Battle of Nazareth, 1801), *Le Pes-tiférés à Jaffa* (The Pesthouse at Jaffa, 1804), and *Charge de cavalrie, executée par le général Murat à la bataille d'Aboukir en Egypte: 25 juillet 1799* (Sketch for "The Cavalry Charge under General Murat at the Battle of Abukir, Egypt: 25 July 1799," 1806). The basic ingredients of these works included a French general of mythic proportions, a relatively small number of victorious European troops, and a rabble of defeated Muslim forces—except in *Pesthouse at Jaffa*, which was peopled by plague-ridden French soldiers.

War was one theme of French Orientalist art, sex was another. In *The Snake Charmer* (ca. 1870) by Jean-Léon Gérôme, an aged man in turban and flowing robes looks longingly at a naked male youth who holds a phallic-like snake while courtiers leer. The painting, kept under a protective layer of glass in a Williamstown, Massachusetts, museum to keep viewers from touching the boy's naked buttocks, became the arresting cover illustration for Edward Said's book *Orientalism*.[26] *Le Bain turc* (Turkish Bath, 1862) by Jean Auguste Domi-nique Ingres (1780–1867) was a signature piece of another type of Orientalist painting. Ingres, like Gros, never ventured south of Italy, but in this work, and in *L'Odalisque et l'esclave* (Odalisque and Slave, 1842), he combined a meticu-lously prepared Middle Eastern setting with nude women as subjects. A turn of an arm or of the head or a bit of curving flesh became sexually suggestive, rep-resenting the permissive East, a theme never far below the surface in such works. Languid women with fetching smiles, their nipples covered with see-through gauze, sans pubic hair, and reclining in inviting positions on com-fortable divans became staples of the Orientalist artistic repertoire; and in the works of artists less skilled than Gérôme, were the stuff of popular erotic art as well.

The opening of the Suez Canal in 1869 brought an increase in travel to the Middle East and Far East. Escapist adventure literature and art grew, as did sex tourism, such as Flaubert and Oscar Wilde wrote about. With the growing availability of cameras, postcards of overseas scenes came quickly to European markets, and postcards of nude women in Oriental settings were sold on Paris boulevards. Malek Alloula, an Algerian poet living in France, later catalogued such sexually explicit postcards of Algerian women taken during the early twentieth century.[27] Many women were shown in degrading poses, dressed in traditional garb but with breasts exposed, kept behind barred harem walls, forcibly looking longingly toward the camera.

Women in such harem photographs were given generic names like Fattmah or Mouquère ("Arab woman" and "prostitute"). Necks were craned, arms bent at unusual angles, while the subjects faked drinking coffee, or

Typical of Orientalist paintings of late-nineteenth-century European artists was this *Odalisque* (1870) by Auguste Renoir (1841–1919). The work contains usual themes for such works: a languid, sensual woman in an inviting pose, imprisoned in a harem as a slave or a concubine to a sultan. Powerful dark men dominating vulnerable white women represented one theme of Orientalist painting. (National Gallery of Art, Washington; Chester Dale Collection)

smoking cigarettes or a hookah—a water pipe rarely used in Algeria. Such crudely arranged photographs did not realistically represent Algerian life, but fed the sexual fantasies of a market of European viewers, reflecting the long-standing sexual underside of Islam's image in the West.

The harem or seraglio was a much-employed symbol in the art and poetry of this time; it was represented as a prison guarded by eunuchs or menacing black guards; inside it was a site where languorous, nearly naked white women guarded by Nubian slaves lounged about waiting for the sultan to take his pleasure. Victor Hugo described the opulent setting in *Les têtes du Sérail:*

> To the harem . . . that night it quivered joyously
> To the sound of gay drums, upon carpets of silk
> The Sultan's wives danced beneath its sacred dome,
> And, like a king bedecked with festive jewels,
> Superb, it revealed itself to the children of the Prophet.[28]

So numerous were the French Orientalist painters that by 1894 they organized a salon of their own works. The school continued after World War I, but soon it produced largely colonial art; after World War II it ceased to exist.[29]

"Woman in a Harem" could be the title for innumerable French late-nineteenth-century photographs. Many of these obviously posed photographs had sexual themes, such as women kept captive behind bars in a harem, or women permissively smoking, or partially undressed, suggesting "the wilder shores of Barbary." (From Malek Alloula, *The Colonial Harem* [Minneapolis: University of Minnesota Press, 1986])

As we enter the twentieth century, Etienne Dinet (1861–1929) represents the various strains of French Orientalist art. Dinet spent almost forty-five years moving between France and Algeria, and was a skilled realist given to intricate detail and obvious message. After his wife's death, the artist lived for many years in the village of Bou Saada in Algeria's south among the Ouled Nail people. He learned Arabic, converted to Islam, made the hajj to Mecca, and produced detailed canvasses about local life, *Tableaux de la vie arabe* (Scenes of Arab Life, 1908), as many of the works were called. His paintings and drawings contained not only arresting portrayals of religious subjects, like *Imam Leading the Prayer: "At Tahia"* (1921), but erotic subjects as well, as in *Au Ouled Nail* (1906), where a lightly clad woman with beckoning eyes stands on a lush stream bank, fingering a phallic-like branch, delicately covering her crotch with a bejeweled hand and thin veil.

Among the most successful of Dinet's canvasses was a painting of his longtime friend and interpreter, *Sliman ben Ibrahim at the Place de la Concorde* (before 1908). The artist's Algerian companion was pictured caught in a Paris winter storm with Napoleon's obelisk at the Place de la Concorde in the background, an early study of a subject trapped between cultures.[30]

Henri Matisse (1869–1954) visited North Africa in 1906, 1912, and 1913. Like other European artists, he had an eye for North African light, color, and shapes, and in his visits to Morocco Matisse found subjects and themes that he reworked throughout his career. Rugs, opulent interiors, and lush vegetation appeared in works like *Moroccan Garden* (1912) and *Landscape Viewed from a Window* (1912–1913). His Tangiers art contained only hints of North African design and setting in works like *The Standing Riffian* (1912) and *Zora on the Terrace* (1912–1913). Matisse painted a number of odalisques, mostly in his Nice studio, for nude models were hard to come by in North Africa. Matisse described Algeria as a wrecked country, "vile, disgusted, ugly."[31] As for Morocco, Matisse said little; his impressions of it were influenced by being stuck for a month and a half in a small Tangiers hotel room during the rainy season, something he and his wife spoke of for years afterward.[32]

Orientalism in British Arts and Letters

Contradictions were numerous in British images of Islam that evolved during the nineteenth century. And not all of the steady outpouring of literature and art on the Orient was received enthusiastically. When a new edition of William Henry Bartlett's *Footsteps of Our Lord and His Apostles* appeared in 1851, a jaded critic for *Tait's Edinburgh Magazine* wrote: "Once more the east! the everlasting east! that standing dish of literary cookery, which is forever being served up till it ceases to gratify the mental palate or nourish the intellectual stomach. Let us suppose we read only a few of these all but daily Oriental productions. Alas! We read them all! Yes: there they are: the same Arabs, camels, deserts, tombs and jackals that we journeyed with, rode on. Traversed, dived into and cursed respectively, only a week ago, with some other travelers."[33]

In the vanguard of those who found good things to say about Islam was the popular writer-lecturer Thomas Carlyle (1795–1881). On Friday, May 8, 1840, he gave a much-heralded talk in his London series, *On Heroes, Hero-Worship, and the Heroic in History*. The lecture's subject was "The Hero as Prophet. Mahomet: Islam" and it soon earned a place in history as the first major public presentation of its kind unqualifiedly supportive of Islam and the Prophet.

This was an age of heroes in literature, and Carlyle had chosen Frederick the Great, Napoleon, Shakespeare, Luther, and Carlyle's fellow Scotsman, Robert Burns, for other places in his pantheon. Carlyle's hero was a person of vision, who saw through the confines of gross materialism around him, creating new hope for humanity, and becoming a lasting figure in the process. Picking heroes was risky business; Carlyle solved it by calculating the endurance of a hero's memory as well as the length of time the hero had been dead. Muhammad was a safe choice; he had both cast a long shadow and been dead for centuries. For Carlyle, Muhammad was neither a heretic nor an imposter, but a legitimate world religious leader:

> The word this man spoke has been the life-guidance now of a hundred-and-eighty millions of men these twelve-hundred years. A greater number of God's creatures believes in Mahomet's word at this hour than in any other word whatever. Are we to suppose that it was a miserable piece of spiritual legerdemain, this which so many creatures of the Almighty have lived by and died by? I, for my part, cannot form any such supposition. A false man found a religion? Why, a false man cannot build a brick house! It will not stand for twelve centuries, to lodge a hundred-and-eighty millions; it will fall straightaway.[34]

Carlyle praised Muhammad's sincerity, and described his history, personality, and teachings. But he called the Koran "a most wearisome confused jumble," yet one worth pursuing, for it showed "the confused ferment of a great rude human soul."[35] Muhammad was an ascetic who subsisted on barleybread and water several months at a time, lived frugally, and mended his own shoes. The author closed his talk with these words: "The Great Man was always as lightening out of Heaven; the rest of men waited for him like fuel, and then they too would flame."

Carlyle was pleased with the response: "I gave my second lecture yesterday to a larger audience than ever, and with all the success, or more, than was necessary for me. It was on Mahomet. I had bishops and all kinds of people among my hearers. I gave them to know that the poor Arab had points about him which it were good for all of them to imitate; that probably *they* were more of quacks than he. The people seemed greatly astonished and greatly pleased."[36]

An opposite point of view was expounded by John Henry Newman (1801–1890), remembered for his conversion to Roman Catholicism, the hymn "Lead, Kindly Light," and his sermons while still a leading Anglican cleric at St. Mary the Virgin Church, Oxford. As a child, Newman remembered, he had wished the magic stories of the *Arabian Nights* were true, but as an adult he had nothing favorable to say about Islam in *The Turks in Their Relation to Europe,* nine lectures Newman gave at the Catholic Institute of Liverpool in October 1853. Newman's Turks were the original Evil Empire, and he hoped they would be "surrounded, pressed upon, divided, decimated, driven into the desert by the force of civilization."[37]

As a writer, Newman invites comparison with Gibbon, whom he sometimes cited, and in omniscience of viewpoint Newman presented Turkish history with magisterial sweep but inaccurate information. His categories of civilization versus barbarism, North versus South, tropical versus temperate climates, were ones imaginative writers had employed since the Middle Ages. "Science, literature and art refuse to germinate in the frost, and are burnt up by the sun" (Lecture 3.5.31), Newman reported.

The lectures were set against the backdrop of the Crimean War, a new crusade against the Turks, who Newman said had been a threat to Europe since at least the eleventh century. Civilized Europe was called to rescue the barbarous East. The Turks were "the enemy of God and Man" but could only menace a divided Europe that had deserted Catholicism and the pope: "The terrible races which I have been describing, like those giants of old, have ever been enemies of God and persecutors of His Church. Celts, Goths, Lombards, Franks, have all been converted, and their descendents to this day are Christian; but, whether we consider Huns, Monguls, or Turks, up to this time they are in the outer darkness."[38] Newman made a distinction between Islamic Turks and Arabs, and the latter came out a bit more favorably. If the Turkish caliphate was the capital of barbarism, its Arab counterpart was once a source of leading philosophers and scientists before its various factions fell on one another in Cordova, Cairo, and Baghdad.[39] Predictably, Newman recalled the Crusades with nostalgia, but in a curiously inaccurate twist said they represented Christian European warfare against the Turks, not the Arabs.

The Turks' political flaws were inextricably linked to Islam, that is, a warlike temperament, polygamy, and a corrupt, decadent court antithetical to centuries of scientific and humanistic progress. Still, Islam was not all bad in Newman's schema. It stood at a crossroads, a halfway point between paganism and Christianity. Other Eastern superstitions were far worse than Islam, but compared to Christianity, its adherents were "preachers of a lie, and enemies, not witnesses of God."[40] His final thunderbolts were that Islam's deficiencies were the same as Protestantism's; both were stern, cold, legalistic, and fatalistic religions.[41] Newman's study of the Turks was deeply flawed by both an almost total dependence on inaccurate sources and by bending history, geography, ethnography, and religion to all favor a single thesis—the need for papal supremacy.

By the mid-nineteenth century, the lines of future Western interpretations of Islam were clearly in place. Source materials were now available in Arabic and other Middle Eastern languages, and translations of the Koran and of other documents became increasingly accessible. How was Islam to be interpreted? Basically in two contrasting schools, represented by Sir William Muir and Charles Forster. Muir wrote about 1857, "the sword of Mahomet and the Koran are the most fatal enemies of civilization, liberty, and the truth which the world has yet known."[42] Forster was more moderate, accepting that Islam was a "spiritual religion," albeit a lesser one than Christianity. Still, Muslims "discovered themselves in a reality of belief, a fervor of zeal and a sincerity of devotion which, it has often been remarked, might put to shame the majority of the Christian world."[43] Muir, for all his erudition, would concede no ground, arguing Islam's benefits were few and its debits many. Forster, though maintaining Muhammad was the Antichrist, foresaw a day when the two great religions would somehow converge. Nearly two centuries later these two positions remain, representing opposing camps in Christian contact with Islam.

Sir William Muir (1819–1905) was a high-ranking officer in the Indian Civil Service, Anglican evangelical lay leader, and author of numerous books on Islam. He belonged to the long tradition of British military and civil administrators who, with time on their hands in isolated duty stations, studied local languages and customs. While in India as lieutenant governor of the Northwest Provinces, where he spent over thirty years, he learned Arabic, Urdu, and Persian, and wrote a popular *Life of Mahomet* (1861). Muir's life reflected the paradoxes many colonial administrators faced: he was attracted to the Arabic language and local cultures and had a growing circle of Muslim friends, yet in his religious and political convictions he denigrated Islamic beliefs and institutions. While British government policy was officially neutral on religions, individual officers like Muir supported the work of British missionaries. Muir wrote, "Britain must not faint until her millions in the East abandon both the false prophet and the idol shrines and rally around the eternal truth which has been brought to light in the Gospel."[44] Islam was a dark apostasy. "Could the counsels of the Evil One have devised any more perfect plan for frustrating the Gospel and grace of God?"[45] Of the Koran, he said it was written "in wild and incoherent rhapsodies couched in words of rare force and beauty, with such force and beauty as the Arabs love." He admired the young Muhammad, a searcher for truth, but when the Prophet later spoke in the name of God it was "high blasphemy."[46]

Charles Forster (1787–1871), grandfather of the novelist E. M. Forster, knew Muir's works but approached Islam in a less hostile manner. Forster envisioned the eventual convergence of the two great religions, although Islam was clearly the lesser faith. Like others engaged in the Catholic–Protestant duel of his day, he believed that both the pope and the Prophet Muhammad were Antichrists.

An Irish cleric of wide-ranging interests, Forster became a parish priest in Kent and Essex. Impressionistic rather than systematic in thought, Forster belonged to no theological camp. Concerned that much available literature on the Prophet was crudely prejudicial, he set out to write a factual life of Muhammad, *Mahometanism Unveiled* (1829). The extended title told the book's story. It was *An Inquiry in Which That Arch-Heresy, Its Diffusion and Continuance, Are Examined on a New Principle, Tending to Confirm the Evidences and Aid the Propagation of the Christian Faith.*

Forster believed that Islam would eventually return to the Christian fold. Ahead was "one great consummation—the glorious fulfillment of the twofold covenant of God with Abraham, in its social and intellectual aspect, by the eventual reunion of his sons Isaac and Ishmael as joint civilizers of the world," the ingathering of all peoples foretold in Isaiah 60. Forster explained the rapidity of Islam's rise and spread despite its obscure origins "in a dark age, among a wild and ignorant people" in a political setting of "extreme hostility and internal dissension. . . . But some remarkable features of Mahometanism there questionably are," he wrote, and "criticisms unfavorable to the Mahometan system have been too frequently deduced, under the palpable influence of groundless and sometimes contradictory impressions."[47] Forster saw Islam as resilient, surviving and adapting in countries hostile to it. Christianity and Islam endured, based on God's twofold promise to Abraham, which left a blessing with both Abraham's sons, Isaac and Ishmael. The result was that, after Christianity and Judaism, "Mahometanism with all its errors and absurdities [is] the best and most beneficial form of religion that has ever been presented in the world."[48] The two religions have commendable features in common: "One day the moon of Mahomet resigning its borrowed rays [will] melt in the undivided light of the everlasting Gospel."[49]

A more subtle voice, a harbinger of modern pluralism, also emerged at this time. Few nineteenth-century figures have been more provocative in their widespread religious views than Frederick Denison Maurice (1805–1872), whose writings on world religions, Christian socialism, biblical studies, and philosophy defy categorization. A Unitarian who joined the Church of England at age twenty-six, Maurice was dismissed from his position as professor of divinity at King's College, London, in 1853 for holding heretical views—he urged people to reject the doctrine of eternal punishment for sinners. Maurice started a Working Man's College, helped found Queen's College for the education of women, and was an early advocate for the rights of workers to better salaries, hours, and working conditions. Maurice often employed archeological metaphors; he called himself a "digger" rather than a "builder."[50] The universal Christ had been present in all ages, and Muhammad was an authentic witness of God in Maurice's thought. The spread of Islam, far from threatening Christianity, represented a testimony of "God's overlordship of the earth."[51] He wrote, "You say that Islamism has not fallen before the Cross. No, but Islamism has become one of God's witnesses for the Cross when those who pretended to hear it had really changed it for another standard."[52]

Maurice's views on world religions were published in a short survey, *The Religions of the World and Their Relations to Christianity,* based on a set of 1846 lectures at King's College, London. The manuscript contained only a few pages about Islam, and Maurice never returned to the subject, leaving many possible avenues of exploration incomplete. An oft-discussed question in this heyday of British imperialism was the relationship of religion and empire. Once more, Maurice turned a question on its ear, to the irritation of some and the puzzlement of others. He sought to free Christianity from its institutional and political constraints through the uniting figure of a loving Christ, who he believed was experienced internally in the heart of believers rather than institutionally. He asked: "Might not particular soils be adapted to particular religions? Might not a better day be at hand, in which all religions alike should be found to have done their work of partial good, of greater evil, and when something much more comprehensive and satisfactory should supercede them?"[53]

As for Islam, Maurice systematically rejected the idea that Muhammad was an imposter or that Islam was a deformation of biblical religion. Islam represented the reassertion of the divine presence in history and served the valuable purpose of calling Christians back to the fundamentals of their faith. Maurice believed the Koran was a book of "just and benevolent sentiment" and Muhammad was "one of the great governing and leavening minds of the world."[54] Nevertheless, Islam represented a flawed belief system that offered not hope of progress but "broken, divided, superstitious schemes for propitiating an unwilling and ungracious Being."[55] Absent Christ's divine love, Islam mirrored a once "noble witness of a Personal Being" (Muhammad) now turned "into the worship of a dead necessity."[56] In short, Maurice offered a wider, more encompassing vision of world religions, but Islam fit into such a schema in only a limited way, because of the rigidity of some of its teachings.

Maurice was a precursor of modern pluralists; he looked systematically at the depths of other religions, and tried to accommodate them, while retaining his own Christian faith, concluding, "The grandeur of the Crescent can be understood by the light which falls upon it from the Cross," because Muslims "will not admit that there has been a Man in the world who was one with God— a Man who exercised power over nature, and yet whose main glory consisted of giving up Himself."[57]

Maurice's younger contemporary Sir Richard Francis Burton (1821–1890) was the adventurous prototype of what T. E. Lawrence would later become, a figure on the establishment's margins who calculatingly railed against it. As such, he was neither the first nor the last Oxbridge student to be expelled, join the army, and seek his future in the overseas world, while writing lively accounts of his adventures.

Burton was most remembered for his 1853 trip to Mecca, disguised as a Sufi mystic "Persian Prince" and, in later years for his sexually explicit translations of the *Arabian Nights* (1885–1886) and other erotic classics. Fluent in twenty-five languages, but with an obvious British accent in the spoken ones, Burton was spurred by a Royal Geographic Society offer of two thousand pounds to explore the interior of Arabia. He arranged for a year's leave of absence from his employer, the British East India Company, and set out from Cairo via the Red Sea for Mecca. Burton's overseas activities were always calculated to give him maximum publicity at home, and his *Personal Narrative of a Pilgrimage to Al-Medinah and Meccah* (1855) sold well and created a following for the author. Had he converted to Islam, Burton could have silently joined thousands of pilgrims making the hajj annually. But that would have placed him beyond the boundaries of Victorian society and been of no interest to the public. Instead, he first spent time in Cairo and Alexandria presenting himself as a Persian prince, then as a healer and vendor of medical tonics, born of Afghani parents in India but raised in Burma. His disguise was convincing, at least to himself, and Burton wrote of being "still dressed nigger fashion," allowing him easier sexual access in Egypt than if had dressed as a British officer.[58]

As it would be for Lawrence, the desert was a powerful attraction for Burton, a place of naked purity in contrast to the "hypocritical politeness and the slavery of civilization" left behind in the city.[59] The English author made a favorable case for Islam; it was no more superstitious than Christianity, he said. Polygamy, veiling, and the harem allowed Muslim women freedoms Western women could not know. Polygamy did not promote lust, he argued, and actually made social and economic sense in tribal societies. Though not a declared member of any faith, Burton respected Islam. Writing from Mecca, he said, "I have seen the religious ceremonies of many lands, but never—nowhere—aught so solemn, so impressive as this."[60]

Burton's later life was spent in a string of marginal overseas Foreign Office consular assignments, including the offshore island of Fernando Po in West Africa, the interior of Brazil, a brief, unsuccessful tour in Damascus, and a final seventeen years of isolation in Trieste. He wrote fifty books, became a vice president of the Anthropological Society, and was knighted for lifetime achievement. Many of his works were a mixture of keen observation, lively writing, and the racism of his time and place.

In later life, Burton focused his energies on translating sexual works such as the *Kama Sutra* from Sanskrit and *The Book of the Thousand Nights and One* from Arabic (1885–1886) in ten volumes, followed in 1886–1888 by a six-volume supplement. His translations included detailed footnotes on sexual customs and a closing article on homosexuality in different cultures, causing one critic to remark "Gallard for the nursery, Lane for the library, Payne for the study, and Burton for the sewers."[61] Burton had been working on the translations for several years, and their publication in the 1880s was tied to meeting a growing underground Victorian market for sexual subjects. The author presented the *Nights* as fantasy escapist literature, often erotic in content but also demonstrating access to truths and cultural insights European society would otherwise have left unexamined.[62] A commercial and critical success, Burton's *Nights* went through several editions and remained in print over a century after being originally issued in a private subscription series.

Some seventy years before Burton published his *Nights,* Lord George Gordon Byron's *Turkish Tales,* published in Great Britain between 1813 and 1816, had presented a tolerant, humane portrait of Islam. Byron (1788–1824), nonjudgmental and ahead of his time, saw the common humanity of both Muslims and Christians. Religious beliefs and customs may differ, but human attributes were similar, Byron seemed to say; he was first of all a story-teller, with little interest in theology, but for him Islamic imagery retained a lively interest.

In 1809 the twenty-one-year-old Byron set out on a two-year grand tour of Portugal, Spain, Albania, Greece, Turkey, and the Mediterranean. He had been reading about the East since childhood, and was especially fascinated with Turkish history and culture. "I can't empty my head of the East," he wrote."[63] Elsewhere he spoke of "the brightest and darkest, but always most lively colors" of the Orient.[64] Byron was among the most observant writers of his generation in portraying the flavor of the countries he visited. He spent time at major archeological sites, marveled at the natural splendor of landscapes, and wandered endlessly through cities like Istanbul and Smyrna. Battling chilly waters and strong currents, he swam across the Hellespont from Europe to Asia in an hour and ten minutes, a defining event in his adventurous life. In the East, Byron found the opposite of the constraints of British society, and at a time when his poetic skills were reaching full maturity, it provided him with some of his richest imagery.

Byron, with a jeweler's eye, added to the English language Arabic, Turkish, and Persian expressions ranging from a few obvious religious terms like "Allah" and "Bishmillah" to "gazelle," "camel," and "bread and salt." The Indian scholar Abdur Raheem Kidwai, in an exhaustive study of the sources of Byron's Islamic imagery, mentioned over a hundred such words and expressions.[65]

Byron filled "The Giaour" (1813) with Oriental images, the crescent moon announcing the beginning of a new lunar month, the mosque illuminated at night by lamps, muskets (tophaike) being fired to celebrate the end of Ramadan (Rhamazani), and the start of the Bairam festival after Ramadan with the firing of canon.

> The crescent glimmers on the hill,
> The Mosque's high lamps are quivering still;
> Though too remote for sound to wake,
> In echoes of the far tophaike,
> The flashes of each joyous peal
> Are seen to prove the Moslem's zeal.
> Tonight—set Rhamazani's sun—
> Tonight—the Bairam feast's begun. (222–229)[66]

Byron's *Turkish Tales* moved beyond classical Christian–Muslim stereotypes and plots. His Christians were not triumphalists; like his Muslims they were more caught in humanity's web than they were mouthpieces of their respective doctrinal camps. It was human greed, lust, and evil that caused conflict, rather than religion, Byron believed.[67]

No nineteenth-century writer in English did more to advance a favorable image of Islam and the chivalrous Saladin than Sir Walter Scott (1771–1832), especially in his novel *The Talisman* (1825). Scott had read *The Arabian Nights* as a youth and his imaginative East resembled the lush Orient of Byron's works. Set during the fall of Jerusalem in 1187, *The Talisman* depicted Saladin as a wise, temperate hero whose adversary, Richard the Lion Hearted, represented the West's decadence and tyranny. The book never became a best-seller but opened a favorable window on the study of Islam. An enthusiastic later advocate was Sir Hamilton Gibb. Like Scott, Gibb was a graduate of Edinburgh's Royal High School. He was also a leading historian of Islam whose articles about Saladin the statesman were important to future generations of students of Islam.

English Artists of the Holy Land and Middle East

British Oriental art differed from French art; British artists were more drawn to topographical art, illustrating the lands of the biblical landscape rather than portraying the strictly exotic or militarily triumphant. David Roberts (1796–1864) spent nearly a year sailing the Nile and trekking through the Holy Land in 1838–1839, sketching or painting temples and landscapes. He returned to become one of Britain's best-known artists of the Middle East. Roberts blamed Egyptian indolence and the Muslim religion for creating a country "reduced by mismanagement and the barbarism of the Muslim creed to a state as savage as wild animals by which they are surrounded."[68] A stage-set designer by training, Robert's spacious, carefully planned works attracted a British public; he was responding to both "Egyptomania" and the growing demand for visual representations of the "land where Jesus walked." Roberts was in the tradition of John Martin (1789–1854), a painter of crowd-pleasing biblical tales with obvious messages and titles like *The Fall of Babylon* (1819) and *Belshazzar's Feast* (1821). Most of Roberts's works were vast landscapes composed on a dramatic scale, with contrasting light and shadow—works of desert grandeur, sweeping vistas, and imposing temples. Sumptuously produced books of his colored lithographs provided a generation of midcentury British viewers with their first impressions of the Middle East.[69]

Few of the artists and travel writers had more than the most superficial understanding of the politics of the countries they visited. Those who traveled to Egypt seemed unaware that many of the country's problems originated not with Islam but with the despotic Ottoman ruler Muhammad Ali. What a biographer wrote about Roberts could equally apply to a generation of British artists: "Among the Muslims he met, he had genuinely liked several, but it is impossible to ignore his apparently total misunderstanding of the Islamic world. His sometimes violent comments on the subject should be regarded only as in accord with pretty well all the other superficial English travelers of that era. He simply did not have the time then, nor the desire, to learn, judge and inwardly understand. He had gone to draw, and that he did superbly."[70]

Roberts's contemporary, Edward Lane (1801–1876), was a professional artist and engraver and author of a much-acclaimed *Account of the Manners and Customs of the Modern Egyptians* (1835) based on an earlier trip to Egypt. Lane carried with him one of the recently invented camera lucidas, portable light and lens projectors that allowed an image to be accurately magnified and projected onto a surface, where it could be accurately copied. At the same time, in this era just before motion pictures, English artists produced large panoramic paint-

Egyptian Hall, Piccadilly, 1828. Egyptian, Moorish, and other Middle Eastern–type buildings, mostly theaters or exhibition halls, appeared in many British and American cities during the nineteenth century. As travel increased, photography improved, and travel publications proliferated. A corresponding interest in such imagery became widespread in Europe and America. (Thomas Hosmer Shepherd, "Egyptian Hall in Piccadilly," June 7, 1828 [engraving]. A. McCarthy, engraver, Jones and Company, publisher, Museum of London)

ings in storytelling sequences. Awed publics came to see them in sites such as the Leicester Square Panorama.[71] Stereoscopes and the spread of inexpensive prints helped fuel a market for artists using Holy Land themes; so did the spread of lantern slides, Christmas cards, and Sunday school pamphlets and award publications. Inexpensive Bibles, many of them illustrated, became widely available, and in 1854 a British art publication jested, "the Holy Land was better known in England than the English lakes."[72]

When the British artist William Holman Hunt (1827–1910) sat by the Dead Sea, paint brush in one hand, rifle in the other, to both capture the Holy Land's scenic beauty and ward off local intruders, he reflected the binary view many Europeans held toward the Middle East as a place of mystery and hostility.[73] The work of several artists like Hunt portrayed biblical subjects in careful Middle Eastern settings, complete with period costumes, headgear, and various metal objects. Eventually photography assumed this task of biblical illustration.

Islam and the Music of Empire

In no form of expression was it easier to create impressions of the exotic Orient than through music. Islam as subject matter was a secondary theme in the music of empire, but a periodically identifiable one. The cantata *On Sea and Shore* by Sir Arthur Sullivan (1842–1900) was about war and loss in a conflict between Genoa and the Moors of North Africa, a message that fit easily in Victorian England. A Moorish orchestral interlude, a Muslim chorus, and a sung call to prayer came early in the work. Not to be outdone, the chained Genoese galley slaves sang, "Hold to Christian manhood, firm in Christian faith / Faithful hearts make fearless hands, and faithful hearts have we / The Christian 'gainst the infidel, chained though we be." Then they revolted, seized the ship, and sailed joyfully back to England.[74]

In no setting was the idea of empire more reinforced than in English music-hall songs and Protestant hymns (and likewise in French music-hall songs). Through lively melodies and singable choruses, audiences were captivated and nationalistic sentiments reinforced in both countries. In this the songs represented a mirror of the ordinary person's sentiments about the oversea world, a carefully constructed world of English (or French) superiority, military prowess, *mission civilisatrice,* and *noblesse oblige.* As might be expected, English hymns of the *Onward, Christian Soldiers* category echoed royalist, imperialist, and military sentiments as well. No such work was more representative than Reginald Heber's *From Greenland's Icy Mountains* (1819), which took only twenty minutes to write but endured for over a century as the signature missionary hymn:

> From Greenland's icy mountains,
> From India's coral strand,
> Where Afric's sunny fountains
> Roll down their golden sand,
> From many an ancient river,
> From many a palmy plain,
> They call us to deliver,
> Their land from error's chain.[75]

The exoticism of the Middle East and North Africa was likewise a constant theme in French music, as in George Bizet's one-act opera *Djamileh* (1872), the story of a slave girl purchased in a Cairo market to please an indolent, self-indulgent prince, Haroun, who changed mistresses every lunar month. Djamileh charmed him with a slow, sensual dance, and Haroun fell in love with her. A chorus of Nile boatmen sang, and an Egyptian plot, costumes, and scenes reworked traditional Orientalist themes of the sort Edward Said found most objectionable.[76]

America: The Holy Land without Arabs

Since the Crusades, the Holy Land had been a lodestone for European Christians, who sought the supposed sites of Christ's life and death, even if few such locations were ever authenticated. Gradually a substantial body of devotional pilgrim's literature developed, much of it allegorical in nature. And in the nineteenth century, the Roman Catholic Church preferred to attract pilgrims to Rome, where the successor to Christ lived in the Vatican, instead of having them scatter about the multiple cities of the Middle East. Evangelicals visiting the Holy Land showed little interest in Islam; for one thing, Islam was not mentioned in the Bible, so it remained a subject of marginal interest to Protestants. Most of the accounts were less about the geographic Holy Land and more about what might be called the Holy Land in peoples' minds. Also, because Ottoman law forbade subjects converting to Christianity, a crime punishable by death, most missionary groups in the Middle East concentrated their work on Eastern Christian communities or Jews.

This Holy Land of nineteenth-century popular Protestant imagery was a tranquil, uncluttered setting. Its undisturbed low hills were free of tumult and conflict; only a few Jews appeared in written accounts and paintings to add local color, and rarely did a Muslim appear. Such "foreigners," when mentioned, were usually busy at agriculture, raising animals, or engaged in colorful local trades, but otherwise they kept out of the way. "We know far more about the land of the Jews than the degraded Arabs who hold it," a magazine writer said of the Holy Land in 1855.[77] More a mental than a geographical construct, this Holy Land was basically any part of the Middle East linked to the Bible, cartographically following the motto of the Jerusalem YMCA that "Where the feet of Jesus have trod is the Holy Land."[78]

Artists produced panoramas of the Holy Land. Church sandboxes and gardens in America replicated its landscapes, and scaled-down reproductions of its features were built at missionary gathering places like the Palestine Park at the Chautauqua Assembly in New York state. A few Muslims appeared in tableaux vivants at the Assembly's "Oriental House," where the call to prayer was chanted twice a day in season, and an "Oriental Funeral Service" was depicted on stage, with wailing women and mourners circling the stage and beating their breasts. At the 1904 St. Louis World's Fair an elaborate Jerusalem exhibit covered eleven acres and contained over three hundred buildings set

The lectures, lantern slides, and travel books of John L. Stoddard aroused the curiosity of late-nineteenth-century Americans about the overseas world. The copiously illustrated lecture books depicted scenes like (clockwise from top): "Between Stanboul and Galata," "A Turkish Lady," "An Arab at Prayer," and "An Egyptian Sheik." (From *John L. Stoddard's Lectures*, vol. 2 [Boston: Balch Brothers, 1898])

along twenty-two streets. The cast of characters included "Turkish cavalry, Rabbis, dealers of Assyria, Arabia, Jews, Moslems, Christians, and the hoi polloi of that life."[79]

As reverence for the almost mystical Holy Land landscape grew, Jews and Arabs continued to have little place in it beyond providing local color, and became ready subjects of negative comment. "They are entirely out of harmony with the character of the land," an American photographer said of the "repulsive peasants" he photographed living near the Sea of Galilee.[80] And in hundreds of captions in the photographic work *Earthly Footsteps*, Arabs were described as predatory and lawless. Islam was "organized sensualism"; its adherents "have reduced begging to a science."[81]

So it went, and the writings of American missionaries from the "degenerative Orient" were no more favorable to Islam. Henry Harris Jessup, an American Presbyterian, spent fifty-three years in Syria and Lebanon (1857–1910). He documented familiar charges against Islam from his own "I was there" accounts. Women were "slanderous, capricious, never trained to control their tempers. The rod, the scourge is the only instrument of discipline. Women are treated like animals, and behave like animals." Elsewhere Jessup wrote what had become a theme to his extensive and unchanging comments on Islam, "The good works of Islam are of the lips, the hands, and the outward bodily act, having no connection with holiness of life, honesty, veracity, and integrity."[82] There was always something defective about Islam; if not its beliefs, then it was the flawed human beings who espoused them. Its adherents ranged from the duplicitous to the ignorant. Although some late-nineteenth-century missionary writers were more tolerant and informed about Islam, their influence would not register among Western readers for decades.

The real or mental pilgrimage to the Holy Land became a staple of Protestant thought, traceable at least to John Bunyan's *The Pilgrim's Progress* (1678–1684). The pilgrim, Christian, representing humanity, trod through the Valley of the Shadow of Death to the Celestial City (also called Mount Zion), the Promised Land, and the Land of Milk and Honey. Both English and Americans braided their political journeys into these religious pilgrimages, reinforced by heroes like General Charles Gordon of Khartoum (1833–1885), who spent his vacation in the Holy Land, using his Bible as a geographic guide. An outpouring of Zion and Canaan hymns reinforced the imagery of the "green hill far away," and the building of a new Jerusalem in "England's bright and pleasant land."

Naturally this new vision of the Holy Land was accompanied by an outpouring of hymns with titles like "I Walk Today Where Jesus Walked" and James Montgomery's "Hail to the Lord's Anointed" (1821), whose third verse has been discreetly retired from later hymnals:

> Arabia's desert-ranger
> To him shall bow the knee
> the Ethiopian stranger
> His glory come to see.

And ending with:

> Kings shall fall down before him,
> And gold and incense bring,
> All nations shall adore him,
> His praise all people sing.[83]

In reality, the Holy Land had been under nominal Ottoman Turkish control since at least the sixteenth century, administered through a string of loosely autonomous local governors, sanjaks. Christians, especially in Jerusalem, enjoyed a large measure of autonomy. But American travelers generally were oblivious to the Ottoman presence, which they regarded as an irritant at best.

One of the few mid-nineteenth-century Christian travel writers interested in Islam was Bayard Taylor, a popular American circuit lecturer, who greeted small-town audiences in flowing Arabic robes and turban, and employed colorful props like water pipes and scimitars. Taylor spent ten months in Egypt in 1851 and sent home travel letters to the *New York Tribune*. Collected as *The Lands of the Saracen*, they became the most widely circulating travel account of biblical lands in mid-century America.[84] Taylor's work was not particularly religious, but the author had an eye for the colorful, "the standard Orientalist subjects of baths, hashish, and the deserts of the Nile," and he had the popular lecturer's skill in whetting the appetites of Protestant middle-class audiences.[85] As steamship travel became a reality, many would tour the Holy Land, returning with vials of water from the River Jordan for baptisms and Roman coins for parlor "whatnot" cabinets.

The Holy Land connection had also become a passport to American exceptionalism, providing a religious raison d'être for the imperialistic ideology then in formation. Interest in Islam had spread to North America in the eighteenth century, inflamed by the raids of Barbary pirates, as I discuss below. The New England preacher Cotton Mather (1663–1728), minister at Boston's North Church, for instance, had nothing good to say about Islam, and in two sermons vividly pictured the Barbary pirates as satanic agents against helpless Christian captives. The pirates were "Hellish Pirates," "the Monsters of Africa," originating with the "Powers of Darkness."[86]

Several lines of thought were at work here. Mather called Massachusetts Governor John Winthrop "Governor Israel." English kings were "Pharaohs,"

George Washington was "Moses," and like others he saw Americans building a new Jerusalem in their country, an American Zion. Over a thousand American towns were given biblical names such as Bethlehem, Canaan, Jericho, Bethany, or Zion. Such "shining city on the hill" imagery, often employed by early American writers, endured, and in recent times has become a staple of Republican presidential speechwriters of the Reagan and Bush eras. It was given full expression in a section on the influence of Puritanism in Samuel Eliot Morison's Oxford History of the American People (1965): "Little Ali, who attends a missionary school and goes on to Robert College in Istanbul, got his chance for an education because little John and Elihu in the colonial era attended Boston Latin or the Hopkins Grammar and went on to Harvard or Yale. And Ali's right to vote and be elected to the Turkish parliament owes much to the fact that Englishmen in New England and Virginia managed to make representative government work."[87]

If one main source of American impressions of the Muslim world in the nineteenth century was the Holy Land, then the other was the Barbary pirates; a leading diplomatic historian of the United States called them "as ruffianly a lot of cutthroats as history can offer."[88] The Barbary pirates, who probably seized more than a million Europeans as slaves, as noted in an earlier chapter, were America's first major overseas national security problem. From about 1785 to 1815 the United States, seeking to open the Mediterranean to commerce, warred with the governments in Morocco, Algeria, Tunisia, and Libya over their state-sponsored piracy. The key issue was payment of ransom for captured ships, sailors, and tribute, the maritime equivalent of protection money, something the United States opposed—hence the popular slogan "Millions for defense, not one cent for tribute." In March 1794 Congress created an American navy of six frigates, and in the following year authorized almost a million dollars, the largest single item in the young nation's budget, as tribute and ransom payments to the Dey of Algeria.[89] Later, in 1801, the American ship Enterprise defeated a Tripolitanian vessel, and the United States promptly declared victory. A play, The Tripolitanian Prize (1802), celebrated the triumph, and a popular novel, History of the Captivity and Suffering of Mrs. Maria Martin (1807), told another fictional story about a vulnerable white woman captured by a menacing Turk. John Riley's lurid Authentic Narrative (1817) sold over a million copies in twenty-eight editions.[90]

And in 1805, as the American troops were returning, Francis Scott Key wrote a patriotic song, "When the Warrior Returns," to a well-known British drinking song "Anacreon in Heaven." He used the tune again in 1814 for "The Star Spangled Banner." The original lyrics contained this verse:

In conflict resistless each toil they endured
Till their foes shrunk dismayed from the war's desolation:
And pale beamed the Crescent, its splendor obscured
By the light of the star-spangled flag of our nation.
Where each flaming star gleamed a meteor of war,
And the turbaned heads bowed to the terrible glare.
Then mixt with the olive the laurel shall wave,
And form a bright wreath for the brow of the brave.[91]

American Writers

No nineteenth-century writer did more to create an interest in Islam as a subject for Americans than Washington Irving (1783–1859), best known for a string of popular early fictional works including "The Legend of Sleepy Hollow" and "Rip Van Winkle." Irving arrived in Madrid in 1826 on a diplomatic assignment, was intrigued with Moorish Spain, and by 1827 began writing *Life of Mohammed,* an overripe work of pure invention, a boldly drawn portrait filled with long-circulating legends about Muhammad. Irving's was a deeply melancholic work, unlike the growing stream of religious travel writing of his time. True male followers of Muhammad, Irving wrote, believed they would "rise from the grave in the prime of manhood, at the age of thirty, of the stature of Adam" with all their "faculties improved to preternatural perfection, with the abilities of a hundred men, and with desires and appetites quickened rather than sated by enjoyment."[92] How is it that Muhammad, the industrious worker, wise teacher, and skilled organizer, became such a changed person, a cruel despot in later life? "We find no other satisfactory mode of solving the enigma of his character and conduct," Irving wrote, "than by supposing that the ray of mental hallucination which flashed upon his enthusiastic spirit during his religious ecstasies in the midnight cavern of Mount Hira, continued more or less to bewilder him to the end of his career, and that he died in the delusive belief of his mission as a prophet."[93]

Ralph Waldo Emerson (1803–1882) dabbled in Eastern imagery during his long career as poet, Unitarian cleric, and religious writer in midcentury New England. He had read the *Arabian Nights* as a young person and Gibbon's *History of the Decline and Fall of the Roman Empire* with its generally favorable history of Muhammad and the Arabs. Shortly after graduation from college he wrote in 1822, "I was the pampered child of the East. I was born where the soft western gale breathed upon me fragrance of cinnamon groves, and through the seventy windows of my hall the eye fell on the Arabian harvest."[94]

After he had left Boston's Second Church in a doctrinal dispute in 1832, Emerson made his living as a lecturer and writer, and often employed Islamic illustrative material in his plea for greater understanding and wider horizons by American audiences. During a trip to England, Emerson met Thomas Carlyle, who had written about the Prophet Muhammad as a hero—a theme Emerson echoed in an 1869 lecture on *Natural Religion,* where he spoke of the Prophet's "spiritual elevation" and the Koran's "abundance of noble sentences."[95] Beginning in 1850, Emerson started a personal journal he called *The Orientalist,* an intellectual scrapbook culled from "the philosophy of India, the poetry of Persia and Arabia, and the wisdom of all the Oriental countries at once."[96] He was attracted to Muslim Persian poets such as Hafiz, whose work he said "abounds in pregnant sentences which might be engraved on a sword-blade."[97] Emerson admired Hafiz's "pure theism" and saw himself as resembling the priest-poet, a creative artist and unfettered religious voice. Emerson had access to few critical sources on Islamic history and beliefs, and his comments, while admiring in the Romantic tradition, are generally embellishments to his already established ideas. Life in the East lacked the complexity of European and American existence, he wrote, and "every word in Arabic is said to be derived from the camel, the horse, and the sheep."[98] Emerson's only journey to Egypt was at age seventy-two, when he lamented his lack of knowledge of Arabic and Islamic history and culture.

Herman Melville (1819–1891), a brooding figure of unconventional Christian beliefs, visited and wrote about the Holy Land in 1857, as he had earlier written about the South Seas and South America. Melville spent only three weeks in Palestine and Syria and suffered from both depression and physical ailments, and for him Jerusalem was a "city besieged by [an] army of the dead," and the Judean landscape was a place with "no grace of decay—no ivy—the unleavened nakedness of desolation—whitish ashes—lime kilns. Crossed elevated plains, with snails that [leave] tracks of slime."[99] More interested in camels than Arabs, Melville was physically and spiritually exhausted by the time he reached the Holy Land; his images were of decay, heat, flies, and stones. The waters lapping at the edge of the Dead Sea reminded him of the "slaver of a mad dog," and the hypocrisy and commercialism of beggars and tour guides only confirmed his growing skepticism about Christianity.[100] His morose outlook would be reconfirmed twenty years later in *Clarel,* a lengthy, melancholy poem of 150 cantos about emptiness and the loss of faith, symbolized by the barren spiritual quest of an American student moving about the holy sites of Jerusalem.

The distinctive feature of Mark Twain (1835–1910), a younger contemporary of Emerson and Melville, was his satirical style. Works like William

Cowper Prime's colorfully exaggerated *Tent Life in the Holy Land* (1857) were easy prey for him. He wrote of Prime in *Innocents Abroad*, "He went through this peaceful land with one hand forever on his revolver, and the other on his pocket-handkerchief. Always, when he was not on the point of crying over a holy place, he was on the point of killing an Arab."[101] *Innocents Abroad* (1869) caught the post–Civil War American middle-class market for entertaining travel literature, and sold over half a million copies by the time of Twain's death. It was an account of the pilgrims from the "Quaker City," the first organized overseas tour of its kind, with Twain watching their every step; they blustered forth, breaking locks to enter sacred sites, ignoring quarantines, and chipping stones from historic buildings for souvenirs. Twain wrote, "Heaven protect the Sepulchre when this tribe invades Jerusalem."[102]

Despite its popular appeal, Twain's book had no fresh insights about the Middle East, its people, or religions. "The people of this region in the Bible were just as they are now—ignorant, depraved, superstitious, thieving vagabonds."[103] *Innocents Abroad* was a work of boat-deck humor and anecdotes. The author had to file two entertaining newspaper columns a week for two different newspapers. It is difficult to quarrel with one critic's observation of the passengers with whom Twain traveled: "They came looking for a Sunday School supplement; they found a near desert Middle Eastern country, and they preferred the image they brought to the one they found."[104]

Twain, who had gained popularity as a newspaper writer in the rough and tumble of frontier America, used the same exaggerated techniques in describing the inhabitants of the Holy Land, whom he equated with American Indians. Other writers employed the same theme, contributing to the formation of early racial typologies. Twain wrote, "They reminded me much of Indians, did these people. They had little but clothing, but such as they had was fanciful in character and fantastic in its arrangement. Any little absurd gewgaw or gimcrack they had they disposed in such a way as to make it attract attention more readily. They sat in silence, and with tireless patience watched our every motion with that vile, uncomplaining impoliteness which is so truly Indian, and which makes a white man so nervous and uncomfortable and savage that he wants to exterminate the whole tribe."[105]

4

"Nous Revenons, Saladin!" (We Return, Saladin!) (1900–2000)

The West's understanding of Islam in the twentieth century represented major changes from earlier times. The sheer growth of Islamic numbers—over a billion Muslims by 2005, only about 18 percent of them living in the Arab world—required a new perspective in the West. Islam had become a major force in Asia from Pakistan to the Philippines. Muslims may have included six million persons in France, 10 percent of the population, and possibly six million people in the United States of America. By century's end, over three million Muslims from all over the world made the hajj, the pilgrimage of the faithful to Mecca, annually. Islam was clearly an established global presence, although the popular image of it often seemed stuck in a composite Middle East of earlier times.[1] The easy accessibility of world travel and the spread of the Internet meant that by century's end it was possible to speak of cyber Islam and of the Internet *ummah* (community of Muslims) as identifiable, though constantly changing, realities. At the same time, scholarship in everything from linguistics and anthropology to the study of Islamic law and mysticism resulted in an outpouring of new studies, transforming what had been a limited focus on the Middle East to the study of global Islam in all its complexity.[2]

The perception of Islam in the West thus became increasingly different from what had gone before, creating a more subtle, expansive, and complex image than that previously held, but one in which the twin elements of attraction and repulsion remained as enduring aspects of the East–West encounter. For those who saw the encounter as primarily a clash of cultures, the issues and much of the language remained the same. Yet another factor in this century was the growing presence of Islam on the silver screen. Such presentations of Islam differed little in content from those of the Punch and Judy shows of an earlier era, and spilled over into the political arena, as films like *Casablanca*, *Khartoum*, and *The Battle for Algiers* attest.

The Middle East after World War I

In earlier centuries, a few basic sources contributed to creating the way Westerners perceived Islam, such as the reports of returned Crusaders, travelers, diplomats, and missionaries, and the works of creative artists, including fabulists, painters, and poets. In the twentieth century the vectors expanded exponentially. Islam was now a demonstrable global reality; the rise and fall of European imperial countries that occupied Muslim lands and the spread of nationalism around the world all affected how Westerners interpreted Islam, as did the discovery of oil in the Middle East, World War II and the coming of the cold war, and the Palestine-Israel problem in all its complexity. Militant Islam became the dominant Islam in many people's perception—the Islam of jihads, riots, and fatwas, exacerbated by prolonged and costly wars in Afghanistan and Iraq.

Early in the century, the collapse of Ottoman rule had sent shock waves through the Middle East. Turkey became a secular state ruled by Mustafa Kemal Atatürk at the end of World War I, and Iraq became a monarchy with a British-appointed king in 1921. Reza Khan Pahlavi, an army officer, seized control of Iran and named himself Shah of Shahs in 1925, establishing a dynasty that lasted until it was violently replaced by the Ayatollah Ruhollah Khomeini in 1979.

Britain and France dominated the Middle East in the interwar period, fortified by a League of Nations mandate to administer conquered lands that "were inhabited by people not yet able to stand by themselves under the strenuous conditions of the modern world." "Advanced nations" would administer them "until such times as they were able to stand alone." And when in 1920 the commander of French troops in Damascus marched to Saladin's tomb in the Great Mosque and announced "Nous revenons Saladin!" (We return, Saladin!), it highlighted the complex, often contentious relationship between Islamic countries and the West, one that persisted throughout the twentieth century. In its crudest form it represented a revival of the West's Crusader mentality, a reflection of imperialism in its wide-ranging political, military, economic, and cultural forms.

The return of the crusaders was a part of both British and French political policy and provided the political imagery on which they drew. Shortly after General Edmund Allenby, head of the Egyptian Expeditionary Force, entered liberated Jerusalem on foot on December 9, 1917, the British humor publication *Punch* published a black-and-white illustration of "The Last Crusade." It showed an armor-clad Richard the Lion Hearted, sword in hand, looking triumphantly over Jerusalem, exclaiming, "My dream comes true." Two major British commanders claimed descent from the Crusaders, and the Department of Information released a propaganda film, "The New Crusaders," that explained British policy in the Palestine Front.[3]

The road was never smooth. The creation of the state of Israel in 1948 and the festering Palestinian problem became flash points in Islamic–non-Islamic state relations and played a lasting role in shaping Western impressions of the Islamic world. Additionally, the discovery and production of oil in Saudi Arabia in the 1930s led to an inflow of petrodollars by the end of World War II. This helped promote an image in the West of a country whose leaders were Cadillac-driving fundamentalists who spent much time in Geneva and London, and so on, but who must be assiduously courted just the same for their oil and oil money.

Oil was not effectively flowing from Saudi Arabia until the mid-1930s, and large Western-dominated multinational oil companies controlled Middle East production until the 1950s, when local countries increasingly demanded more profits and greater power in controlling their resources. In 1975 Kuwait and Dubai totally took over oil production in their countries, as did Saudi Arabia in 1980. American policy toward access to Middle East oil has always been preemptive, based on the desire to keep the communists out while retaining constant access to sources of oil, although Middle East oil in recent times has accounted for only about a fifth of American oil imports (but a third of Europe's oil imports, and 80 percent of Japan's).[4]

In the period following World War II, the United States and Great Britain became increasingly obsessed with the Soviet Union's potential for invading Western Europe as well as the Middle East. Strategic geopolitical interests were the key to American thinking, and in 1948 a Joint Chiefs of Staff survey argued for a Western air base in Egypt: "If we antagonize the Mohammedan World, we shall not only be unable to obtain the facilities for this base which we require in Egypt, but we shall be unable to get facilities in Pakistan" and elsewhere. British appraisals of potential Egyptian allies were blunt. "These Egyptians are fundamentally cowards," a ranking British military official wrote. "They will march about the streets yelling slogans, insulting individuals and breaking up property," but if challenged, "they will pick up at once."[5]

Also, by now there was the wild card of Arab nationalism. The United States supported the emergence of independent nations in the Middle East and elsewhere while simultaneously retaining historic ties with Great Britain and France. But when the new nationalisms produced unpredictable actors like Iran's Prime Minister Mohammad Mossadegh in 1951 and Egypt's Colonel Gamal Abdul Nasser in 1952, cautionary signals went up. Mossadegh, *Time* magazine's man of the year in 1951, nationalized Iran's oil fields, and Nasser seized the Suez Canal and proclaimed his brand of Arab socialism as an alternative to Western democracy.

The politics of such leaders were suspect, as was Islam, the religion from which they emerged, and which was seen by many in the West as a regressive, reactionary force, detrimental to economic and social progress. Muslims were not procommunist, in this view, but were easy to manipulate by communists through clever promises, and strident Arab state opposition to Israel made it difficult for most Western governments to find sympathy with Islamic governments or with Islam.

Emblematic of the new, unpredictable generation of Middle Eastern nationalists was Mohammad Mossadegh (1882–1967), scion of a distinguished family of Iranian civil servants. Like many Iranians, he was enraged at the 1919 Anglo-Persian Agreement that reduced Iran to the servile status of a British protectorate. Equally vocal against the subsequent reign of Iran's two shahs, the popular orator and charismatic politician led parliamentary efforts to nationalize the Anglo-Iranian Oil Company in 1951; for this he incurred the wrath of the British and American governments. A 1953 CIA coup led to his arrest, and he died while under house arrest in 1967. Mossadegh was a conventionally religious Iranian nationalist; a silk-screen print in the dining room of his old house carried the inscription "As I am an Iranian and a Muslim, I oppose anything that is against Iran or Islam."[6]

Once the shah had fallen in 1979, the next major Iranian irritant for the West was the Ayatollah Ruhollah Khomeini (1902–1989), descendent of a prominent Shia clerical family and a longtime anti-Western voice. Khomeni wanted an Islamic Republic with unquestioned clerical control over its major functions through organizations such as the Supreme Judicial Council. He vilified Israel and called the United States the "Great Satan" and Great Britain the "Small Satan"—trash talk that in turn revived the most inflammatory anti-Islamic images in the West. Particularly controversial was his February 14, 1989, declaration of a fatwa (an influential legal decree by a respected cleric) ordering the death of Salman Rushdie, an Indian-born, nonpracticing Muslim writer, who lived in Great Britain, for his novel *The Satanic Verses*.

A distinctly inflammatory vocabulary was a feature of the Iranian model of Islamic government that resonated throughout the Islamic world. Clerical leaders were repressive of human rights and free speech, corruption was widespread, and the Iranian regime's early attraction to some Westerners substantially faded by century's end.[7]

In Egypt, caution and distrust characterized British and American postwar policy. The most suspect figure was Gamal Abdul Nasser (1918–1970), who rose to power in a 1952 officer's coup and remained a charismatic global personality until his death on September 28, 1970. Impulsive, unpredictable, and vindictive, Nasser nationalized the British-operated Suez Canal Company in 1956, harbored and trained anti-French Algerian revolutionaries, and crafted an eclectic brand of Arab socialism. Nasser was basically a military-political secularist with little interest in Islam beyond manipulating its adherents. As he was putting down the Muslim Brotherhood, with which he once actively collaborated, Nasser told the press in December 1953, "I really don't know how one could possibly govern according to the Koran."[8] The Egyptian leader also actively wooed Soviet Union and eastern bloc support, and his warfare with neighboring Israel and constant dabbling in Third World politics, from which he tended to emerge with headlines in places like the 1955 Bandung Conference, made him a constant irritant to Western leaders. In 1955, with typical grandiloquence, Nasser wrote in his *Philosophy of the Revolution*: "For some reason it seems to me, that within the Arab circle there is a role, wandering aimless in search of a hero. And I do not know why it seems to me that this role, exhausted by its wanderings, has at last settled down, tired and weary, near the borders of our country and is beckoning to us to move, to take up its lines, to put on its costume, since no one else is qualified to play it."[9]

The Beginnings of a New Policy Approach

On May 3, 1957, several U.S. foreign affairs agencies completed a secret *Inventory of U.S. Government and Private Organization Activity Regarding Islamic Organizations as an Aspect of Overseas Operations*.[10] The working group assumed that global Muslim political groups were religiously motivated, and that Islam and Christianity shared a common spiritual basis, unlike atheistic communism. The Soviet Union was making a largely successful effort to attract Muslim support in the Middle East, the study concluded. "As a militant missionary faith, the ultimate aim of Islam is world conversion," the paper argued, noting that sixteen of eighty-one United Nations member states had Muslim majorities, and another thirty-two had significant Muslim minorities. Except for the changing numbers and a few other dated topical references, the document could have emerged from a similar task force a half century later. American government personnel were poorly trained to serve among Muslim populations, it said; "exchange of persons" programs were greatly underfunded; and although Islamic schools, political, and cultural groups, and brotherhoods existed around the globe, little was known about them. Of the often politically involved religious groups, the report said, "It is improbable that any U.S. agency or organization has contacts with these orders that have millions of followers."[11]

The era of seeing Islam as the political-military battle ground of the democracy versus communist 1950s slugfest was gradually overlaid in the 1960s and 1970s by one where economic development became the weapon to move Middle Eastern and other Islamic countries away from communism and socialism, freeing them from the darkness of religiously informed traditional behavior, supposedly to become successful modern democratic states. Developmental and modernization theory offered a new way of looking at the overseas world and became a cornerstone of international relations between the West and many Middle Eastern countries for a few decades. Works such as MIT Professor Daniel Lerner's *The Passing of Traditional Society* (1958) and White House advisor Walt W. Rostow's *The Stages of Economic Growth* (1960) were blueprints for building this new world.[12] Richard W. Bulliet, Columbia University historian and former director of the Middle East Studies Association, wrote of such works, "As students we learned that tradition was a murky and impenetrable maze, and modernization a straight path to a luminous future."[13]

The century's end was a time of increasing violence, and many Westerners saw Islam and violence as inseparable. Violence clothed in religious language occurred both within and among states; "a disturbance of spirits" is what the historian Albert Hourani called the post-1967 period.[14] Some of its manifestations were the Israeli-Egyptian War of 1967, the Israeli-Lebanese conflict of 1982, the Turkish-Kurdish conflict that simmered throughout the twentieth century, and the devastating eight-year war between Iraq and Iran that began in 1980, followed by the emergence of the Taliban in Afghanistan and al-Qaida elsewhere, with their sustained use of assassinations, bombings, and other forms of violence for political ends.

The list was a long one, including the seizure of sixty-six American embassy hostages in Iran in November 1979, attacks on American diplomatic establishments in Libya and Pakistan, and the October 23, 1983, suicide bombing of 241 American Marines at their Beirut headquarters. Bombings of American embassies in Kenya and Tanzania on August 7, 1998, with a collective loss of 224 people killed and over 4,000 wounded, served to underline the global aspect of such terrorism. Islamic terrorism came to American soil with the 1993 attack on the World Trade Center in New York and the devastating attacks of September 11, 2001, in New York and Washington.

It is not that positive steps were lacking. Anwar Sadat's journey to Jerusalem on November 19, 1977, and the September 1978 talks at Camp David, Maryland, between Sadat, Menachem Begin, and Jimmy Carter showed prospects for a changed climate of relations. But Sadat's assassination in October 1981 by Egyptian extremists once again threw relations into disarray.

While extremists claimed the limelight in recent years, far more significant in its long-term implications was the Islamic activism of moderate, middle-of-the-road clerics, teachers, merchants, professionals, and government workers. This growing population throughout the Islamic word and elsewhere contained many members who consciously disavowed the West for its arrogance, materialism, and hedonism. At the same time, their desire was not to live in a world of jihads and fatwas but to hold productive jobs, educate their children, and live securely with access to better standards of living, which would include the benefits of Western technology.

Disenchanted also with their own corrupt, unresponsive governments that failed to deliver basic public services such as safety, education, and medical services, such people increasingly turned inwardly and outwardly to Islam as a source of hope. This was part of the message of the bumper stickers on bolt-rattling northern Nigeria taxis that proclaimed, "Islam Is the Answer."

A Reorientation of Perceptions

A new understanding was emerging of Islam as a coherent, comprehensive world religion capable of standing on its own with the other major global faiths. However, the scale of Islamic studies in the West was fragile for most of the twentieth century, when compared to other historical, linguistic, or religious and cultural disciplines. The transmission of knowledge initially could be compared to a *silsila,* a chain of individual teachers and students that eventually became a small network of European colleagues. In Paris early in the century, over a hundred students were studying various forms of Arabic, while at Oxford only a single student took an honors degree in Arabic and Persian in the five-year period of 1910–1914. A handful of language teachers taught one-year courses preparing British civil servants for work in the Levant, Egypt, the

Sudan, or India.[15] When H. A. R. Gibb, frustrated by the limited opportunities to develop Islamic studies at Oxford, moved to Harvard University in 1955 to head a newly founded Middle East Studies Center, it marked the expansion of Islamic studies in the United States. In the post–World War II and cold war period, several major foundations and the U.S. government supported what were called area studies programs, and in 1967 more than 2,344 National Defense Education Act fellowships were awarded in language and area studies at several major universities now teaching multidisciplinary programs in international studies.[16]

The harbingers of a new approach to Islam in the late nineteenth and early twentieth centuries were the Hungarian Jewish scholar Ignaz Goldziher, the Dutch linguist–colonial policy adviser Christiann Snouck Hurgronje, the German linguist Carl Heinrich Becker, Hartford Theological Seminary's Duncan Black Macdonald, and the French sociologist-mystic Louis Massignon. What emerged from their collective early-twentieth-century work, and that of their students and professional collaborators, was a fundamental reorientation of Western perceptions of Islam. The scholars of this new academic generation were often proficient in Semitic languages, wrote independent studies of their subject matter, and interacted over a number of years with Islamic counterparts.

Among the most influential of the earliest European generation of scholars on Islam in this century was Ignaz Goldziher (1850–1921).[17] Born on June 22, 1850, in a Hungarian village, the son of a Jewish leather merchant, he was raised in a pious Jewish intellectual family, attended Hungarian Cistercian and Calvinist schools, and studied Turkish, Persian, and Arabic. In 1868 Goldziher left for Berlin, Leipzig, and Paris, where he broadened his studies in Semitic languages and received a doctorate at age twenty. Goldziher taught Hebrew in Budapest's Calvinist Faculty of Theology in 1873, and was one of the first Europeans to study at Cairo's al-Azhar University, where he gathered a large collection of Arabic manuscripts that he sent back to Budapest.

In 1876 Goldziher became secretary of Budapest's Jewish community, a position he held for the next thirty years. During this time he wrote articles on Muslim law, the cult of the saints in Islam, and detailed Koranic studies. Declining a position at Cambridge University, he helped launch the *Encyclopedia of Islam* (1908), to which he contributed thirty articles. By 1912 he was an active collaborator with Hurgronje, Becker, Massignon, and Douglas Black Macdonald. The First World War was hard on the Hungarian Jewish scholar, who suffered from depression and the loss of many friends and family. He died in 1921, having been a major figure in introducing the new scholarly tools of linguistic analysis and intellectual history to the study of Islam. Before Goldziher, as we have seen, much Western writing about Islam was unrelievedly polemical, sometimes with touches of romance. Goldziher, on the other hand, in a series of articles and lectures, and in widespread contact with other scholars and students, methodically traced the development of Islam as a prophetic religion, explained its intellectual and religious unity, and the appeal of Sufi mysticism as a counterbalance to the legalistic Sharia.[18]

In the Netherlands, meanwhile, the son of a Dutch Reformed pastor, Christiaan Snouck Hurgronje (1857–1936), abandoned ministerial studies for work in Arabic and Armenian, and wrote a doctoral thesis on the origins of the hajj, a biography of the Prophet Muhammad, a history of Islam, and a study of Islamic law.[19] From 1881 to 1887, Hurgronje taught a course preparing future colonial administrators for the Dutch Netherlands. And from February to August 1885, at the request of a community of leading Arab religious figures, he lived for several months in Mecca, a rarity for a non-Muslim, and from which his two-volume history of Mecca emerged in 1888. Increasingly, given the Dutch presence in Indonesia, Hurgronje focused attention on Muslim populations there, and in 1889 he left for two years in Indonesia. The heart of his work was interpreting Muslim society and Muslim traditional law to Dutch colonial authorities and explaining Dutch policies to the local Muslim community. He spent seven months in 1891–1892 in the troubled Aceh region, a place of numerous armed insurrections. Recommendations he prepared to reduce friction in the region's colonial administration were rejected by the Dutch government, which favored an expanded military presence. Although close to several high colonial figures because of his knowledge of local languages and customs, Hurgronje faced opposition from established conservative planters and settlers who wanted to retain maximum political and economic control without offering more than minimal salaries to exploited local populations.

Hurgronje disputed Christian missionaries' arguments that Islam and traditional religions could be eliminated and totally replaced by Christianity. Islam was deeply rooted in local societies, even while it was finding growing links to global Islam through publications and travel to Mecca, connecting Indonesians to a wider world. The Dutch scholar believed international Islam represented a peaceful community drawn to the ancient idea of the Dar-al-Islam, the territory of Islam, and that no political pan-Islamic union would result, nor would a global jihad. He said a Dutch policy toward Islam should respect religious freedom, support local Islamic institutions, and encourage their evolution along Western lines. At the same time, the Dutch should strictly keep meddlesome external influences out, principally the Muslim Brotherhood and Islamic groups from other countries.

In 1907 Hurgronje accepted a post as professor of Arabic language and literature at the University of Leiden and continued his role as advisor on

Islamic affairs to the government. In a 1922 lecture on "Islam and the Problem of Races" he praised Islam's universality and its adaptability to different races, a relatively new and controversial concept for a Westerner in the 1920s. He retired in 1927 and died in 1936.

The counterpart of Goldziher and Hurgronje in Germany at this time was Carl Heinrich Becker (1876–1933), who was raised in a German Lutheran family and in Lausanne and Heidelberg studied theology, including the two new disciplines of biblical criticism and comparative religions. After learning Arabic, in 1900 Becker visited Egypt, Sudan, Palestine, and Syria, and by 1907 he had taught future German colonial administrators in Hamburg. Becker was founder of the scientific periodical *Der Islam* in 1910, and in 1913 became professor of Arabic studies and Islamology at the University of Bonn. With Hitler's rise to power, the liberal democratic world Becker knew was shattered, and he died in 1933.

Much of Becker's work was of a preliminary nature. He did little original fieldwork and had no special interest in law or theology, but kept up a lively interest in the work of colleagues such as Goldziher and Hurgronje. Nevertheless, he was a significant figure in promoting the serious study of Islam in Germany, and in training a generation of colonial administrators.[20]

The Twentieth Century in Great Britain and the United States

In addition to the work of the Hungarian, German, and Dutch figures just discussed, the study of Islam also grew in Great Britain and the United States, and produced a range of contrasting, and at times contradictory, conclusions. Among the people involved were W. H. T. Gairdner, a prominent missionary working in Egypt at the same time as Lord Cromer, proconsul at the turn of the century; Samuel M. Zwemer, Gardiner's colleague in Cairo; Sir Thomas Arnold, who taught in India for some sixteen years; and Lord Cromer himself. For decades these figures expressed opposition, partial opposition, or partial acceptance of Islam.

William Henry Temple Gairdner (1873–1928), an Oxford-trained Arabist and missionary to Egypt, represented a new tendency in British religious attitudes toward Islam. Gairdner's views of Islam were spelled out in *The Reproach of Islam* (1909). "Reproach" ("Rebuke" in the revised 1920 volume that sold over twenty thousand copies), meant that what was missing in Christianity was an understanding of the unity, personality, and spirit of Jesus, all expressions he employed frequently. "The spirit of Jesus is the only asset of the Church," he said repeatedly. "We need the *song* note of the joyous in our message to the

Muslims, not the dry crackle of disputation, but the song note of joyous witness, tender invitation"—an approach rare in missionary literature.[21]

Gairdner first arrived in Egypt in 1899 to work among Egyptian students and intellectuals, primarily through weekly discussion groups. He rode his bicycle about Cairo, handing out pamphlets in Arabic at public beaches and on streets. His approach was not confrontational. Muhammad, he said, was "a very great man, with the mixed character of light and shade which the natural great man ever displays."[22] With brush strokes that could grace a staircase painting in the Victoria and Albert Museum, he portrayed a universal Islamic empire where daily over two hundred million members formed a global circle of prayer and turned to Mecca and "spread out in the form of an enormous Cross, the arms of which reach from the Pacific to the Atlantic, its uprights from Siberia to the Zambezi, and its center and focus, physically as well as spiritually, Mecca in Arabia."[23]

"Islam and Christianity are incompatible," Gairdner stated, reflecting the missionary outlook of his time, but he also pleaded against senseless Muslim–Christian competition for power. "Christianity has always cut its most pitiful figure when seen trying to meet Islam with Islam's weapons, or competing with it on its own ground. . . . We owe to that great host that follows the great Mohammed the realization, final and definitive, that the Spirit of Jesus is the only asset of the church."[24]

Formative to Gairdner's attitudes toward Islam was a sabbatical leave of seventeen months he took beginning in 1910. After three months in Germany, he spent five months at the Hartford Theological Seminary in Connecticut with Duncan Black Macdonald, who remembered Gairdner saying, "I came here thinking that I would get from you knock-down arguments"—that was the exact phrase—"to use with Muslims and you are teaching me only to understand them."[25] Next was a month in Budapest with Ignaz Goldziher. After their conversations Gairdner began translating The Niche of Lights, a mystical commentary on the meaning of "light" by the Persian poet al-Ghazali (1058–1128). Finally, he headed for Aleppo, and spent many hours in mosques talking with Islamic scholars. After returning to Cairo, Gairdner recommenced a busy round of daily work that continued until his death in 1928. There were understandably incomplete and contradictory elements in his writings, as was true of many other missionary scholars of his era. Some ultimately rejected the teachings of Islam as incompatible with Christian belief but, at the same time, others acknowledged that Islam contained a deep spirituality of its own. The two religions remained wide apart, and Gairdner never found the put-away arguments he sought to triumph in discussions with Muslims. Instead of a frontal attack on Muslim beliefs about Christ and the Bible, Gairdner wrote:

The primary call to the Church of Christ in the Near East is to atone
to the Muslim and Jewish peoples for the centuries of misrepresen-
tation of the person of her master, and to reveal Him as Savior
and Lord, by life and by word. There is no other way to win the
peoples of Palestine and Egypt to Christ than the way of the incarnate
and crucified Lord, the way of love and the way of suffering...here
there can be no measurement of missionary work in terms of
numbers, whether of stations occupied or of converts won, but only
in terms of the quality of spirit and life.[26]

Gairdner's Cairo colleague, Samuel M. Zwemer (1867–1952), who lived in
Egypt from 1913 to 1929, was less conciliatory. Despite his doctrinal rigidity,
however, Zwemer was a highly productive scholar who traveled extensively
from Iran to China, and to many cities in the Arabian Peninsula. He wrote
more than fifty books, and for thirty-six years was also editor of *The Moslem
World,* eventually renamed *The Muslim World.* After leaving Egypt, he became
a professor of church history and missions at Princeton Theological Seminary
from 1929 until his death in 1952.[27]

A realistic analyst of problems facing missionaries, Zwemer called Islam
"the most baffling of all missionary problems."[28] As a way to avoid dealing with
the ultimate difficulties in the Muslim–Christian encounter, he kept saying that
Islam was dying in its home territories. "There is now abundant evidence that
the religion of Islam is slowly disintegrating," he concluded, without producing
any real evidence.[29] And, like Christian apologists since the seventh century, he
found the Prophet a morally flawed character. Islam had "a flabby moral nature," he said.[30] Zwemer kept metaphorically getting stuck in a sand dune; he
acknowledged Christianity was making few converts through confrontations
with Muslims, but his advice was to keep trying just the same.

Sir Thomas Walker Arnold (1864–1930), in *The Preaching of Islam* (1896),
emerged as one of the English-speaking world's most informed historians of
Islam at the turn of the century. Islam was for Arnold a missionary religion;
this he attributed to the zeal and energy of Muslim lay missionaries. He cited
the example of "school masters, government clerks in the canal and opium
departments, traders, and a dealer in camel-carts, an editor of a newspaper, a
bookkeeper in a printing establishment" in Lahore.[31]

After studying Arabic and Sanskrit at Oxford and Cambridge, Arnold was
posted to India in 1888–1898 as teacher of philosophy at the Muhammadan
Anglo-Oriental College at Aligarh. He dressed like a local Muslim and eagerly
joined a group of Indian reformers trying to merge Western scientific thought
with Koranic beliefs. Arnold returned from India to London in 1904, taught

Arabic at University College, and became first holder of the chair of Arabic and Islamic studies at the School of Oriental Studies at the University of London in 1921.

Arnold presented Islam as a distinctly new movement in Arabia when it was introduced, diametrically opposed to the ideals of existing society, a movement that stressed a universal appeal without racial or social distinctions. He was clear: Islam was not a religion of forcible conversions, and the use of religious warfare was carefully circumscribed. He pointed out that the verb jahada, from which jihad was derived, meant "to strive, labor, toil, to exert oneself; to be diligent, or studious, to take pains."[32] *The Preaching of Islam* was one of the first works to chronicle the spread of Islam in Central Asia, Africa, India, and China. Western authors were gradually becoming aware of Islam as a global presence.

In contrast to the measured acceptance of Islam by the scholar-administrator Arnold, an even more important figure and an unyielding opponent of Islam was Evelyn Baring, Lord Cromer (1841–1917), who spent twenty-four years in Egypt, from 1883 to 1907 as a British administrator and later consul general. Cromer could have been central casting's model of a Victorian proconsul. "Islam as a social system is moribund," he wrote. Its failures included the subjugation of women, the cruel and unusual punishment allowed by the Sharia law code, the encouragement of slavery, and intolerance toward other religions. "It is absurd to suppose that Europe will look on as a passive spectator whilst a retrograde government, based on purely Mohammedan principles and obsolete Oriental ideas, is established in Egypt," he wrote in *Quo Vadis,* his valedictory on "The Egyptian Question," adding that "The ideal of the Moslem patriot is, in my opinion, incapable of realization." England could establish sound civil government in Egypt, but could never expect gratitude in return. "Neither by the display of sympathy nor by good government, can we forge bonds which will be other than brittle."[33]

Cromer, a former military officer, was an administrative and fiscal reformer for much of his career. He called his system a veiled protectorate, since it placed a layer of British administrators behind their Egyptian cabinet counterparts. Although he had pronounced views on all aspects of Egyptian life and society, Cromer never learned Arabic and had few contacts among the growing class of reform-minded Egyptian middle-class intellectuals.

His *Modern Egypt* (1908) became a surprise best-seller on both sides of the Atlantic. Cromer intended the book, dense with details of administrative reforms, to be a handbook on Oriental administration, and a way to introduce "the commonplace requirements of European civilization" to Egyptians.[34] One looks in vain for a hint of appreciation of Egyptian achievements. Peasants were "sunk in the deepest ignorance" and the country's al-Azhar-trained leaders would only demonstrate "corruption, misgovernment, and oppression" if the reins of government were turned over to them.[35] In 1907 Cromer wrote, "It will not take years but probably generations, to change the moral character of the Egyptian people. They are heavily weighed by their leaden creed and by the institutions which cluster around the Koran."[36]

Cromer could always find an anecdote to make his point about Egyptians as "childlike" subject peoples, and he cautioned against instituting a system of local government that would allow "a small minority of natives to misgovern their countrymen" when what was needed was a system that "will enable the mass of the population to be governed according to the code of Christian morality." Fundamentally he had no interest in Islam or any other religion. [37] "He had not an ecclesiastical mind," a friend said of him.[38]

As the twentieth century progressed a new, more comprehensive under-standing of Islam was coming into place in the West, represented by popu-larizers like the enigmatic T. E. Lawrence in England and a new scholarly generation that included Duncan Black Macdonald, a Scottish scholar working in America; David Samuel Margoliouth of New College, Oxford; and James Thayer Addison of the Episcopal Theological School in Cambridge, Massa-chusetts. Other academics like Annemarie Schimmel in Germany and Amer-ica, H. A. R. Gibb and W. Montgomery Watt in the English-speaking world, and Louis Massignon and Jacques Becque in France collectively presented a new picture of Islam in all its complexity.

Most of these writers were basically orthodox Christians, but they displayed sympathy for Islamic beliefs even when they did not agree with them. Because the study of Islam as a popular subject attracted only limited interest, their best-read works were largely books of the "What Is Islam?" and "Who Was Mu-hammad?" nature, but such volumes were far less polemical than their pre-decessors. The foundation stones for the comparative study of religions were being laid, and Islam increasingly gained respect among Westerners for its religious depth.

T(homas) E(dward) Lawrence (1888–1935), at once representative of British relations with Islam in the Middle East and at the same time an eccentric who stood alone, was a contradictory figure, a sometime rebel within the Estab-lishment, like Sir Richard Burton a century earlier. His *Seven Pillars of Wisdom*, first published privately in 1926, became the gateway to "the Arab mind" for many Westerners.[39] And when the popular lecturer Lowell Thomas wrote a book in 1924 and made a film describing Lawrence's Middle Eastern adven-tures, Lawrence gained a celebratory status usually reserved for film stars.[40] Lawrence was later alternately a hero for some readers and the personification

Sometimes T. E. Lawrence (1888–1938) wore his British army officer's uniform while working in the Arab Bureau during World War I in Cairo, but often he dressed in a composite costume of what the lecturer Lowell Thomas called "an oriental potentate." Thomas helped make Lawrence famous in his adventure memoir, *With Lawrence in Arabia* (1924). (Getty Images)

of an imperialist for others. But if Lawrence is considered in the context of the times he spent in the Arab world and those when he worked as a political advisor to the British government, a more nuanced verdict emerges. He was often ahead of his day in his appreciation of Arabic life and culture, and was simultaneously the product of mainstream early-twentieth-century British imperialist thought. The inescapable conclusion in reading him now is of both Lawrence's acute sensitivity and his advocacy of British benevolent paternalism that carried with it the seeds of its own eventual destruction.

The psychosexual literature on Lawrence is considerable, and this account will not attempt to deal with issues in Lawrence's makeup, such as his birth out of wedlock, unsettled relations with demanding parents, or difficulties in relating to women. Doubtlessly they influenced his personality and helped spur his desire to lose himself in an alien culture.[41]

Lawrence's involvement with the Middle East began during his Oxford years. An early interest in French medieval epic poetry was followed by thesis work on the architecture of Syrian crusader castles, which led to his first research trip in 1909. Lawrence soon constructed a fantasy realm where heroic Bedouin chiefs waited to ride out of the desert and rule, just as altruistic knights once provided leadership to an unruly Europe.

Lawrence had a deaf ear for religion, and his comments on Islam were largely about the character of Arab men, who displayed a universal clearness or hardness of belief. He wrote, "The gospel of bareness in materials is a good one, and it involves apparently a sort of moral bareness too. They think for a moment, and endeavor to skip through life without turning corners or climbing hills. It is a race trained out, and to avoid difficulties they have to jettison so much that we think honorable and grave."[42] For Lawrence, Islam belonged to a region of vast deserts, pure air, starlit skies, and few cities or people. Its hero was the Bedouin, not the town dweller. Like others who dreamed of the future shape of empire, he envisioned an extended commonwealth of free people, "a new nation of thinking people, all acclaiming our freedom, and demanding admittance into our empire."[43] No other possibility existed for countries like Egypt and India, and Lawrence foresaw an Arab Dominion as part of the British Empire. But he was not only a dreamer but also enough of a realist to know how fragile were the political sandcastles Britain was building.

Lawrence was among the early-twentieth-century Europeans whose concept of Islam was at heart a political-strategic one. The Middle East was a hoped-for possession for the West in the great power game of global expansion, and an understanding of Arab culture, customs, and belief would help ease the way to expanded European influence. But when the captains and the kings departed, Lawrence, like other players in the great game, realized that imperialism was a chimera. Lawrence, for all his dreams, concluded, "Arab unity is a madman's notion—for this century or the next probably. English speaking unity is a fair parallel."[44]

The Scottish Presbyterian cleric and scholar Duncan Black Macdonald (1863–1943), sometime fellow of the University of Glasgow, arrived at the newly founded Hartford Theological Seminary in 1892 to teach Semitic languages, and stayed fifty years. In 1902 he published *Development of Muslim Theology, Jurisprudence, and Constitutional Theory.*

Macdonald was also remembered for recommending the *Arabian Nights* as a doorway to understanding Muslims and other Semitic peoples, calling the tales "the great mirror of mediaeval Muslim life."[45] Macdonald wrote the article on the *Nights* in the *Encyclopedia of Islam* and the *Encyclopedia Britannica*

(1929). The tales, which he had known since childhood, opened the way to "the Muslim mind," he believed:

> Such books must always, for the home-staying student, take the place of contact with the Moslem world itself, and the best known of them all is, of course, the *Arabian Nights*. They do not mislead or misinform. . . . I would bear testimony now that when I did meet the Moslem world face to face, the picture of its workings and ideas and usages which I had gained from these romances, poems and religious tales needed modification in no essential point—almost, even, in no detail.[46]

Emblematic of a storybook Orient, the *Nights* required little exegesis or commentary. "The world of the *Arabian Nights* is God's world," he told an audience in 1906, even with "All his belief in magic and his sense of the power of the enchanters, the Muslim is a man" who "stands on God's earth, beneath his sky, and at any time can enter that presence and can carry his wrong to the highest court. Between him and Allah there stands nothing, and he is absolutely sure of Allah."[47] Macdonald was skilled in languages and encyclopedic in his knowledge of Islamic law and theology, although his portrayal of the Prophet Muhammad was conventional even for its time, with its "good moralist but weak person" imagery.

Like many other Westerners, Macdonald found in the Persian philosopher, poet, and mystic al-Ghazali (1058–1111) a figure that could bridge both cultures. He called the Persian poet "the greatest, certainly the most sympathetic figure in the history of Islam," the equal of Augustine in philosophy and theology.[48] Many other people who wished to absorb something of Islamic spirituality and find a congenial intellectual figure also settled on al-Ghazali or the Persian mystic poet Jalaluddin Rumi (1207–1273). It was a bit like trying to understand Western civilization through a study of John Donne or George Herbert, brilliant but hardly representative figures.

According to Macdonald, the effective missionary must be "a large, all-round man of personality, and if possible of mystical tendency" who realizes that "when Muslims accept Christianity they will have to make it over for themselves; they will have to construct their own theology." All the missionary can do is "the help them discreetly in the development of their own system. By no means should he attempt to force any system upon them or be surprised at any deviations which they may develop."[49] His primary missionary strategy was not to frontally attack Islam or engage in polemical arguments but rather to build clubs and associations with lecture series and discussion groups. Beyond that, the most effective thing the missionary could do was to give young Muslim men copies of an Arabic-language Bible. "Face to face with the Bible, we can safely leave the Muslim. When he needs help he will seek it."[50]

The religious encounter, for Macdonald, was anything but a one-way street. He had a special interest in the lives of the saints, Muslim and Christian, and favorably recalled the Sunni custom of visiting saints' tombs, then placing a right hand on the rail surrounding them, and reciting the Fatihah, "In the name of God, the Merciful, the Compassionate. . . ." He experienced "feeling the nearness of the spiritual kindred of all that call upon the Lord." Muslims who saw him at prayer "felt that here was a spiritual unity, that this man, Christian though he may be, reverenced their saint and knew what it meant to recognize holiness and the life hid in God."[51] Considering his time and setting, Macdonald would have to be considered a progressive figure, certainly in regard to earlier generations of missionaries actively hostile to Islam.

Increasingly, Western scholars found more balanced things to say about Islam and displayed a more tolerant attitude toward this major world religion. Representative of the new scholarship on Islam in early-twentieth-century Great Britain was David Samuel Margoliouth (1858–1940), a fellow of New College, Oxford, and holder of the Laudian Professorship of Arabic for forty-eight years. His Jewish father had converted to Christianity and become a missionary to Jews in England, and his father-in-law was dean of Canterbury Cathedral and a well-known Syriac scholar. Margoliouth, also an ordained Anglican cleric, was at home in several classical and modern languages and self-taught in Arabic. His popular biography *Mohammed* (1905), published in a *Heroes of the Nations* series, went through several editions and became a standard work for a quarter century. Despite the laudatory title given the series, Margoulieth's basic position was one of balanced realism. He regarded Muhammad as a great man "who solved a political problem of appalling difficulty— the construction of a state and an empire out of the Arab tribes."[52]

In his cautious approval of Muhammad, Margoliouth called him "a genius equal to the emergencies, but . . . not too great for them. Security for his person he wisely regarded as the first condition of success: a crown would be useless if he had no head to wear it. He allowed no scruple to stand between him and success. He estimated accurately what the emergencies required, and did not waste his energies in giving them more."[53]

Margoliouth presented Islam as a positive social force, especially for women. He understood veiling to be a result of polygamy. "If by the introduction of the veil Mohammed curtailed women's liberty, he undoubtedly secured for them by laws the rights of inheriting and holding property, which under the older system was precarious."[54]

Like Gairdner, Margoliouth surveyed the global spread of Islam, using the geography and climate arguments then in vogue, "In the main, then, Islam is a religion of the Heat Belt, the part of the earth's surface which lies between 30 degrees N. latitude and 30 degrees S. latitude, with a mean temperature of 68 degrees F."[55] Democratic government would have a hard time catching hold in constantly hot countries, Margoliouth believed, "since the demand for wide-spread intellectual activity which constitutional government makes cannot easily be met."[56] Albert Hourani, writing about Margoliouth, said, "there was a streak of fantasy, perhaps of irony, which led him to sometimes to propose untenable theories."[57]

A later missionary strategist in the Gairdner tradition was James Thayer Addison, an American seminary teacher, who wrote *The Christian Approach to the Moslem* (1942).[58] Addison (1887–1953) taught church history at the Episcopal Theological School in Cambridge, Massachusetts. His approach was historical, with separate discussions of several countries in the Middle East; he had no polemical axe to grind against Islam and Muslims. Were missionaries shock troops aggressively seeking to convert Muslims, he asked? Or were they heralds of a coming new religious future? "Shall they view the non-Christian religions as works of Satan or as incomplete revelations or as permanent alternatives to Christianity requiring only modification through Christian influence? ... Is their mission to be an anxious search party looking for the truth with the aid of local search parties or is it to be a royal embassy bearing good tidings to all men?"[59] Islam, he said, "has a rigid bony structure. It does not deal in shades of gray, but in blacks and whites." He then listed, but saw no resolution to, a set of well-enunciated issues: the Koran versus the Bible, the place of Jesus, the Crucifixion, and the Trinity.[60]

Addison was convinced of the missionary imperative to preach Christ to the Muslims, but could find no points to build on between the two faiths. Still, he was not disparaging of Islam; rather, it represented an enigma. "In place of a frontal attack launched on the intellectual level, the best of modern missionaries to Islam pursue a mode of approach which was seldom neglected by their predecessors but which was never quite trusted to bear full fruit—the method of intimate personal fellowship, of loving service, of sympathetic testimony, and of united prayer." This, he believed, would lead Muslims to conversion because it would appeal to a Muslim's deepest religious aspirations.[61] Faced with a theological impasse, Gairdner and Addison and other missionary figures of their generation saw no real way to bridge the problem of the Muslim–Christian divide, but did advocate sustained loving contact as a mechanism for dialogue.

The leading German-language student of Islam in the next generation was Annemarie Schimmel (1922–2003), who taught at Harvard from 1970 to

1992. The author of eighty books, she spoke ten languages, and was an expert on Islamic mysticism, religion, the poetry of Rumi, and the religious thought of the important Pakistani political leader Sir Muhammad Iqbal. Schimmel gained instant notoriety in 1995 when, as a leading Western scholar of Islam, she criticized Salman Rushdie for publishing *The Satanic Verses*. Although she made it clear she did not support the fatwa against Rushdie, she said the book was still harmful to Muslims by insulting the faith of many pious believers.

Schimmel was singularly successful in promoting Western interest in Sufi mysticism and poetry. Of Muhammad she said that Westerners "will be amazed to witness the powerful mystical qualities that are ascribed to this man in the Sufi tradition.... Even the most recent studies of the Prophet, which show his honesty and profoundly religious attitude, betray nothing of the mystical love that his followers feel for him. A Prophet who was so certain of being God's instrument must indeed have been a great man of prayer; for precisely through prayer he could sense over and over again the presence of the God who had sent him."[62]

A voice of moderation and academic balance, Sir Hamilton Alexander Rosskeen Gibb (1895–1971) was the leading English-language scholar of Islam in the mid-twentieth century. Born in Egypt of Scottish parents, he studied at Edinburgh University and later at the University of London's School of Oriental and African Studies (SOAS), where he perfected his skills in Arabic and several other Semitic languages. In 1937 he was named to succeed Margoliouth in the Laudian Chair of Arabic at Oxford, where he stayed until departing for Harvard in 1955. From Gibb's pen came a steady flow of major works, including *Modern Trends in Islam* (1947), and (with Harold Bowen) *Islamic Society and the West: A Study of the Impact of Western Civilization on Moslem Culture in the Near East*, vol. 1, (1950); these were followed by *Studies on the Civilization of Islam* (1962), *Arabic Literature* (1963), and the widely used text *Mohammedism*, which Hourani said would remain for over a generation the first book most English-speaking students would read about Islam.[63]

Not all constructs Gibb used to explain Arab society endured. His division of Islamic societies into "ruling" and "religious" classes, and some of the discussions of the supposed corporate nature of Arab provincial society, possibly drawn from Louis Massignon, were products of their time.[64] Like others of that era, Gibb employed concepts like "the Arab mind," the "Muslim mind," and the "Western mind," but saw Islam as "a living and vital religion," expressed through poetic speech unaffected by Western logic or rationality.[65] In the preface to his *Modern Trends in Islam*, Gibb explained his religious beliefs as they related to Islam. Christianity as a concept held believers together, as did Islam. Both religions underwent constant renewal, although this was rarely discernable from the outside because of the rigidity of their outward forms of expression. Gibb wrote, "I see the church and the congregation of Christian people as each dependent on the other for continued vitality.... My view of Islam will necessarily be the counterpart of this. The Muslim church and its members constitute a similar composite, each forming and reacting to the other so long as Islam remains a living organism and its doctrines satisfy the religious consciousness of its adherents."[66]

The Scottish cleric-historian W. Montgomery Watt (1909–2006) was another major twentieth-century writer on Muhammad and Islam in the tradition of Margoliouth and Gibb. Watt studied at Edinburgh, Jena, and Balliol College, Oxford, and returned to Edinburgh, where he taught from 1934 until his 1979 retirement as professor of Arabic Literature and Islamic Studies. *Muhammad at Mecca* (1953) and *Muhammad at Medina* (1956) were two seminal works, along with *Muhammad: Prophet and Statesman* (1961), *Companion to the Koran* (1967), *The Majesty That Was Islam: The Islamic World, 661–1100* (1974), and *Muslim–Christian Encounters* (1991). Much of Watt's work was an endeavor to bring about a rapprochement between Christians and Muslims, and he acknowledged that "For Westerners none of the world's religious leaders is so difficult to appreciate as Muhammad, since the West has deep-seated prejudices against him."[67]

For over half a century, Watt sorted out fact from legend, plausible judgment from prejudicial speculation on one of the most controversial of historical subjects, the life and times of the Prophet Muhammad. The Prophet had been both denigrated and idealized. Muhammad was called an imposter, treacherous, and lustful—these were the main objections to his character. Watt answered each charge: if Muhammad was an imposter, how could he have commanded the allegiance of so many followers of upright moral character? "If in some respects he was mistaken, his mistakes were not due to deliberate lying or imposture." Watt referred to the Prophet's marriage to the youthful Zaynab, the divorced wife of his adopted son, but asked, "Was the marriage with Zaynab a yielding to sexual desire or a mainly political act? "Sufficient has been said about the interpretation of these events to show that the case against Muhammad is much weaker than is sometimes thought." Of the Prophet he said, "Was Muhammad a prophet? He was a man in whom creative imagination worked at deep levels and produced ideas relevant to the central questions of human existence, so that his religion has had a widespread appeal, not only in his own age but in succeeding centuries. Not all the ideas he proclaimed are true and sound, but by God's grace he has been enabled to provide millions of men with a better religion than they had before they testified that there is no god but God and that Muhammad is the messenger of God."[68]

France: Louis Massignon

The person most responsible for writing the Roman Catholic Church's landmark Vatican II (1964) conciliatory declaration toward Islam was the French
spiritual original Louis Massignon (1883–1962), who died just as the first
council session convened in October 1962. The final "Declaration on the Relationship of the Church to Non-Christian Religions" deserves quoting in its
entirety, for in a short statement it reversed more than a millennium's officially
sanctioned religious hostility toward Islam.

> Upon the Muslims, too, the Church looks with esteem. They adore
> one God, living and enduring, merciful and all-powerful, Maker of
> heaven and earth and Speaker to men. They strive to submit whole-
> heartedly even to His inscrutable decrees, just as did Abraham, with
> whom the Islamic faith is pleased to associate itself. Though they do
> not acknowledge Jesus as God, they revere him as a prophet. They
> also honor Mary, His virgin mother; at times they call on her, too,
> with devotion. In addition they await the day of judgment when God
> will give each man his due after raising him up. Consequently, they
> prize the moral life, and give worship to God especially through
> prayer, almsgiving, and fasting.
>
> Although in the course of the centuries many quarrels and
> hostilities have arisen between Christians and Muslims, this most
> sacred Synod urges all to forget the past and to strive sincerely
> for mutual understanding. On behalf of all mankind, let them make
> common cause of safeguarding and fostering social justice, moral
> values, peace, and freedom.[69]

The council's original preparatory documents made no mention of Islam or
other world religions, but in its September–December 1963 meetings discussed
what to say about Judaism. Several Middle Eastern bishops, including the
Greco-Melkite Patriarch Maximos IV, responded that if a section on Christian–
Jewish relations was included, there should be one on Christian–Muslim relations as well, especially considering the sensitivity of Israel as an issue among
Arab states. It was during the third council session (September–December
1964) that the document *Nostra Aetate* was approved, containing Massignon's
conciliatory statement about Muslims.

Louis Massignon's religious journey was a circuitous one filled with numerous surprise "curves" (his oft-used phrase) and was likewise controversial.
Purist Muslims and Catholics could find his attempts to unite the descendents

of Abraham threatening, and always there was the unyielding figure of Massignon railing against French policy, first in the Middle East, then in Algeria. A half century after his death, followers and detractors were still sorting out the contributions of France's most influential twentieth-century figure in Islamic–Christian relations.[70]

Massignon was born of an old Breton family in comfortable circumstances in Paris, to a devout Roman Catholic mother and nonbelieving successful sculptor father. A gifted linguist, Massignon became fluent in at least ten Semitic languages, including Arabic and Hebrew. He went to Algeria in 1901 at age eighteen to improve his Arabic, and completed a Sorbonne degree that year. At the Collège de France, Massignon taught the sociology of Islam, a chair he occupied from 1926 until his retirement at age seventy-one in 1954.[71]

In Baghdad, in May 1908, Massignon was jailed and interrogated as a spy. His arrest and interrogation triggered a conversion experience. Massignon prayed in Arabic "*Allah, Allah, as'ad du'fi* (God, God! Help my weakness!"), after which he reclaimed his earlier Catholic faith. "I remember that my first prayer to God in prison, when I was bound, fettered, naked, and had nothing to wear on my back, was in Arabic. Indeed, what possible interest could I have had in speaking to men who were interrogating me about things which I never did."[72] He experienced an "unimaginable encounter" that included the apparition of a divine guest who silently stayed with him during his ordeal. When he returned to the Baghdad Muslim family with whom he was staying, his hosts had prepared for him a small glass seal on which was engraved "Louis Massignon, the servant (*abduhu*) of Him (God)."

On January 28, 1950, Massignon was secretly ordained a priest in the Byzantine-Melkite Rite in Cairo. Like most everything else in his life, this was a complicated journey. Massignon, married and the father of three children, in 1949 had transferred his affiliation from the Latin to the Melkite rite of the Greek Catholic Church, with the personal permission of Pope Pius XII. Meanwhile, an old friend, Mary Kahil, an Egyptian Catholic, arranged for his ordination. The Greek Catholic Church permitted married clergy, but that was not the reason for Massignon's attraction to it. He was determined to experience the life of the Arab Christians among whom he had lived and with whom he had shared his religious life. Never interested in parish ministry, he intended to say the mass in Arabic for the deeper unity of Muslims and Christians each day at dawn in the small study of his Paris apartment.

Massignon's consuming work of over fifty years, and one that deeply influenced his own perspective toward religious faith, was the *Passion d'al-Hallaj,* the account of the life and death of a martyred tenth-century Persian mystic. Massignon saw in Hussein ibn Mansur al-Hallaj (857–922) a co-sufferer with

Christ, "a visible image of the Crucified Christ." The Iranian Sufi figure was revered by some Turkish and Persian Muslims as a popular saint and denounced by others as a heretic. Hallaj made three pilgrimages to Mecca with increasing numbers of followers, but preached a controversial doctrine that an acceptable pilgrimage to Mecca could be made in the human heart rather than as a physical journey. Proclaiming, "I am the Truth," Hallaj returned to Baghdad in 908 and was held in a palace prison for nine years, where he continued to receive visitors, but he was finally sentenced to death for heresy, tortured, and crucified on March 22, 922.[73]

Massignon also founded the *Badaliya* movement in Egypt in 1934 to bring Muslims and Christians closer together through mutual understanding and works of charity. Its members were mostly from the small number of Greek and Arab-speaking Christians in predominantly Muslim countries. Its goal was to "Let Jesus Christ, truly God and yet truly man, be blessed in Islam."[74] This was not a project to convert Muslims, but rather an effort at substitution and intercession on their behalf. "We incessantly ask God for the reconciliation of these dear souls for which we want to offer ourselves up as substitutes, *fil badaliya* [in compensation or in exchange], paying their ransom out of our own pockets and substituting ourselves for them."[75] The way of substitution became a central concept for Massignon. "Only then can we discover all of the demands of charity. We have to substitute ourselves completely for other people, take their sins and their defects upon ourselves, even suffer with them, in their stead, the limitations of their dogmas and canonical practices."[76]

Massignon's mystical theology and ascetical practices deepened French Catholic appreciation of Islam, though it resolved no doctrinal issues. The twin desires to bring Muslims to Christ while respecting Islam as a valid way of salvation were obviously contradictory. Catholics could appreciate the depths of Muslim theology without buying into an Islamic schema of salvation. Still, acceptance of the concept that God provided multiple roads to salvation for different people represented a radical departure for Catholics of the 1960s. The twin beacons of generous hospitality and sacrificial expiation—of holding oneself hostage for Muslims—offered a depth of interfaith contact not realized before in France. Abraham was the paradigmatic biblical guest and host, and through the martyrdom of Hallaj and Jesus' Way of the Cross, the possibility of a mystical unity was made available to representatives of the two great faith traditions, even if few would avail themselves of it.

French perceptions of Islam later in the twentieth century were colored by the dismal failure of the French colonial-military presence in Algeria, climaxing in the French-Algerian War, 1954–1962. The myth of the seamless web of France's *mission civilisatrice* was shattered, the Fourth Republic fell, and accusations of torture and brutality ended the fiction of a North African fertile land of happy inhabitants on which the warming sun never set. Several Algerians or Moroccans who wrote in French described the resultant wounded relationship, a shared history severely fractured by sudden decolonization. Tahar Ben Jelloun, a Moroccan writer living in France, called for "making a clean break. We must do this to shock people and make them think. Later we must look for common ground." Also writing of the colonial encounter, Albert Camus has a French farmer in Algeria say, "We do share the same blood as human beings. We'll kill each other a little while longer, cut off each other's balls and torture a bit more and then we'll start to live together as men, which is what the country wants."[77] And with the French defeat in Indochina at Dien Bien Phu in May 1954, the loss of most of France's overseas positions, and the shrinking of its place in Europe, the image of the exotic overseas world, which included Islam, diminished in French public consciousness. It would be kept fleetingly alive by a small community of nostalgic excolonials, but gone now were the verbal portraits of Flaubert, the paintings of Matisse, or the operas of Bizet with their colorful, exotic overseas subjects.

Islam of the Stage and Silver Screen

Motion pictures, a new and influential cultural force, spread across the globe by mid-twentieth century. With magic wands, motion picture directors, writers, actors, and musicians gave a waiting world instant images of overseas worlds. The technology was there, as were waiting audiences, yet the messages were—for all their technical skill in presentation—surprisingly conventional, they reproduced images of Islam as a pagan religion thriving in backward cultures peopled by romantic desert chiefs on powerful steeds.

Several themes were worked and reworked in such films—the desert as a place of romance in *The Garden of Allah* and *The Desert Song;* the casbah as a place of mystery and lawlessness, in *Algiers* and *The Battle of Algiers;* and the Arab chief as sexual conqueror in *The Sheik* and *The Son of the Sheik.* Arabs were backward, comic figures in *Casablanca* and *Raiders of the Lost Ark;* there was the Magic Carpet Orient in *Harum Scarum* and *Alladin,* and Arabs as ruthless killers in *Rules of Engagement.* A few films, such as *Lawrence of Arabia* and *Khartoum,* made an honest effort to portray strengths and weaknesses in the colonial-indigenous relationship. None of these created a new image of Islam in the twentieth century; all drew on existing material, presented graphically in the new medium.

The desert as a place of romance was a theme developed by Robert Smythe Hichens (1864–1950), an English journalist-playwright whose many popular works included *The Coastguard's Secret* and *The Green Carnation*, a satire about Oscar Wilde. Increasingly drawn to North Africa, where he had gone to recuperate from an illness, Hichens turned out a string of Orientalist romances, thin on plot and characters, but lively with action. His most sustained success was *The Garden of Allah* (1904), initially a novel that went through more than forty editions; it became a long-running play, complete with camels and onstage sandstorms, on Broadway and in London. Marlene Dietrich and Basil Rathbone starred in a 1936 film, one of three screen versions of the book.[78] Garden of Allah perfume became popular in department stores, where costumed cast members circulated in the aisles to help promote its sale. *The Garden of Allah,* along with *The Sheik* and *The Desert Song,* did much to popularize the "Sheik of Araby" romantic Orient imagery popular in America and Great Britain in the 1920s and 1930s, and whose aftereffects lingered for decades.

The Garden of Allah was the Sahara, a place of timeless beauty, and the object of the quest of an uptight English heiress, Domini Enfilden, daughter of the late Lord and Lady Rens. The family were devout Catholics, until the mother ran off with a passionate Hungarian violinist. Domini's father quickly became an embittered atheist and, following his death, Domini set off for the Sahara. In the tiny inland Tunisian village of Beni-Mora she visited the well-kept garden of an Italian, Count Anteoni, and fell in love with a mysterious stranger, Boris Androvsky, a Trappist monk. Androvsky had spent twenty happy years at the coastal el-Largani monastery, and was the only brother who knew the secret recipe for a potent herb liqueur that was the order's main source of revenue. The couple's wedding night was spent in a carpet-covered bed carried by a camel. Soon Boris disclosed his secret to his bride, and while they were on their way to Tunis after their honeymoon, the strong-willed Domini ordered the carriage to head for the monastery. Outside its gates were two signs; "This is the Gate of Heaven" was written over the main portal, and a smaller "Women do not enter here" was tacked on a nearby wall. Domini, pregnant now, returned alone to Beni-Mora, where she settled near the garden. Later she watched her child, Boris, grow, content that her former spouse had found the inner peace for which he was searching.

Islam was never a serious topic in *The Garden of Allah;* Muslims were bit actors in the book and film, providing local color through Batouch, the wise porter-interpreter, and a cast of gardeners, musicians, waiters, and a fortune-

The Garden of Allah souvenir book (1911). The play, based on a novel by the English writer Robert Hitchens, enjoyed a long run on Broadway. It featured camels and a sandstorm onstage. Also, costumed actors and actresses promoted "Garden of Allah" perfume in New York department stores. (Edward Leffingwell Smith Collection, West Redding, Ct.)

teller. Early in the novel Hitchens described Domini's quest in florid language that could fit other period works: "She wanted freedom, a wide horizon, the great winds, the great sun, the terrible spaces, the glowing, shimmering radiance, the hot entrancing noons and bloomy, purple nights of Africa . . . the nomad's fires and the acid voices of the Kabyle dogs . . . the roar of the tom-toms, the clash of cymbals, the rattle of the negroes' castanets."[79] Hitchens both drew from and added to a romantic vision of Islamic culture that would endure for decades.

Almost sixty years later, the Walt Disney blockbuster film *Aladdin* (1992), the studio's top-grossing film that year, opened with the following lines.

> Oh, I come from a land
> From a faraway place
> Where the caravan camels roam.
> Where they cut off your ear

> If they don't like your face,
> It's barbaric, but hey, it's home.

After protests from the American Arab Anti-Discrimination Committee, the last three lines were softened:

> Where it's flat and immense
> And the heat is intense
> It's barbaric, but hey, it's home.[80]

The text could have been lifted from any one of innumerable twentieth-century films about the Middle East, from Rudolph Valentino's *The Sheik* (1921) and *The Son of the Sheik* (1926) to Douglas Fairbanks's *The Thief of Bagdad* (1924) and more modern works like *Raiders of the Lost Ark* (1981).[81] Little about Islam as a religion or culture was mentioned in such films, but writers, actors, and directors drew from the ancient storehouse of stock images, presenting them with increasing technical mastery and storyteller's refinement. In *The Sheik,* the adventurous Lady Diana Mayo conducts a tempestuous relationship with an imperious bronzed Arab chief. Lady Diana is kidnapped from the coastal city of Biskra and carried by Ahmed Ben Hassan (Rudolph Valentino) to his tent in a desert oasis, where she is told by Hassan, "When an Arab sees a woman that he wants, he takes her." Stubborn Lady Diana falls quickly in love with her captor and learns that Hassan was Paris educated, keeps a French valet, and is the friend of a famous French writer, who visits him in the desert and tells Lady Diana that Hassan's parents were European: lost and near death, an English man and his Spanish wife had been saved by a kindly sheik, along with their son, whom the sheik chose as his successor and sent to Europe for a proper education. Valentino, lithe and muscular, and dressed in flowing robes that could have come from Muammar al-Qadafi's wardrobe closet, was unrivaled as a matinee idol. The characters in *The Sheik* brought existing stereotypes into the new film medium, although the décor could have come from an Oxfam used furniture shop, and the presence of Islamic beliefs was left to a few lines like "All things are with Allah."

Kidnapping and rape-to-find-fulfillment were unstated themes in many such works; but not miscegenation, which remained a taboo. Hassan's parents were Europeans, and he received a proper education in France. Frigid white European women could meet virile Arab chiefs, and romance and sexuality were ingredients in the encounter, but there was always an escape clause in the script: the captor was European or at least educated in Europe.

Often employed as subject matter in these early- to mid-twentieth century films was the magic-carpet Orient, peopled with charming street urchins and genies, followed in the 1960s by ruthless, rich oil sheiks; crazed, power-mad

RUDOLPH VALENTINO & VILMA BANKY.   236 P.
IN "THE SON OF THE SHEIK".   BEAGLES POSTCARDS
FAMOUS CINEMA STAR SERIES.

Rudolph Valentino was the virile, dominant Arab chief Ahmed, and Vilma
Bánky was Yasmine, the vulnerable daughter of a local Frenchman, in the
immensely popular silent film *The Son of the Sheik*. The 1926 work portrayed
prevalent Orientalist stereotypes, café exoticism, low-life comedy, betrayal,
rape for revenge, and reunited lovers riding off into the endless desert. (Mary
Evans Picture Library)

political leaders; and, in the post-9/11 period, terrorists. Elvis Presley, with a
bath towel wrapped around his head, starred in one such film, *Harum Scarum*
(1965), the décor of which was Main Street in Las Vegas, with a few Moorish
arches and costumes for effect. Presley leapt from his horse in the Nevada
desert and chased two menacing Arabs who had tied a white woman to a
stake. Presley sang:

> I'm gonna go where the desert sun is; where the fun is; go where
> the harem girls dance; go where there's love and romance—out
> on the burning sands, in some caravan. I'll find adventure where I
> can. To say the least, go East, young man. You'll feel like the sheik,
> so rich and grand, with dancing girls at your command. When
> paradise starts calling, into some tent I'm crawling. I'll make love
> the way I plan. Go East—and drink and feast—go East, young man.[82]

All the usual themes were there: easy access to sex, the desert, the harem, and endless adventure.

One of the most egregiously anti-Muslim political films of recent times was *Rules of Engagement* (2000).[83] Written by James Webb, secretary of the navy in the Reagan administration and later a U.S. senator from Virginia, the script was originally set in Latin America, but the film was moved to an Arab country when it became apparent that America's large Hispanic population would find the story offensive. African Americans, Jews, Hispanics, and Native Americans were no longer fair game for racial film profiling, but Muslims remained to provide fodder for humanity's dark underpinnings of racism.

The film began with the American embassy in Yemen besieged by a screaming, rifle-wielding mob of local people, including many women and children. No reason was ever given for the demonstration. The timorous American ambassador was safely evacuated by helicopter by Colonel Terry Childers, played by African American actor Samuel L. Jackson, who returned to the embassy, rescued the American flag, and, lying on the embassy roof under fire, told his troops "Waste the motherfuckers." What followed was an extended high-tech drama of war and carnage where eighty-three Yemeni were killed and over a hundred were wounded. Then the footage in Yemen ended. The film's second part, an extended court-martial drama, took place in Washington, raising the ancient issue of clear-cut rules of engagement versus risky decisions in the heat of combat. Paramount Studios dodged the racial issue with a stiffly worded press release saying that the film was just a "dramatization and fictional account of the consequences of extremism in all its forms," and not an indictment of any particular culture. It just happened to be set in Yemen, whose ambassador to the United States subsequently received numerous inquiries from Americans asking for details of the actual battle.[84]

It would be wrong to find all films dealing with Islamic subject matter deficient. *Khartoum* (1966) was generally accurate in its portrayal of the positions of the Mahdi and General Charles Gordon, although they never actually met in person. *Lawrence of Arabia* (1962) was a carefully presented portrayal of British political ambitions in the Middle East. In 2005, director Ridley Scott took on the Crusades in a controversial film, *Kingdom of Heaven*, which presented the Muslim military commander Saladin as a wise and judicious leader. In this film, Christians were presented as being at times deceptive, Muslims at times noble and godly.

But possibly the most significant film on an Islamic-related theme to emerge during the second half of the twentieth century was *La Bataille d'Algers* (The Battle of Algiers, 1965), a controversial film about the French-Algerian conflict from 1952 to 1957. Edward Said called it one of the greatest political films of all time. Banned successively in France and Algiers, it was used later by

U.S. forces in Iraq as a training film on how insurgency groups organize and operate. In the film, declarations of the Fronte Nationale de la Liberation (FLN) alternated with French army statements of how Algeria was really part of France. Scenes from the European town and the casbah alternated as the director, Gillo Pontecorvo, a former Italian communist, used a newsreel style and mostly local actors to juxtapose Ali-la-Pointe, an Algerian revolutionary leader trying to outsmart Colonel Mathieu, with this experienced French officer, Resistance hero, and Vietnam veteran.

Gradually the insurgents established their informal rule in the unsettled town, issued decrees against prostitution, alcohol, and drugs, and conducted clandestine marriage ceremonies. They were equally busy with terrorist acts, such as bombing the Air France office, a crowded café, and shooting French police officers. Insurgents organized into three-person cells, and only one cell member had contact with members of any other cell. If a cell member was interrogated, he would thus have only limited information to divulge. Colonel Mathieu said the FLN was like a tapeworm with a great number of links. An idealistic Algerian political leader, later captured and killed, told young Ali, "It is difficult to start a revolution, even more difficult to sustain it, and still more difficult to win—and then the real difficulties begin." Increasing violence was a feature of both French and FLN terrorism, accompanied by justifications for their actions by both sides. Algerians exclaimed "May God be with you" as they set out to bomb ice-cream bars; the French called their intensified torture campaign "Operation Champagne." The film ended with the French paratroopers, led into the casbah by Colonel Mathieu, destroying Ali-la-Pointe's hiding place and declaring a victory.[85] European and Islamic audiences watched this film with unease, for while clearly supporting the insurrection it showed the strengths and flaws of both sides.

Films triggered visceral emotions in the hearts of viewers, and on subjects such as religion and race the results were always emotionally charged.[86] Islam provided the trimmings, the exotic setting for the story of such films, but rarely was a subject explored in its own right, except periodically in documentaries. It is ironic that, as Western scholarship on Islam grew more detailed and balanced, popular films continued to portray old myths and images of inferiority and backwardness when dealing with Islamic themes.

Islam and the Music of Empire

In music halls, vocal artists like Peter Dawson in Great Britain and Maurice Chevalier and a host of music-hall singers in France wove themes from the

Middle East and North Africa into their performances. In no form of expression was it easier to create impressions of the exotic than through music. Arabs and Islam as subject matter were secondary themes in the music of empire, but periodically identifiable ones.

England's most representative voice of empire was that of the Australian bass-baritone, Peter Dawson (1882–1961), whose parents were originally Scottish and who trained as a singer in England. Possessed of a powerful voice and a refined, expressive technique, Dawson frequently toured the British Isles and the empire, and became an early BBC wireless favorite and gramophone bestseller. His Orientalist repertoire included such popular numbers as *The Bedouin Love Song, The Garden of Allah, Till the Sands of the Desert Grow Cold,* and his personal favorite, *A Lover in Damascus,* complete with jingling camel harness.[87]

Numerous French music-hall artists of the 1920s and 1930s, including Joséphine Baker, Fernandel, Édith Piaf, Maurice Chevalier, and Charles Trenet, contributed to that country's Orientalist repertoire. Their works made little distinction between ports of call. Arabs, West Indians, Africans, Chinese, and Vietnamese were all subjects of comic representation. With tiles like *Sahara* (Nitta-Jo), *Chez les Bédouins* (Georgius), *Ali Ben Baba* (Maurice Chevalier), and *Nuit d'Alger* (Joséphine Baker) the songs portrayed the most obvious sentiments of empire, heroic French legionnaires, loyal or scheming natives, the vast desert, pitiless sun, romantic nights, and doomed temporary liaisons with indigenous women (but not the other way around). Moorish women were generically called "fatima," men "sidi," and they were usually identified with flute music, although at times African tom-tom drums were added as well.

Representative of such works was a French patriotic song, *Sidi-Ferruch,* named for the place where French forces originally landed outside Algiers in 1830:

> Sidi-Ferruch! Du coq français
> Observant les lois suzeraines,
> Italians, Espagnols, Maltais,
> Juifs, Mzabits des regions lointaines,
> Fiers gars, libres gars algériens,
> De l'amour fort de la Patrie,
> Musulmans autant que Chrétiens
> Chérissez tous votre Algérie.[88]

(Sidi-Ferruch! The French cock / observes sovereign laws / Italians, Spaniards, Maltese, / Jews, Mzabits [Berbers] from distant regions / loyal guys, free Algerian guys, / for the strong love of the country, / Muslims as well as Christians / all cherish your Algeria)."

American Orientalism

Eclecticism was a feature of American Orientalism, not only in films but also in other public manifestations such as architecture and popular culture. In the nineteenth century, the Chicago architect Louis Sullivan (1844–1900) employed Middle Eastern themes in many buildings. And in many cities movie houses were designed to look like Egyptian or Babylonian monuments; Sheik and Ramses condoms were for sale, as were Fatima and Salome cigarettes.[89]

One of the best-known newscasters and foreign correspondents of his time, Lowell Thomas, toured Great Britain and the United States in the 1920s with a travelogue about Lawrence of Arabia, whom he turned into a cult figure. His state-of-the-art technology included three projectors, specially shot film segments mixed with 285 colored slides, and a ton and a half of equipment that Thomas lugged to cities on two continents for several years. The performance opened in an Egyptian setting—the Nile, the pyramids illuminated by moonlight, and a dancer with seven veils. "Come with me on a magic carpet," Thomas said, stepping on stage, to launch the two-hour extravaganza.[90]

Orientalism in American popular culture in the late nineteenth and early twentieth centuries was most widely evident in the Shriner movement. Its Masonic halls carried Arab-type names, elaborate temples went up in places like Wilkes-Barre, Pennsylvania., and Richmond, Virginia, and dentists and bankers straight out of Sinclair Lewis novels traded their business suits for Zouave-like costumes and scimitars, and marched in local parades to tunes such as John Philip Sousa's *Nobles of the Mystic Shrine March*.

The Ancient Arabic Order Nobles of the Mystic Shrine, founded in 1870, claimed a half million members by 1922. A parallel African American Shriners organization emerged during this time as well, and in 1923 the Shriner legions descended on Washington, D.C., for a three-day convention; its theme was "Park your camel with Uncle Sam." Shriner meeting places were "mosques," members wore red felt fezzes decorated with tassels, gold-thread inscriptions, and rhinestones. Members traced a spurious linage to Ali, son-in-law of the Prophet, and greeted one another with "as-Salam Aleikum" (Peace be with you).

The spread of such popular cultural inspirations was spurred on by the Chicago World's Fair of 1893, which featured Turkish, Tunisian, and Algerian displays and a "Streets of Cairo" that attracted more than 2.5 million visitors with bazaars, snake charmers, and belly dancers.[91] One viewer said the Egyptian dancers were "formless as badly-stuffed animals, as homely as owls, and graceless as stall-fed bovines ... their abdominal muscles were the only portions of anatomy or mind which showed any cultivation."[92] A new invention,

American composer John Philip Sousa (with fez) on the cover of his *Nobles of the Mystic Shrine March* (1923). By the 1930s the Masonic Ancient Order of the Nobles of the Mystic Shrine, with their Middle East–type costumes, claimed over half a million members in the United States. (Collections of the Chancellor Robert R. Livingston Masonic Grand Lodge, New York City)

the camera, helped spread impressions from the fair through postcards, picture books, and camera rentals, sending photos of a visitor on a camel or of Oriental buildings or costumes to folks back home all over America.

Although the Shriner rituals, dress, and symbolism contained an overlay of Oriental motifs, none had any real links to Islamic culture. Cultural historians and psychologists may eventually have a field day with the subject, but some obvious explanations are possible. There was an escapist quality to the Shriners, as there was to the Orient in films and music halls of the period. Also part of the allure was belonging to a secret society, enjoying male camaraderie, horseplay, and living for a brief while in a fantasy world, for which a fantasy "Orient" provided a setting. It was a bit like entering the world of Oz, but for middle-aged white American males rather than for Dorothy and her companions.

5

The Summing Up

The basic image of Islam in the West was in place by the Middle Ages and continues to the present. It contains four elements: religiously, Muhammad was either the Antichrist or a fallen Lucifer-like figure, a cardinal who failed to be elected pope, so he turned on the church. Personally, he was a flawed human being, unable or unwilling to contain his sexuality; he was polygamous or a predator, depending on the account. Politically, he was either a major leader who united the desert tribes for the first time ever or a greedy despot. Finally, and contradicting what had been said before, he was an original source of the wisdom of the East for some and the last and greatest prophet of divine revelation for others, giving Muhammad a lasting place in history.

While these basic constructs—in shorthand heretic, sensualist, ruler, and religious leader—endured as the four pillars around which the Western image of Islam was formed over the centuries, gradually new, more informed appraisals were added in successive epochs; they were added, however, as layers or overlays to the extant images of Islam long in place, and not as full replacements for the older prejudices and fears Westerners held about Islam. These never fully disappeared, but were submerged to reappear at various times of real or imagined threat. Conceptually, increased tolerance and understanding of Islam was not linear and upward but resembled more the contrasting themes and variations of a musical composition that, after once being played, may reappear later in a somewhat different form.

Early Times and the Middle Ages

The negative image of Islam appeared early in Europe's history, even before the Prophet's birth. As early as Greek and Roman times, Westerners partially defined themselves by seeing themselves in opposition to the roving bands of armed, unknown tribesmen on Asia's frontiers. This created a self-perceived division between liberty-loving "civilized" Europeans and despotic "barbarian" strangers. The Bible became the great anti-Islamic text, although it was compiled centuries before the Prophet's birth and never mentioned Muslims. Still, its apocalyptical passages were filled with vivid warnings about the "abomination that desolates" from the Prophet Daniel (9:27, 11:31, and 12:11). Later Matthew (24:15–31) warned of the coming of false prophets and messiahs cleverly resembling Christ. Willing minds quickly connected these forces of evil with Islam, a theme theologians of the Middle Ages would squeeze for all its possible use.

But gradually the anti-Islamic arguments of religious writers like John of Damascus, Isidore of Seville, and Peter the Venerable were modified by a new generation of commentators. By the late twelfth century the archenemy Saladin was represented as a legendary and often chivalrous figure, and the Holy Roman Emperor, Frederick II of Hohenstaufen (reigned 1212–1250) displayed an independent outlook toward Islam and a curiosity about Arabic science and philosophy. Meanwhile, widely scattered communities of Muslim traders settled throughout southern Italy and elsewhere along the Mediterranean coast, and from the eighth to the fifteenth centuries vibrant Jewish, Arabic, and Christian communities lived together in Spain in relative harmony. During this time the contributions of Arab sciences, mathematics, medicine, and philosophy became widely known and adopted in the West.

The Sixteenth, Seventeenth, and Eighteenth Centuries

Other positive strains of interpretation about Islam emerged by the sixteenth century. Michael de Montaigne's widely circulated *Essais* (1580) were relatively free from the strident dogmatism of his predecessors and included numerous factual references to Turkish history and customs. Additionally, European traders visited Turkey, Persia, and North Africa in increasing numbers, established embassies, expanded commercial relations, and imported coffee, tea, spices, precious metals, and cloth in increasing quantities.

Meanwhile, creative artists invented an Islam of their own. Muslim imagery became widely employed in European music and drama. Muslim–Christian plays and operas often took the form of carefully staged crusader combats. Christians always won, but usually after bloody fighting, and sometimes with brief but compassionate encounters with Muslim opponents, as in Claudio Monteverdi's one-act opera, *Combattimento di Tancredi e Clorinda* (1624).

Despite the gradual increase in new information about Islam and the Orient, European perspectives were always filtered through the prism of local needs and interests. By the seventeenth century, Europeans had invented a carefully constructed Orient to serve their own purposes. But as political and economic contact with the Orient increased, more scattered information about its people, beliefs, and cultures emerged and was selectively integrated into Western beliefs about the overseas world. And this imaginary Orient allowed Europeans to help shape their identity in opposition to it. Such an Orient never engaged in dialogue as an equal partner of the West, and remained the passive background, the canvas on which Europeans painted whatever they imagined the distant world to be.[1] At the same time, French writers fashioned an Islam for their own use; the clever opinions of Montesquieu's imagined "Persians" provided a convenient way of suggesting political reforms for France while avoiding the censors.

The scientific study of Islam was now established, primarily through the study of Arabic and other Oriental languages in Paris, Leiden, Rome, Oxford, Cambridge, and elsewhere. In England, a chair of Arabic was created at Cambridge University in 1632 and another was established at Oxford in 1636. The Koran had been inadequately translated from French into English in 1649; George Sale, a London layman-solicitor, produced his own widely disseminated translation in 1734. Sale called the Prophet "a man of at least tolerable morals, and not such a monster of wickedness as he is usually represented."[2] Simon Ockley, a Cambridge cleric-linguist, produced *The History of the Saracens* (1718), the first comprehensive history of its kind in English. Such early scholars laid the foundations for what became an increasingly informed understanding of Islam.

During the eighteenth century, several English writers presented a more informed image of Islam than had been available previously, and gradually popularized Islam to wider audiences. For the English historian Edward Gibbon, Islam contained several positive attributes; Gibbon's *The History of the Decline and Fall of the Roman Empire* (1788) included an accessible biography of Muhammad, memorable for portraying the changing complexity of the Prophet's religious growth and evolving political role. Muhammad was described as an admirable person during his Mecca years, but once he fully accepted his religious leadership role after the hijrah to Medina, he became an ambitious impostor.

Of growing, sustained popularity were *The Thousand and One Nights*, sometimes called the *Arabian Nights*, colorful and suspenseful Oriental tales. The tales, which appeared in French and English versions by the late eighteenth century, were in turn bawdy, misogynous, virtuous, adventurous, and comic in content. Slowly, the image of Islam was being transformed from being one primarily about the Antichrist to a portrayal of a lively, exotic, spice-and-silk-filled civilization.

In addition to religious representations of Islam, two roads were now open to Western observers of Islam: the exotic and the political-commercial. The exotic East was an imaginary realm, a place of mental escape and for the projection of images of the sacred and profane, and of a multitude of racial and sexual images, themes that became increasingly important during the nineteenth century. The political-commercial Orient was the locus of a growing trade with Europe and real geographical features, including archeological ruins to be explored and shipped back to London, Paris, and Berlin. It would soon become the battleground where European imperial powers would fight one another, make alliances with local rulers, and subjugate countries for more than a century.

The Nineteenth Century

During the nineteenth century, a new school of thought on Islam emerged. Thomas Carlyle's famous 1840 lecture on "The Hero as Prophet" marked a major shift in European representations of Muhammad, whom Carlyle portrayed as a genuine world leader alongside Napoleon, Frederick the Great, and Shakespeare. Muhammad saw through the gross materialism surrounding him and created a new hope for humanity through his life and teachings. Neither a heretic nor an impostor, he was a great world religious leader. "A greater number of God's creatures believes in Mahomet's word at this hour than in any word whatever," Carlyle wrote.[3] Yet the old negatives remained. Cardinal Newman's sustained attacks on Islam in a set of nine lectures in 1853 were but one example, answered, though not directly, by a more inclusive and tolerant Anglican writer, F. D. Maurice.[4]

"Tourist Islam" also became a distinct reality. Steamship travel to the Middle East, the opening of the Suez Canal in 1869, the invention of photography, and the growth of popular newspaper and magazine journalism accounted for the spread of widespread curiosity about the Middle East and the more distant Orient. The weekly newspaper accounts of Mark Twain and the popular novels of Pierre Loti are but two examples of such works. Loti, a career naval officer, wrote thirty-nine published volumes that sold over a million copies. The content of his works was generally the same—an exotic setting and a passionate, ill-fated romance between two people of different races, usually a white-skinned dominant male and a darker-skinned vulnerable native woman who left their own cultures, often with fatal consequences.

Contradictions were numerous in nineteenth-century British interpretations of Islam. Sir Thomas Muir, a prominent linguist-colonial administrator with long service in India, found it a regressive force while Charles Forster, an English cleric and author of *Mahometanism Unveiled*, said that after Christianity and Judaism, Islam represented "the best and most beneficial form of religion" to emerge in the world. Islam was portrayed by European artists in similarly contradictory ways, with reverence and disdain, as the world of pious Muslims or sensual Arabs. Jean-Léon Gérôme painted mosques and Muslims at prayer in hushed, seemingly timeless settings as well as innumerable harem scenes of reclining white women lounging on lush divans.

For American Protestants, on the other hand, the Holy Land of nineteenth-century popular imagery was a tranquil setting often uncluttered with people. A few Jews and Arabs appeared as props, busy at farming or local trades, but otherwise they kept out of the way. "We know far more about the land of the Jews than the degraded Arabs who hold it," a magazine writer said of the Holy Land in 1855. More a mental than a geographical construct, the land "Where the feet of Jesus have trod is the Holy Land" is how the Jerusalem YMCA defined its boundaries.[5] Sandboxes in Protestant Sunday schools across America rebuilt miniature versions of its hills and temples. Catholics, however, urged their pilgrims to spend their tourist dollars and find spiritual edification in Rome, the residence of the pope and of the great basilica of St. Peter's, the mother church of Roman Catholicism.

In those rare instances when they were mentioned, Muslims were presented as scheming heathen, not unlike American Indians. Mark Twain elaborated on this theme, as did other writers, who to the list of suspect persons added the Barbary pirates, who represented a real threat to the young American republic. This helped create an "us" against "them" mentality on the part of Americans, God's elect, regarding foreigners—civilized, peaceful Christians against the uncivilized, warlike heathen foreigners. This theme, borrowed in part from the European past, was carried unhesitatingly into America's global future. The Holy Land connection thus became an informing image for American expansionism, providing a religious raison d'être for the imperialistic ideology then in formation. Americans saw a new Jerusalem emerging in their country, an American Zion, which American diplomats, military, and missionaries would extend in various ways to the world's ends.

By the late nineteenth century, biology, anthropology, and other sciences had combined in the hands of some practitioners to produce a relative ranking of world civilizations along racial lines. Islam did not fare well. Typical of early racial profiling was the work of French scholar Ernest Renan. On a superior-inferior scale, for Renan Christianity was the leading religion, the product of the higher Aryan race. Islam, of lower Semitic origin, represented an inhibiting "iron circle" around the heads of believers, and kept them from absorbing modern advances in human knowledge.

Such relative ranking of races and civilizations was as elaborate as it was wrong. In the twentieth century, Arnold Toynbee elaborated on it in voluminous writings, constructing a panoply of competing world civilizations, each with distinctive characteristics of ascendancy or decline. But the chimerical data used in his rankings faded away when examined closely. This West versus the rest overview of history was abandoned by most mainstream historians as an interesting but failed experiment, retained only by a handful of "clash of civilization" proponents who struggled to infuse it with oxygen long after its demise.

The Twenty-First Century: Violence and Global Islam

The West's understanding of Islam in the twenty-first century represents both continuity and change from what has gone before. Continuity in that scholarship in everything from linguistics and anthropology to the study of Islamic law and mysticism has produced an outpouring of new studies, transforming a limited focus on the Middle East to the study of global Islam in all its complexity. There is continuity as well, in that the persistence of long-standing prejudices remain about Islamic societies, their beliefs, and practices.[6]

Change has come through the easy accessibility of world travel and the spread of the Internet, and means that by the early twenty-first century it is possible to speak of cyber Islam and the Internet *ummah,* a global electronic community. Additionally, the sheer growth of Islamic numbers—over a billion Muslims by 2005, only about 18 percent of them living in the Arab world, requires a new perspective in the West. Islam has become a major force in Asia from Pakistan to the Philippines.

The image of Islam no longer exists as mainly a passive construct in Western minds; it has emerged as a global presence to contest the West, and the basic conditions of the encounter are often hostile. When the governor of Baghdad said, "We are like a razor blade stuck in the throat. The U.S. cannot swallow us or spit us out," his language suggested the present moment's difficulties.

What has emerged is a new image of Islam in the West, an active, not a passive force, as a global political-militant presence seemingly preaching a brand of extremist religion and ideologies that appears to be in sharp conflict with Western values. Yet while extremists claim the limelight, far more significant in its long-term implications is the Islamic activism of what might be called with some accuracy "shopkeeper Islam," the religious expressions of moderate, middle-of-the-road clerics, teachers, merchants, professionals, and government workers. Representing a growing population throughout the Islamic world, many of such members consciously disavow the West, at least in its present relationships, for its secularism and militarism, but do not condone violence. Disenchanted with their own corrupt, nonresponsive governments that fail to deliver jobs, basic public safety, or educational and medical services, such people increasingly see Islamic-governed societies as a source of hope. When bumper stickers on dust-covered northern Nigerian taxis proclaim "Islam Is the Answer," the not-so-hidden message is that corrupt, ineffective state governments should give way to Islamic-ruled ones.

This complex relationship is portrayed by the British playwright David Edgar in *Pentecost* (1994), mutatis mutandis, a medieval morality play written for modern times.[7] The play's ostensible theme concerns the (fictional) discovery of an amazing medieval fresco on the walls of a decrepit Balkan church of disputed ownership. The fresco, representing Europe's past, is possibly as important a discovery as the Pompeii ruins, for it employed three-dimensioned perspective long before it was known in the West. Additional drama is added when it appears than an unknown master artist from the East might have been the fresco's painter and inventor of this revolutionary advance in art. The issue is never resolved, for just as the discovery is made, a band of armed refugees seizes the church. Their numbers symbolically include a Palestinian, a Kuwaiti, an Azeri, a Mozambican, a Bosnian, a Russian, a Ukrainian, an Afghan, a Kurd, a Sri Lankan, and a Bosnian Roma. Fleeing their conflict-ridden homelands, they want access to Europe, representing jobs, stability, and the prospect of a new life. As tensions mount, one of the group, an armed Middle Eastern male, threatens to destroy the fresco. But its real destruction comes moments later, when government-sponsored German-speaking commandos burst through a hole they have hacked through the wall, destroying the masterpiece, and shoot some of the refugees and a European art professional.

At the play's end a local curator says the ancient structure that had symbolized Central Europe has endured until now as "Church. Mosque. Stable. Torture center. Foodstore. Fortress. Cemetery ... Middle Europe theme park?" A Jewish American art historian summarizes the basic East–West

Osama Bin Laden and Ayman al-Zwahiri, Saudi and Egyptian terrorists, pose with an automatic weapon propped between them in this shot for al-Jazeera television. The background cave symbolizes the site on a hill outside Mecca where Muhammad prayed during the Night of Power and received the initial revelations of the Koran. Responsible for the 9/11 attacks, Bin Laden and al-Zwahiri coauthored a February 23, 1998, fatwa urging Muslims everywhere "to kill the Americans and their allies, civilian and military." (Associated Press Images)

relationship: "We are the sum of all the people who've invaded us. We are, involuntarily, each other's guests."[8]

In summary, two aspects, violence and reciprocity, have come to characterize the dominant image of Islam in the West in recent times: violence in the widespread prevalence of targeted killings, riots, bombings, and warfare that have devastated parts of the world; reciprocity in that Islam is no longer the passive tableau on which Westerners fashion an image. The Western image of Islam is now the subject of constant modification on the basis of sustained, complex, almost instantaneous global contact.

Pope Benedict XVI

Misunderstandings between Islam and the West with serious consequences continue unabated to the present day. During the autumn of 2006, Pope Benedict XVI returned for six days to the Bavaria of his youth. The leader of

1.1 billion Roman Catholics visited several south German church sites, and on September 12 delivered a lecture at Regensberg University, where he had once been a theology professor. It was a lengthy, convoluted discourse on the relationship of faith and science, and the loss of religious belief in Europe, much of it in the code language of professional theologians and philosophers of religion. But early in the speech the seventy-nine-year-old pontiff interjected a section about Islam that hardly related to the topic and that, within hours, resulted in protests throughout the Muslim world. The pope quoted from a conversation between a fourteenth-century Byzantine Christian emperor of a small territory, Manuel Paleologos II, and an educated Persian about the differences between Christianity and Islam: "The emperor comes to speak about the issue of jihad, holy war," Benedict remarked. "He said, I quote, 'show me just what Muhammad brought that was new, and then you will find things only evil and inhuman such as his command to spread by the sword the faith he preached.' "[9]

Benedict neither endorsed nor disagreed with the statement. The larger question was why ever he chose it, for it did not fit with the rest of his remarks, most of which were about "dehellenization." It was not that Benedict was being intentionally anti-Islamic; two Christian experts he referred to in his speech, the Lebanese Arabist Theodore Khoury and the French Islamic scholar Roger Arnaldez, had both written mainstream works on the interaction of Islam and Christianity. And Benedict's larger message was that violence solves nothing.

Responses to the pope's comments were instantaneous. Cyber Islam and the Internet *ummah,* the worldwide Islamic community linked by state-of-the-art telecommunications, were now realities in international political and religious discourse, aided by the Internet, cell phone, and television. Palestinian Muslims set fire to five churches in the West Bank, including an Anglican and a Greek Orthodox church. The grand sheik of Cairo's al-Azhar Mosque said the pope's comments "reflected ignorance" and broke off talks with the Vatican. Morocco recalled its ambassador to the Vatican, the rarely heard-from Sudanese and Algerian parliaments passed resolutions of outrage. Egyptian demonstrators chanted "Oh Crusaders, oh cowards," and a Hamas official remarked, "This is another Crusader war against the Arab and Muslim world."[10] Still others compared Benedict's talk to Pope Urban's launching of the Crusades in the late eleventh century.

A planned papal trip to Turkey later in the year was still scheduled. Benedict, at a hastily called meeting with ambassadors from Islamic countries, said the quoted section did not reflect his personal opinion and he was "deeply sorry" about the furor it created. Dialogue was a "vital necessity" for the future, he said, adding, "the lessons of the past cannot fail to prompt us to seek out the path of reconciliation." Central to the Catholic position, he continued, was the earlier Vatican Council statement that "the Church looks with esteem on the Muslim world, which believes in one sole God." Finally, he descended from his gold and red velvet throne to shake hands with each envoy.[11]

But indignation continued to spread. A sixty-five-year-old Italian nun was killed in riots in Somalia, and by month's end more than 2,500 items had been posted on one global news Web site about the pope's remarks. The range of such reactions fit predictable categories. Responses ranged from angry slurs at the pope and "the Crusaders" to "let's get this behind us and move on." The secretary general of the Organization of the Islamic Conference said, "the confrontation is neither in the interest of Islam nor in the interest of Christianity and humanity."[12] Jihadist groups threatened to "destroy the Cross and the jug of wine" and called the pope "the donkey of Rome." Conspiracy theorists sprung up like mushrooms; one said the pope was being extorted for his Nazi Youth membership.[13] Others read the pope's September 12 speech as a carefully planned post–September 11 anniversary attack on Islam. An Iranian commentator somehow managed to tie Americans and Zionists to an orchestrated anti-Muslim plot that included the pope's address, Salman Rushdie's novel The Satanic Verses, and Danish cartoons that included caricatures of the Prophet.[14]

But other more moderate voices, such as those of the Muslim presidents of Indonesia and Malaysia, said the pope's apology allowed all parties to "end the global outcry among Muslims." A Saudi writer observed, "We need to be strong in confronting this issue, but burning flags and images and insulting the Christian religion is not the way."[15] An Egyptian Muslim Brotherhood leader remarked, "While anger over the Pope's remarks is necessary, it shouldn't last for long."[16] Italian Muslims added, "The Pope did the most that we could expect of him." But Italian and German Ministry of Interior officials took a different position, saying there was nothing wrong with the pope's remarks, and that Islam had a strong fundamentalist strain to it and Muslims didn't know how to interact with Europeans in a constructive way.[17]

The incident raises the larger issue of how Muslims and Christians might engage in a healthy dialogue. Widespread ignorance and misunderstanding about Islam exists in the West, but the reverse holds true as well. Additionally, many Muslims live in countries where active discussion of differing political and religious viewpoints is either suppressed in the media or repressed by those in power. But Singapore's Prime Minister Lee Hsien Loong said that social cohesion in societies would weaken unless active steps were taken to increase cooperation among different faith communities. He added that the increased activities of individual faith communities should be matched by heightened cooperation among different religious groups at the local level. Such activity should include socializing and making friends with persons of different faiths, and preserving public spaces such as schools, parks, and workplaces as "shared places where everyone belongs and feels comfortable."[18]

Although the pope's four-day visit to Turkey in late November 2006 successfully touched all bases, making contact with Muslim and Orthodox religious leaders, it otherwise opened no new doors. Islam was still held in "esteem," a Catholic code word, in use since the 1960s, for respectful distancing. But a month later, when Spanish Muslims petitioned the pope to use space in Cordoba Cathedral, a former mosque, for periodic worship, they were flatly turned down. The cathedral, a UNESCO World Heritage site, was one of the world's largest and most architecturally imposing mosques during the Cordoba Caliphate. When the region was reconquered by Christians in 1236, it was consecrated as a Roman Catholic cathedral. Gradually Spanish Gothic,

Reconquista Festival, 2006. Spanish villagers dressed like Moors parade through Cervillente, Valencia, in one of the many elaborate such festivals held annually throughout Spain. Some mock battles include an effigy of the Prophet Muhammad being thrown off castle ramparts or having his firecracker-filled head blown off to commemorate the Christian victory over the Moors in 1492. In recent years, the content of such festivals has become less violent, following protests by Spanish Muslims. (Reuters Images)

Baroque, and other architectural features were crowded into its once unified and harmonious space.

The Spanish Islamic Board, in petitioning the pope, said it did not desire to take over the holy place, "but to create in it, together with you and other faiths, an ecumenical space unique in the world." Mansur Escudero, general secretary of the Spanish Islamic Board, said such a gesture by the pope would help "awake the conscience" of followers of both faiths and help bury their warlike past. He said that in the present day security guards often prevent Muslims who visit the former mosque from praying there. Rome's answer came via the local bishop of Cordoba, Juan Jose Asenjo. He replied that the faithful would only be confused by the joint use of places of worship and that such an action would not contribute to the peaceful coexistence of the two world religions. The shared use of worship space might be appropriate in an airport or Olympic village, the bishop reasoned, but not in a consecrated Catholic cathedral.[19]

Representative Keith Ellison in Congress

Another recent illustration of the complexities of contemporary intercultural, interfaith relations occurred in America. When Keith Ellison, the first Muslim member of the U.S. Congress, was sworn in as part of the 110th Congress on January 4, 2007, it became both a historic and controversial event. The Michigan Democrat and African American descendent of slaves had converted to Islam while a student at Detroit's Wayne State University.

Opposition to Ellison, a long-established Minneapolis attorney and community leader, and to the use of the Koran in Congress was voiced by Rep. Virgil Goode, a Republican legislator from rural Virginia, who wrote constituents, "The Muslim representative from Minnesota was elected by the voters of that district and if American citizens don't wake up and adopt the Virgil Goode position on immigration there will likely be many more Muslims elected to office and demanding the use of the Koran."[20] Members of Congress actually were sworn in as a group by simply raising their right hands and repeating the oath of office. Individual swearing-in photos were later taken in the office of the Speaker of the House on a Bible, Torah, no book at all, or, in Ellison's case, an English translation of the Koran that once belonged to President Thomas Jefferson. Ironically, Jefferson was born in Albemarle County, Virginia, now part of Goode's congressional district.

Goode tied his opposition to Ellis and the Koran to fears of Middle Easterners immigrating to the United States, adding "I fear that in the next

The first Muslim member of the U.S. Congress, Representative Keith Ellison, a forty-three-year-old attorney and Minnesota Democrat, used Thomas Jefferson's copy of the Koran for this swearing-in photo with his wife, Kim, and Speaker of the House Nancy Pelosi, on January 4, 2007. Jefferson's copy of the Koran was a 1734 English translation by George Sale kept in the rare book collection of the Library of Congress, Washington, D.C. (Michaela McNichol photo, Library of Congress)

century we will have many more Muslims in the United States if we do not adopt the strict immigration policies that I believe are necessary to preserve the values and beliefs traditional to the United States of America and prevent our resources from being swamped."

The use of the Koran "undermines American civilization," Los Angeles radio talk show commentator Dennis Prager remarked. Other commentators said that only the Christian Bible should be used in such ceremonies, but other, more moderate voices were heard as well. A congressman from New Jersey, whose district contains a large number of Muslims, took issue with Goode's position. Rep. William J. Parscrell, Jr., a Democrat, wrote, "Your letter wrongly equates the issue of immigration with a fear of Muslim integration in our society. I take your remarks as personally offensive to the large community of Muslim-Americans I represent." Muslim American groups protested as well. James Zogby, president of the Arab American Institute, said the swearing in on the Koran both reflected the religious tolerance of founders like Benjamin Franklin, George Washington, and Thomas Jefferson, and represented "a great American story. It deserves to be celebrated. It is now part of our history. In becoming the first, Ellison, like Jackie Robinson [the first African American major league baseball player] makes us all richer and better."[21]

Following the group swearing-in ceremony, Ellison walked over to shake Goode's hand while proponents of the two positions continued to spread their arguments.

Prince Charles and the "Unity of Faiths"

One of the most impressive efforts in recent times to bridge the gap between Muslims, Jews, and Christians came in a speech on the "Unity of Faith" that Crown Prince Charles of Great Britain gave at historic al-Azhar University in Cairo on March 21, 2006. Drawing on the common roots of the three Abrahamic faiths, he noted, "I do not want you to imagine for one moment that I think they are one and the same. There are differences, and we should celebrate them. But in the things that matter most, we have a common root." His speech was also about the challenge of interpreting sacred texts, the "difficult and subtle art that gave rise in Islam to great principles of interpretation and great schools of jurisprudence." Clearly having current disputes in mind, he stated, "Between the text and the meaning of the text—between the meaning of God's word for all time and its meaning for this time—falls the act of interpretation.... Today, too often, there seems to be a tendency to read texts as if they needed no interpretation, as if we could read their meaning on the surface. That does violence to the Divine word, and violence to the word eventually leads to violence to the person, and to the world."

He concluded with a thoughtful passage that could serve as a starting point among those who would work for greater understanding among Muslims, Jews, and Christians:

> When all we can hear in sacred texts is simple certainties, when all we can see in God's multicolored world is black and white, we begin to divide humanity into simple oppositions: the good and the evil; the pious and the profane; us and the enemy. And this then leads to hatred and violence. For it is then that we lose the single most important principle that unites the Abrahamic faith: In Judaism, "Love your neighbor as yourself"; in Christianity, "All things whatsoever you would that men should do to you, do you to them"; and in Islam, "No-one of you is a believer until he desires for his brother that which he desires for himself."[22]

Appendix

"Am I Not Your Lord?" Kenneth Cragg
on Muslim–Christian Dialogue

No person in modern times has contributed more to an understanding of Islam in the non-Muslim world than Kenneth Cragg, who turned ninety-four on March 8, 2007. During an Oxford sabbatical in 2003 I spent several sessions interviewing Cragg, who was generous with his time and hospitality despite a busy schedule of writing and speaking. His base was a dining room table with a small 1960s portable typewriter. Near it was a yellow pad and fountain pen, polished with years of use, and carefully arranged folders, all in a tidy ground-level apartment in Pegasus Grange, Whitehouse Road, Oxford.

The Call of the Minaret, one of his thirty books, was a path-breaking work half a century ago, which described the basis of the Islamic faith to Western audiences, and urged Christians to respond with love, inclusiveness, and patience. It was now in its third printing, and from Cragg's pen poured a series of related volumes, including *The Event of the Qur'an, Jesus and the Muslim, Readings in the Qur'an, Islam among the Spires: An Oxford Reverie,* and *Am I Not Your Lord?*

"It was considered enemy country," Cragg said of the Middle East he first visited as a young missionary in 1939 and from which he officially retired as an Anglican bishop in 1985. He was born in 1913 in the northern seacoast city of Blackpool, where his father was a struggling but devout shopkeeper who wanted to apprentice young Kenneth as an errand boy to a local pharmacist. A master at the local school persuaded Cragg's parents to let Kenneth continue his education, which led to a scholarship to Jesus College, Oxford, where he read modern history and took his first degree in 1934. Financially, Oxford life was "pretty much near the bone." The youth could not afford to join the social life of the Oxford Union, but after some hesitation joined the Christian Union, an evangelical group, and "it seemed to be the right thing." He began to think about ordination after graduation, took a short course at Bristol, and was ordained on his twenty-third birthday in 1936.

His first Middle East posting was to Beirut, where he spent eight years, and on New Year's Eve 1939 married Milena, his companion for forty-eight years. His assignment was as head of a Christian hostel, St. Justin's House, at American University. Cragg added Arabic to Latin, acquired an Arabic concordance, and became fascinated with the Koran and the richness of Islamic spirituality and culture. Eighteen months later he could preach in Arabic. The next sixty years were spent studying, translating, and writing about Islam and Christianity. In 1947 the Craggs and their two young sons returned to Oxford, where Kenneth became vicar of a small church near Oxford and completed a D.Phil. in 1950 on "Islam in the Twentieth Century: The Relationship of Christian Theology to Its Problems." From 1951 to 1956 he was professor of Arabic at Hartford Theological Seminary in Connecticut, and editor of *The Muslim World* quarterly. He returned to Jerusalem in 1957 as study secretary for the Near East Council of Churches and residentary canon at St. George's Cathedral, Jerusalem, where he established a series of seminars and other educational programs. From Jerusalem he moved to Canterbury to become part of the faculty and eventually warden of the Central College of the Anglican Community at Canterbury, until it closed in 1967.

Cragg next served as an Anglican assistant bishop in the Jerusalem jurisdiction, based in Cairo but covering a string of parishes from Morocco to the Arabian Peninsula. A visit to a city meant a meeting with local Islamic leaders, and the bishop was one of a handful of Western Christians to actively seek an open exchange with Islamic counterparts. Not all his clergy were similarly inclined.

From 1974 to 1978 he taught comparative religions at the University of Sussex, and also continued as an honorary assistant bishop, visiting the Middle East periodically. At various times he held visiting lectureships abroad, including in Lebanon, Egypt, the United States, and Nigeria. Cragg is an honorary fellow at Jesus College, and was a Bye Fellow of Gonville and Caius College, Cambridge, where he had a year free to do research. He presently is honorary assistant bishop in the Diocese of Oxford, and is active many Sundays.

In public presentations, his clear Lancashire accent and strong preacher's voice fill a room. Not far from his home is St. Matthew's Church, a large, bustling evangelical congregation that considers the distinguished scholar an active pastor in its midst. More than sixty persons gathered on a Wednesday night for his presentation on "At School in the Middle East." This was a play on words, suggesting there is always something more to learn about Arab history and religion. "Those who drink of the Nile always return," he quoted an Egyptian proverb. Presiding over a Sunday Eucharist, he resembled an eighteenth-century divine, with reflective countenance and sparse gestures, dressed in a simple long-sleeved white bishop's gown, as in a period engraving. The only hint of his international presence was a plain olivewood cross.

Cragg was one of the leaders who helped launch Oxford's Center for Islamic Studies, a controversial undertaking in the 1980s and beyond. Local residents and some conservative Christians did not want to see a mosque and minaret among the town's ancient stone spires, and only a tie-breaking vote by the City Council's chair allowed the project, even though it has the enthusiastic backing of its royal patron, Prince Charles. In 2006 construction was well advanced in Magdalen College's old Deer Park. The completed center includes space for thirty scholars, a library and lecture hall, plus a place of worship for Oxford's growing Islamic community. Centers for Jewish and Hindu studies exist already as satellites to Oxford's colleges.

Our questions and answers were compiled during several meetings from February 18 to March 18, 2003, and during the summer of 2004 in Oxford, supplemented here by occasional quotations from Cragg's books.

What do you think the shock waves of the Iraq war will be on Arab–Christian relations?

"I think they will set things back quite a lot. I feel very unhappy about this. Within the Koran there is a warrant to retaliate in a collective sense, and the whole concept of jihad—you must respond if you are attacked. It's giving democracy's opponents an excuse to censor, to display enmity and apathy. America is playing into the hands of hostile people. Even if the conflict goes well in terms of brevity, I think it will intensify the feeling that this is an enormous power resorting to bullying." As for violence, "It is no good politicians saying 'This is not Islam!' It is *an* Islam, just as Christianity was marked by the violence of the Crusades, Inquisition, and the Wars of Religion."

Is it possible for Muslims, Christians, and Jews to find a greater religious convergence than they have found to date?

"What I have always thought is there is a genuine, honest, real overlap between Muslims and Christianity, so that the attitude many people had of 'them and us' alienation is misleading. It is important not to let that sense of otherness dominate; we can fraternize over what is genuinely mutual. The concept of creation, human creaturehood, the divine stake and human response, and the whole concept of prophethood are concepts we share.

"An approach can come through a greater appreciation of the mystery of God. 'Am I not your Lord?' (Surah 7.172). The question is asked in the Koran. It is at the heart of all theology. All of the progeny of the sons of Adam are congregated like a vast audience, and are addressed with this question. A negative question, I learned as a young student in Latin class, expects a 'yes' answer. All humanity answers, almost in anticipation, 'Yes, we bear witness to it.' Although for Islam and Christianity the patterns of response are both significantly akin and yet in crucial ways different." In *Muhammad and the Christian,* the author wrote, "This is a deep and unifying truth that we all share. There is no doubt of our common Muslim/Christian theism. Where we differ is about the divine involvement this entails. It seems clear God cannot create and be as if He had not.... It is a divine enterprise hinged on man, an intention on God's part, staked in a human concurrence...to which the divine calls and the human responds."[1]

What do you say to those whose goal is to see the entire world become Islamic or Christian?

"Religions have to coexist and witness, but not demand to dominate in universal terms. Islam has to coexist. The modern world can not be properly addressed as something to be Islamized. One-fourth of all Muslims are in dispersion, and can not realistically anticipate Dar-al-Islam, an Islam exercising unilateral power. They need to ask themselves: what does it mean to be a British Muslim or an American Muslim?

"The Koran should not be taken like a telephone directory where every line is considered authoritative by itself. Also the Bible should be considered both a book of revelation and one written by several authors across a considerable span of history. Today we would regard ethnic cleansing in the Book of Joshua as obsolete, though we still have it in the text." The goal is, "to keep an honest realism and not be patronizing. To balance our apprehension of others considering not only what defines them but what commends them. So much depends on how we present our faith, at its core it is a mystery.

"What about the theology here? The question is how to diminish reliance on power. It is always a principal of Koranic exegesis that the content of the message reflects the temporal situation from which it emerges. The sequence of the Koran follows episodes of Muhammad's life. The occasions of revelation have to be interpreted in the context of 'time when' or 'place where' over twenty-three years."

Mission is common to both Islam and Christianity, but must it result in conflict?

"Mission is not fixed and static, it is something learned as we go along. The ten lepers learned of Jesus as they were cleansed, as they ministered they received.

"The Great Commission, the idea of making disciples out of all peoples, is in the plural. 'Peoples' means cultures, languages, and religions. The object of the Christian religion is to bring the individual into faith. The symbol of that is baptism. I wouldn't for a second suggest that we forsake that, but we must ask, 'Is there a discreet and compassionate Christian relationship we can establish with other religions as such, realizing they are going to be part of the scene?' They are not going to disappear. They are going to stay.

"These great religions have so much in their care. They preside over peace and war as we can see today. Plus questions of poverty, malnutrition, emigration. Christianity of itself cannot monopolize the answers to these human issues. Therefore surely other faiths are part of a genuine communication of meaning. I think part of the lesson of 'Go ye and make disciples of all nations' is can we possibly approximate the Muslim understanding of itself to the understanding of the love of God we have in the church?"

How do you respond when some Christians or Muslims are unyielding that their God is the only God? Is there any way to move beyond such an impasse?

"I don't think they are right. The ultimate power is not in doubt. But both faiths have the clear concept, it is over to you, you humans to have dominion of the earth. It is very clear there humanity is set over the 'middle state' of nature. We control the plow, wheel, and what we do with what there is shows dominion. Nature is susceptible to our intelligent control. This is the raw material of consecration. That is a Judeo-Christian-Islamic concept."

Repeatedly Cragg stressed cherishing creation as a religious concept common to the three Abrahamic faiths, one that could give them grounds for closer cooperation. He said, "We speak of 'The Holy Land' but it is a usage I do not favor because no land can be holy unless all lands are holy."

The bishop concluded, "I like to come around to it this way, you have to have an idea of divine power that is consistent with the givenness of creation. This is quite genuine. This is where environmental issues are so deep. If one accepts this argument, the handing over of relative control, of stewardship of the earth, leaves no question of the source of ultimate control.

"I sometimes use the analogy of education. In a descent school there is no doubt about who is presiding, but the subject matter is constantly adjusted to the ongoing business of education. A student has the possibility to err. That is a condition of education. Any teacher in a classroom is controlling, but in such a manner that students may make mistakes or come up with wrong answers."

Does my God win over your God? both sides might ask.

"My concern is that Muslims should be ready to appreciate those dimensions of the nature of God that are distinctively present in God in Christ. Michael Ramsey's phrase was 'the Christlikeness of God' and that is a distinctive Christian offering." Elsewhere the author wrote, "We have to surrender copyright ownership of that to which we witness. There is a sort of monolatry latent in aggressive witness or theology, if we are implying that we only possess God truly or that the truth of Him is copyright to us alone. . . . Monolatry, adopting one God, is distinguished sharply from monotheism or belief in the Oneness of God.[2]

"Some might conclude that witness is at an end. I don't think that would ever be true about the New Testament, but this witness should reflect that there are things we hold in trust for our tradition, so that the truth of them shall not perish from the earth. Yet, at the same time we should be happy to acknowledge that this to which they witness is in part a common territory. Other religions can come to a greater understanding of God through the Christian experience."

In *The Call of the Minaret* he wrote, "Those who say that Allah is not 'the God and father of our Lord Jesus Christ' are right if they mean that God is not so described by Muslims. They are wrong if they mean that Allah is other than the God of the Christian faith."[3]

Could Christians say Allah is God's Prophet, Christ is the Son of God, and leave the final disposition to the "God of Gods, Light of Lights, Very God of Very God"?

Cragg drew on linguistic examples for several answers. God is the same in the nominative in Islam and Christianity, but not quite the same in the predicate, the verbal forms used to access the noun. "A simple grammatical illustration; in Arabic grammar

God is subject of all predication, yet different in different predicates, yet all predicates lead to same subject. In English we can say 'Manchester is a city in Connecticut or a city in England.' The two predicates can be the same, but are different, leading to the same subject, the same word."

An important feature of both traditions is prophethood. "Prophethood is a tribute to the dignity of creaturehood. You would not send prophets to puppets. According to the Koran the human trustee is fickle, lacking in staying power, liable to forget. We are summoned to our vocation before God, but we forget or ignore our role. Creation, creaturehood, and prophecy are all related in the great religions."

What about the "You only" passages in the Bible, such as John 13:4–11, those that say that Christ is the only way to God?

"Again the noun-predicate illustration is helpful. In the Gospel of John he that has the son has the father. The father is fully and finally expressed in sending the son. When we appreciate the nature of Christhood we then see the nature of the God from whom that Christhood comes. No one comes unto this fatherhood except through the Son, just as no one comes to Shakespeare except through his plays, or no one comes to Beethoven except through his symphonies. That is the father-son relationship."

He switched the discussion's focus away from in-and-out scriptural barriers, observing, "The ultimate unbelief is ingratitude, never saying 'Thank you.' It is not the God we deny, it is the God we ignore." Part of the understanding of God, he continued, comes from the nature of divine-human interaction, "God, Allah, Deus, Yahweh, what sort of a word is it? It is a relational word, like friend. You can't be a friend unless you have someone to be friendly with. You can't be a host without guests. These are relational words. The heart of the Christian faith is that we are in a relationship with God. I'm not saying that the meaning of God is exhausted there. There are ninety-nine names of Allah, just as Christ is seen as savior, liberator, the lamb of God, etc."

How difficult is communication between religions?

"You can't be sure the other party has got what you said, but a misunderstanding can also be an occasion for learning for all people." Cragg recalled the example of a Christian missionary who was shocked when a Turkish girl said, "How disgusting!" of the concept of the lord as a shepherd in Psalm 23. "They are illiterate, outcasts, very much on the margins of society. I would never marry one!" she stated emphatically. A central Christian concept meant nothing in a Muslim society, unless the missionary could explain that the relationship of the sheep to the shepherd was one of trust, dependence, guidance, and protection, like the relationship between people and their God." Cragg was quick to tell audiences that a common vocabulary and metaphors are not shared by the worlds' religions, and that patient dialogue held in an atmosphere of mutual trust and respect is a requisite of a meaningful interfaith encounter.

He acknowledged that such encounters take place in a highly charged world, one of political, military, economic, and cultural disruptions. "These immense changes have occurred within two generations. We have absorbed these changes in the West since the Industrial Revolution, but in the Arab world people whose grandfathers were diving for pearls or driving camels are studying computers. But the twenty-first century is not like the sixth, and the world community is not like early Arabian society. Islam is final; therefore it must be interpreted in a way that is abreast of the present time. Islamic political thought is yet to adjust fully to the idea of the modern secular state. Traditionally, Muslims would and should be ruled by Muslims. The political dimension is integral to the completeness of Islam.[4] Thus, to live in the fullness of faith, Islamic peoples want to live in a state immersed with an Islamic worldview, sustained by Islamic law; living outside such a setting can leave a Muslim with strong feelings of being deeply uprooted.

How important are the Mecca-Medina differences in Islam?

"I am working on a book on the tragic in Islam. Sunni Islam often extols the amazing spread and success of Islam. Suffering is a minority concept, left largely with the Shia, who recall the immolation of Hasan, victim of the massacre perpetrated against Muhammad's direct lineage and followers. Many people do not realize that during the Meccan period Muhammad was a genuine sufferer. During those thirteen years he was up against the vested interests of a pagan shrine, and the pride of the custodians from whose tribe he came as a junior member. The situation was not unlike Paul in Ephesus, where the people were making shrines to Diana, asking what would happen to their Goddess if this new message was accepted?

"He was completely powerless. He bore this situation with very few results. He was in a kind of potential Gethsemene, mutatis mutandis. The light at end of tunnel was not in Mecca but in Medina, the people invited him to take refuge there. He departed with his followers and gained a wide following. This was the pivotal event. Time in Islam dates from hijrah (622 CE), not his birth date.

"After eight years the Meccans succumbed to his superior power. What had become a transtribal message became an intertribal war. In some senses, the hijrah was a tragedy, because conflict came in its wake. In Mecca, the message was just a religion, the practice of prayer, the beginnings of a caring community, without benefit of power. It was analogous in some ways to the first three centuries of Christianity, the religion in the catacombs before Constantine the conqueror made it an established world religion. The priority of Mecca over Medina is not in doubt; witness the pilgrimage. Mecca is the place to which every mosque points."

War, terrorism and globalization give unique coloration to the Islamic–Christian encounter. Hostility, misunderstanding, and arrogance on both sides historically characterize the exchange. At the same time, the number of those who seriously study the interaction of Islam and Christianity grows. Cragg's numerous works provide a point in medias res for such encounters, representing a half century's work of a conscious, faithful interlocutor between the two faith traditions.

Notes

INTRODUCTION

1. Todd Kontje, *German Orientalisms* (Ann Arbor: University of Michigan Press, 2004).

2. Leonard P. Harvey, *Islamic Spain, 1200 to 1500* (Chicago: University of Chicago Press, 1990) and *Muslims in Spain, 1500 to 1614* (Chicago: University of Chicago Press, 2005); Maxime Rodinson, *Europe and the Mystique of Islam*, trans. Roger Veinus (Seattle: University of Washington Press, 1987); Thierry Hentsch, *Imagining the Middle East*, trans. Fred A. Reed (New York: Black Rose Books, 1992).

3. Bernard Lewis and Peter M. Holt, eds., *Historians of the Middle East* (London: Oxford University Press, 1962), 1.

4. Fitzroy MacLean, *Eastern Approaches* (New York: Penguin, 2004; originally published in 1949).

5. Hans J. Mol, *Meaning and Place, an Introduction to the Social Scientific Study of Religion* (New York: Pilgrim Press, 1983), 117–118. The definition of "image" is derived from *The New Shorter Oxford English Dictionary*, ed. Lesley Brown (Oxford: Clarendon Press, 1993), 1: 1312.

6. John L. Stoddard, *John L. Stoddard's Lectures* (Boston: Balch Brothers, 1897), 224.

7. "Jews 'Apes' in Saudi School Textbooks," *The Sunday Telegraph* (London), June 25, 2006, p. 27.

8. "Falwell Sorry for Bashing Muhammad," CBS News, Internet version, October 14, 2002.

9. "Pat Robertson Describes Islam as Violent Religion," Associated Press, Internet version, February 23, 2003.

CHAPTER I

1. *The World Almanac and Book of Facts 2001* (Mahwah, N.J.: World Almanac Books, 2001), 689. Fourteen different population estimates from as many sources are listed in the Internet entry of Answers.com, "Islam in the United States."

2. "Seeing Islam as 'Evil' Faith, Evangelicals Seek Converts," *New York Times,* May 27, 2003, 1; Don Richardson, *Secrets of the Koran* (Ventura, Calif.: Regal Books, 2003).

3. "For Religious Bigotry," *New York Times* editorial, August 26, 2004.

4. Zbigniew Brzezinski, " 'Some Stirred-up Muslims,' Reflections on Soviet Intervention in Afghanistan "(1998) in *The Middle East and the Islamic World Reader,* ed. Marvin E. Gettleman and Stuart Schaar (New York: Grove, 2003), 274.

5. Samuel P. Huntington, "The Clash of Civilizations?" *Foreign Affairs* 72.3 (1993), 22–49.

6. Bernard Lewis, "The Roots of Muslim Rage," *Atlantic Monthly* 266 (September 1990), 59–60.

7. Ibid., 59.

8. The "Clash of Civilizations" issue is discussed in Zachary Lockman, *Contending Visions of the Middle East: The History and Politics of Orientalism* (Cambridge: Cambridge University Press, 2004), 233–236.

9. Edward Said, *Orientalism* (New York: Pantheon, 1978), 3.

10. "Arabs, Islam, and the Dogmas of the West," *New York Times Book Review,* October 31, 1976, 4.

11. David Kopf, "Hermeneutics versus History," quoted in Alexander Lyon Macfie, ed., *Orientalism: A Reader* (New York: New York University Press, 2000), 195.

12. John M. MacKenzie, *Orientalism: History, Theory, and the Arts* (Manchester: Manchester University Press, 1995), xv.

13. Ibid., 208.

14. Richard W. Bulliet, *The Case for Islamo-Christian Civilization* (New York: Columbia University Press, 2004), 97.

15. Gerald Ackerman, personal communication, February 9, 2006.

16. Bulliet, *Case for Islamo-Christian Civilization,* 49–50.

17. Richard Fletcher, *The Cross and the Crescent: Christianity and Islam from Muhammad to the Reformation* (New York: Viking, 2004), 155–156.

18. Park Honan, *Christopher Marlowe: Poet and Spy* (New York: Oxford University Press, 2005), 29.

19. John Victor Tolan, *Saracens: Islam in the Medieval European Imagination* (New York: Columbia University Press, 2002), xxiii.

20. Hentsch, *Imagining the Middle East,* ix.

21. *Algiers,* directed by John Cromwell, 1938. Alpha Video, Narberth, Pa., 2002.

22. Rodinson, *Europe and the Mystique of Islam,* 11.

23. Lockman, *Contending Visions of the Middle East,* 34–37, 111–119.

24. Quoted in John C. Lamoreaux, "Early Christian Responses to Islam," in *Medieval Christian Perceptions of Islam, A Book of Essays,* ed. John Victor Tolan (New York: Garland, 1996), 9.

25. Fletcher, *Cross and the Crescent*, 3–11.

26. *The Oxford English Dictionary*, 2nd edition, ed. J. A. Simson and E. S. C. Weiner, vol. 14 (Oxford: Clarendon Press, 1991), 470.

27. Quoted in Lockman, *Contending Visions of the Middle East*, 25.

28. Richard William Southern, *Western Views of Islam in the Middle Ages* (Cambridge, Mass.: Harvard University Press, 1962), 13–14.

29. Ibid., 14.

30. Ibid., 28–29.

31. The Bible translation used in this volume is the *New Revised Standard Version, Anglicized Edition* (Oxford: Oxford University Press, 1995).

32. Tolan, *Saracens*, 10–14; Rodinson, *Europe and the Mystique of Islam*, 3–14.

33. Lockman, *Contending Visions of the Middle East*, 32–33.

34. Tolan, *Saracens*, 58–59.

35. Others went native or assumed the second-class status of *dhimmi*, citizens who, though free, had to pay taxes, were forbidden from carrying swords, were limited in their occupations and places of residence, and were required to wear specified types of dress with badges depicting their status, such as honey-colored hoods and belts. Sometimes they were required to nail a wooden image of the devil on their doors.

36. Jean de Joinville, *Life of St. Louis*, translated by M. R. B. Shaw (London: Hamondsworth, 1963), 262.

37. María Rosa Menocal, *The Ornament of the World* (Boston: Little, Brown, 2002), 17–49.

38. Tolan, *Saracens*, 133–134, 174–193.

39. Quoted in Fletcher, *Cross and the Crescent*, 48.

40. Southern, *Western Views of Islam in the Middle Ages*, 25–26.

41. Tolan, *Saracens*, 87.

42. Ibid., 90.

43. Quoted ibid., 92.

44. Quoted in Harvey, *Islamic Spain, 1250 to 1500*, 290.

45. Mark Mazower, *Salonica: City of Ghosts, Christians, Muslims, and Jews, 1430–1950* (New York: Harper Perennial, 2004), 474.

46. "Spain: Moorish Festivals Must Not Offend Muslims," www.westernresistance.com/blog/archives/003105.html; Tolan, *Saracens*, 133.

47. Quoted in Lockman, *Contending Visions of the Middle East*, 28.

48. Thomas Asbridge, *The First Crusade: A New History. The Roots of Conflict between Christianity and Islam* (Oxford: Oxford University Press, 2004), 33.

49. Lockman, *Contending Visions of the Middle East*, 29–30.

50. Quoted ibid., 34.

51. Rodinson, *Europe and the Mystique of Islam*, 23.

52. Ronald C. Finucane, *Soldiers of the Faith: Crusaders and Moslems at War* (London: Phoenix, 2004), 194–195.

53. David Abulafia, *Frederick II: A Medieval Emperor* (London: Allen Lane, Penguin, 1988), 168–171.

54. Rodinson, *Europe and the Mystique of Islam*, 25.

55. Julie Taylor, *Muslims in Medieval Italy: The Colony at Lucera* (New York: Lexington Books, 2003), 177–188.

56. Tolan, *Saracens*, 117.

57. Ibid., xvii.

58. Daniel J. Vitkus, *Turning Turk: English Theater and the Multicultural Mediterranean, 1570–1630* (New York: Palgrave Macmillan, 2003), 79–80.

59. Richard Schwobel, *The Shadow of the Crescent: The Renaissance Image of the Turk, 1453–1517* (Nieuwkoop: B. De Graff, 1967), 13–14.

60. Ibid., 12–13.

61. Ibid., 19–13.

62. Ibid., 85–90.

63. Ibid., 68–72.

64. See Tolan, *Saracens*, 3–20, for a discussion of Isidore.

65. Daniel J. Sahas, *John of Damascus on Islam: The "Heresy of the Ishmaelites"* (Leiden: E. J. Brill, 1972), 127.

66. Tolan, *Saracens*, 54–55.

67. Katharine Scarfe Beckett, *Anglo-Saxon Perceptions of the Islamic World* (Cambridge: Cambridge University Press, 2003), 20.

68. The Venerable Bede, *Ecclesiastical History of the English People* [5:23], translated by L. Sherley-Price [1955] (London: Penguin, 1990), 323.

69. Dorothee Metlitzki, *The Matter of Araby in Medieval England* (New Haven: Yale University Press, 1977), 14.

70. Ibid., 30.

71. Menocal, *Ornament of the World*, 179–180.

72. Tolan, *Saracens*, 156.

73. Quoted ibid., 220.

74. Ibid., 226.

75. Ibid., 234–240.

76. James Waltz, "Muhammad and the Muslims in St. Thomas Aquinas," *Muslim World* 66.2 (April 1976): 83.

77. Quoted in Tolan, *Saracens*, 243.

78. David B. Burrell, "Thomas Aquinas and Islam," in *Thomas for the Twenty-First Century*, ed. Jim Fodor and Frederick Christian Bauerschmidt (Malden, Mass.: Blackwell, 2004), 67–83.

79. Tolan, *Saracens*, 268–274.

80. Rodinson, *Europe and the Mystique of Islam*, 19.

81. Quoted in Suzanne Conklin Akbari, "The Rhetoric of Antichrist in Western Lives of Muhammad," *Islam and Christian–Muslim Relations* 8.3 (1997): 297.

82. Quoted in Kontje, *German Orientalisms*, 39.

83. Johann Sebastian Bach, *Kantaten zu den Sonntagen Septuagesimae und Sexagesimae*, "Gleichwie der Regen und Schnee vom Himmel Fällt," BMW 18 (Leipzig: Bärenreiter Verlag Kassel und Basel, 1956), 124–125.

84. Stefano Carboni, *Venice and the Islamic World, 828–1797* (New York: Metropolitan Museum of Art, 2007).

85. Within Carboni, *Venice and the Islamic World*, see the portrait by Bellini, *Portrait of Sultan Mehmet II*, on page 68.

86. Within Carboni, *Venice and the Islamic World*, see the paintings *The Adoration of the Magi* on page 144; Mansueti's *The Arrest and Trial of St. Mark* on page 126, and Carpaccio's *La lapidation de saint Étienne* on page 27.

87. Within Carboni, *Venice and the Islamic World*, see the painting by Veneziano, *Madonna and Child Enthroned*, on page 32.

88. Carboni, *Venice and the Islamic World*, 183–189.

89. Quoted ibid., 49.

90. Egil Grislis, "Luther and the Turks," part 1, *Muslim World* 64.3 (July 1974): 180.

91. Grislis, "Luther and the Turks," 183.

92. Ibid., 184.

93. Ibid., 276.

94. Quoted in Albert Hourani, *Europe and the Middle East* (Berkeley: University of California Press, 1980), 26.

95. Quoted in Gregory J. Miller, "Holy War and Holy Terror: Views of Islam in German Pamphlet Literature, 1520–1545" (Ph.D. dissertation, University of Michigan, 1994), 146.

96. *Acts and Monuments of John Foxe: With a Life of the Martyrologist, and Vindication of the Work, by the Rev. George Townsend, M.A., of Trinity College, Cambridge, Prebendary of Durham; and Vicar of Northallerton, Yorkshire*, vol. 4 (New York: AMS, 1965), 18–20, 121–122.

97. Clarence Dana Rouillard, *The Turk in French History, Thought, and Literature (1520–1660)* (Paris: Boivin, 1938), 363–376.

98. Galen Johnson, "Muhammad and Ideology in Medieval Christian Literature," *Islam and Christian–Muslim Relations* 11.3 (2000).

99. Rodinson, *Europe and the Mystique of Islam*, 10.

100. Kontje, *German Orientalisms*, 15–32.

101. Ibid., 19.

102. Rodinson, *Europe and the Mystique of Islam*, 27.

103. G. Ronald Murphy, S.J., *Gemstone of Paradise: The Holy Grail in Wolfram's Parzival* (New York: Oxford University Press, 2006), 71.

104. Geoffrey Chaucer, *The Canterbury Tales*, translated with notes by David Wright [1986] (Oxford: Oxford University Press, 1998), 122; Metlitzki, *Matter of Araby in Medieval England*, 198–207.

105. Brenda Deen Schildgen, *Pagans, Tartars, Moslems, and Jews in Chaucer's Canterbury Tales* (Gainesville: University Press of Florida, 2001), 49–52, 55–66.

106. Metlitzki, *Matter of Araby in Medieval England*, 74–75, 80–89, 198–207.

107. Akbari, "Rhetoric of Antichrist," 303–304.

108. Quoted in Samuel C. Chew, *The Crescent and the Rose: Islam and England during the Renaissance* (Oxford: Oxford University Press, 1937), 472. See also "Marlowe's Mahomet" in Vitkus, *Turning Turk*, 44–75.

109. Quoted in Shawkat M. Toorawa, "Muhammad, Muslims, and Islamophiles in Dante's *Commedia*," *Muslim World* 82.1–2 (January–April 1992): 134.

110. Brenda Deen Schildgen, *Dante and the Orient* (Chicago: University of Illinois Press, 2002), 55–61.

111. Philip F. Kennedy, "The Muslim Sources of Dante?" in *Arab Influence in Medieval Europe*, ed. Dionisius A. Agius and Richard Hitchcock (Reading, U.K.: Ithaca, 1994), 79.

112. Tolan, *Saracens*, 275–279.

CHAPTER 2

1. Robert C. Davis, "Counting European Slaves on the Barbary Coast," *Past and Present* 172 (August 2001): 123.

2. Hentsch, *Imagining the Middle East*, 113.

3. Quoted in Hourani, *Europe and the Middle East*, 27.

4. Norman L. Torrey, *Les philosophes* (New York: Capricorn Books, 1960), 41.

5. P. M. Holt, "The Treatment of Arab History by Prideaux, Ockley, and Sale," in *Historians of the Middle East*, ed. Bernard Lewis and Peter M. Holt (London: Oxford University Press, 1962), 298.

6. Chew, *Crescent and the Rose*, 111–115.

7. Quoted in Hentsch, *Imagining the Middle East*, 64.

8. Quoted in Lockman, *Contending Visions of the Middle East*, 43.

9. Julian H. Franklin, *Jean Bodin and the Sixteenth-Century Revolution in the Methodology of Law and History* (New York: Columbia University Press, 1963), 71–77; Henri Baudrillars, *J. Bodin et son temps, tableau des théories politiques et des idées économiques au seizème siècle* (New York: Burt Franklin, 1969; reprint of 1853 edition), 413–418.

10. Lewis and Holt, *Historians of the Middle East*, 300.

11. Jane I. Smith, "French Christian Narratives Concerning Muhammad and the Religion of Islam from the Fifteenth to the Eighteenth Centuries," *Islam and Christian–Muslim Relations* 7.1 (1996): 58.

12. Ibid., 47–61.

13. L. Dedouvres, *Le Père Joseph, polémiste: Ses premiers écrits, 1623–1626* (Paris: Alphonse Picard, 1895), 36.

14. Quoted ibid., 387.

15. Rouillard, *Turk in French History, Thought, and Literature*, 448–455.

16. Minou Reeves, *Muhammad in Europe* (New York: New York University Press, 2000), 144. See pages 139–146 for a discussion of Montesquieu.

17. Marie-Louise Dufrenoy, *L'orient romanesque en France, 1704–1789* (Montreal: Éditions Beauchemin, 1946), 327.

18. Charles de Secondat, baron de Montesquieu, *The Persian Letters* (London: Athenaeum, 1901), 159.

19. Roger Pearson, *Voltaire Almighty: A Life in Pursuit of Freedom* (London: Bloomsbury, 2005), 170–173.

20. Magdy Gabriel Badir, "Voltaire et l'Islam," in *Studies on Voltaire and the Eighteenth Century*, Vol. 125, ed. Theodore Betterman (Banbury, U.K.: Voltaire Foundation, 1974), 141.

21. Quoted in Norman Daniel, *Islam and the West: The Making of an Image* (Oxford: Oneworld, 1993), 31.

22. Quoted in Reeves, *Muhammad in Europe*, 156–157.

23. Pearson, *Voltaire Almighty*, 119.

24. Hugh Trevor-Roper, *Archbishop Laud, 1573–1645*, 2nd ed. (London: Phoenix Press, 2000), 380.

25. Alastair Hamilton, *William Bedwell, the Arabist: 1563–1632* (Leiden: Sir Thomas Browne Institute / E. J. Brill / Leiden University Press, 1985), 4–10, 67.

26. Holt, "Treatment of Arab History by Prideaux, Ockley, and Sale," 290.

27. Nabil Matar, *Islam in Britain, 1558–1685* (Cambridge: Cambridge University Press, 1998), 82.

28. Holt, "Treatment of Arab History by Prideaux, Ockley, and Sale," 290.

29. Joseph Schacht and C. E. Bosworth, eds., *The Legacy of Islam* (Oxford: Oxford University Press, 1979), 36.

30. Matar, *Islam in Britain*, 79.

31. A. J. Arberry, *Oriental Essays: Portraits of Seven Scholars* (London: George Allen & Unwin, 1960), 14–15.

32. Dominique Carnoy, *Représentations de l'Islam dans la France du XVIIe siècle: La ville des tentations* (Paris: L'Harmattan, 1998), 41–44. See also Alastair Hamilton and Francis Richard, *André du Ryer and Oriental Studies in Seventeenth-Century France* (Oxford: Arcadian Library in association with Oxford University Press, 2004).

33. J. A. I. Champion, *The Pillars of Priesthood Shaken: The Church of England and Its Enemies, 1669–1730* (Cambridge: Cambridge University Press, 1992), 104–105.

34. Holt, "Treatment of Arab History by Prideaux, Ockley, and Sale," 298–302.

35. Ibid.

36. Quoted in Byron Porter Smith, *Islam in English Literature*, ed. S. B. Bushrui and Anahid Melikian (2nd ed.: Delmar, N.Y.: Caravan Books, 1939), 68–69.

37. Quoted ibid., 70.

38. Holt, "Treatment of Arab History by Prideaux, Ockley, and Sale," 302.

39. Matar, *Islam in Britain*, 158.

40. Quoted ibid., 153–154.

41. Byron Porter Smith, *Islam in English Literature*, 26.

42. *Oxford Dictionary of National Biography*, vol. 41: 428–430.

43. Arberry, *Oriental Essays*, 45.

44. Quoted in Holt, "Treatment of Arab History by Prideaux, Ockley, and Sale," 430.

45. A roadmap through these controversies is provided in David Womersley, *Gibbon and the "Watchmen of the Holy City": The Historian and His Reputation, 1776–1815* (Oxford: Oxford University Press, 2002), 157–160.

46. Lewis and Holt, *Historians of the Middle East*, 13.

47. Champion, *Pillars of Priesthood Shaken*, 106–111.

48. Ibid., 114–116. Not all the works on Islam at this time were negative. Adrian Reland, professor of Oriental Tongues at the University of Utrecht, produced a work *Of the Mohametan Theology* (1712) that Champion called "a work of profound and impartial scholarship" (116). A. Bobovius's *A Treatise Concerning the Turkish Liturgy* was a similarly balanced work.

49. Reeves, *Muhammad in Europe*, 165.

50. Quoted in P. M. Holt, *Seventeenth-Century Defender of Islam, Henry Stubbe (1632–76) and His Book* (London: Dr. Williams's Trust, 1972), 17–18, 28.

51. Ibid., 28.

52. Matar, *Islam in Britain*, 104.

53. Quoted in Kenneth Cracknell, *Justice, Courtesy, and Love: Theologians and Missionaries Encountering World Religions, 1846–1914* (London: Epworth, 1995), 17–18.

54. Gibbon's views on Islam are discussed in Womersley, *Gibbon and the "Watchmen of the Holy City*,*" 147–174.

55. Edward Gibbon, *The History of the Decline and Fall of the Roman Empire*, ed. David Womersley (New York: Penguin, 1995), 3: 191.

56. Bernard Lewis, "Gibbon on Muhammad," in *Edward Gibbon and the Decline and Fall of the Roman Empire*, ed. G. W. Bowersock, John Clive, and Stephen R. Graubard (Cambridge, Mass.: Harvard University Press, 1977).

57. Quoted in Byron Porter Smith, *Islam in English Literature*, 113.

58. Quoted ibid., 109–110.

59. Southern, *Western Views of Islam in the Middle Ages*, 13.

60. Quoted in Bulliet, *Case for Islamo-Christian Civilization*, 7.

61. Joseph White, *Sermons Preached before the University of Oxford in the Year 1784 at the Lecture Founded by the Rev. John Bampton*, 4th ed. (London: G.G.J. and J. Robinson, 1792), 524–525.

62. Jane Shaw, "Gender and the 'Nature' of Religion: Lady Mary Wortley Montagu's Embassy Letters and Their Place in Enlightenment Philosophy of Religion," *Bulletin of the John Rylands Library* 80.3 (Autumn 1998): 145.

63. Quoted in Byron Porter Smith, *Islam in English Literature*, 59.

64. Quoted ibid., 60.

65. Quoted in *Embassy to Constantinople: The Travel Letters of Lady Mary Wortley Montagu*, ed. and comp. Christopher Pick (London: Century, 1988), 99–100.

66. A Turks Head Public House exists in central London, with two carved heads and a painted tavern sign above the door, at 10 Motcomb Street, Belgravia. Turks Head taverns still exist in many major cities throughout the United Kingdom.

67. Matar, *Islam in Britain*, 115–116.

68. Quoted ibid., 110.

69. Ibid., 117.

70. Ibid., 113.

71. Daniel J. Vitkus, ed., *Piracy, Slavery, and Redemption* (New York: Columbia University Press, 2001), 6–9, 13–16.

72. Robert C. Davis, "Counting European Slaves on the Barbary Coast," 97.

73. Ibid., 87–124.

74. Ibid., 124.

75. Vitkus, *Turning Turk*, 82; Daniel J. Vitkus, ed., *Three Turk Plays from Early Modern England: Selimus, A Christian Turned Turk, The Renegado* (New York: Columbia University Press, 2000), 4.

76. Osman Benchérif, *The Image of Algeria in Anglo-American Writings, 1785–1962* (Lanham, Md.: University Press of America, 1997), 23. In 1884 the British consul general in Algiers, Sir Lambert Playfair, wrote a book about his experiences, calling the Algerian pirates *The Scourge of Christendom*.

77. Quoted in Byron Porter Smith, *Islam in English Literature*, 62–63.

78. The whole lugubrious rite is contained in Vitkus, *Piracy, Slavery, and Redemption*, 361–366.

79. Ibid., 365–366.

80. Benchérif, *Image of Algeria in Anglo–American Writings*, 37. Frédéric Delaméa, "The Noble Death: Pangs of Vivaldian Opera," in Antonio Vivaldi, *Bajazet* (London: EMI Records/Virgin Classics, 2005), 11–14 in the accompanying text.

81. Matar, *Islam in Britain*, 52–53.

82. Quoted ibid., 55.

83. Vitkus, *Three Turk Plays*, 23–28, 151–239.

84. Quoted in Matar, *Islam in Britain*, 52.

85. See "Othello Turns Turk" in Vitkus, *Turning Turk*, 77–106.

86. John W. Draper, *Orientalia and Shakespeareana* (New York: Vantage, 1978), 129–139, 146–157.

87. Schacht and Bosworth, *Legacy of Islam*, 36–37.

88. Robert Irwin, *Arabian Nights: A Companion* (London: Allen Lane, 1994), 241.

89. Robert L. Mack, ed., *Arabian Nights' Entertainments* (Oxford: Oxford University Press, 1998), ix–xx. See also Peter L. Caracciolo, ed., *The Arabian Nights in English Literature: Studies in the Reception of the Thousand and One Nights into British Culture* (New York: St. Martin's, 1988), 1–80.

90. Menocal, *Ornament of the World*, 253–265.

91. Quoted in John Rodenbeck, "Cervantes and Islam: Attitudes toward Islam and Islamic Culture in *Don Quixote*," *Cairo Papers in Social Science* 19.2 (September 1996): 65.

92. Kontje, *German Orientalisms*, 109.

93. Ibid., 72–73.

94. Quoted in Stephen Houlgate, ed., *The Hegel Reader* (Malden, Mass.: Blackwell, 1998), 401.

95. Hentsch, *Imagining the Middle East*, 144.

96. Gotthold E. Lessing, *Nathan the Wise*, trans. Bayard Quincy Morgan (New York: Frederick Ungar, 1955), vi, 75–82.

97. Kontje, *German Orientalisms*, 118–132.

98. One of the few recordings of "Mahomet's Song" is Hyperion CDJ 33024 from Hyperion's Schubert Edition, vol. 24.

99. Kontje, *German Orientalisms*, 122.

100. George Henry Lewes, *The Life of Goethe* (New York: Frederick Ungar, 1965), 139–140.

101. Ibid., 527–528; J. G. Robertson, *Life and Work of Goethe, 1749–1832* (New York: Haskell House, 1973), 263–266.

102. Richard Friedenthal, *Goethe: His Life and Times* (Cleveland: World Publishing, 1963), 432–445.

103. Claudio Monteverdi, *Combattimento di Tancredi e Clorinda*. Tactus Digital CD TC56031101, 1987.

104. Vivaldi, *Bajazet*.

105. Sylvie Bouissou, *Les Indes galantes*, translated by James O. Wooten, Harmonia mundi CD 901367.69, Montpelier, 1991, 50–52 in the accompanying text.

106. Ibid., 108.

CHAPTER 3

1. Eitan Bar-Yosef, *The Holy Land in English Culture 1799–1917: Palestine and the Question of Orientalism* (Oxford: Clarendon Press, 2005), 64.

2. J. Christopher Herold, *Bonaparte in Egypt* (New York: Harper & Row, 1992), 5.

3. Ibid., 69–70.

4. Ibid., 82, 153.

5. Ibid., 145.

6. Ibid., 185.

7. Quoted in Hentsch, *Imagining the Middle East*, 127–128.

8. Quoted ibid., 123.

9. Quoted ibid., 125.

10. Raymond Schwab, *La renaissance orientale* (Paris: Payot, 1950; New York: AMS, 1977), 71–74, 316–318.

11. Francis Steegmuller, ed., *Flaubert in Egypt: A Sensibility on Tour* (London: Bodley Head, 1972).

12. Gérard de Nerval, *Journey to the Orient*, trans. Norman Glass (New York: New York University Press, 1972).

13. Lesley Blanch, *Pierre Loti: Travels with the Legendary Romantic* (New York: I. B. Tauris, 2004), unnumbered photo section and 233. See also Pierre-E. Briquet, *Pierre Loti et l'orient* (Neuchatel: Éditions de la Baconnière, 1945); and Pierre Loti, *Aziyadé*, trans. Marjorie Laurie (New York: Kegan Paul, 1989).

14. Ernest Renan, *L'Islamisme et la science: Conférence faite a la Sorbonne le 29 Mars 1883* (Paris: Calmann Lévy, 1883), 24, 21.

15. Quoted in Hourani, *Europe and the Middle East*, 12.

16. Ibid., 61–62.

17. Joseph Gobineau, *Essai sur l'inégalité des races humaines* (Paris: Firmin-Didot, 1853).

18. Gustave Le Bon, *La civilization des Arabes*, Book 6 (Paris: Firmin-Didot, 1884), 165.

19. Quoted in J. W. Fück, "Islam as an Historical Problem in European Historiography since 1800," in Lewis and Holt, *Historians of the Middle East*, 303–314.

20. Ann Thomson, *Barbary and Enlightenment: European Attitudes towards the Maghreb in the 18th Century* (New York: E. J. Brill, 1987), 72–73.

21. Gerald M. Ackerman, *American Orientalists* (Paris: ACR, 1994), 11.

22. Ibid., 8.

23. Malcolm Warner, "The Question of Faith: Orientalism, Christianity, and Islam," in *The Orientalists: Delacroix to Matisse, European Painters in North Africa and the Near East*, ed. Mary Anne Stevens (London: Royal Academy of Arts, 1984), 8–38.

24. Ibid., 38.

25. Quoted in Stevens, *Orientalists*, 19.

26. Holly Edwards, *Noble Dreams, Wicked Pleasures: Orientalism in America, 1870–1930* (Princeton: Princeton University Press, 2000), 10–11, 130.

27. Malek Alloula, *The Colonial Harem*, ed. Myrna Godzich and Wlad Godzich (Minneapolis: University of Minnesota Press, 1986).

28. Quoted in Reeves, *Muhammad in Europe*, 31.

29. Robert Irwin, "The Orient and the West from Bonaparte to T. E. Lawrence," in Stevens, *Orientalists*, 22; Mary Anne Stevens, "Western Art and Its Encounter with the Islamic World," in Stevens, *Orientalists*, 22.

30. Roger Benjamin, an Australian art historian, surveyed Dinet's works in *Orientalist Aesthetics: Art, Colonialism, and French North Africa, 1880–1930* (Los Angeles: University of California Press, 2003).

31. Benjamin, *Orientalist Aesthetics*, 165.

32. Hilary Spurling, *Matisse the Master: A Life of Henri Matisse*. Vol. 2, *The Conquest of Color, 1909–1954* (New York: Hamish Hamilton, Penguin, 2005), 101–108.

33. Quoted in Debra N. Mancoff, *David Roberts: Travels in Egypt and the Holy Land* (San Francisco: Pomegranate, 1999), 118–119.

34. Quoted in Byron Porter Smith, *Islam in English Literature*, 221.

35. Quoted ibid., 232–233.

36. Quoted ibid., 226.

37. Quoted in Muhammed al-Da'mi, *Arabian Mirrors and Western Soothsayers: Nineteenth-Century Literary Approaches to Arab-Islamic History* (New York: Peter Lang, 2002), 4.

38. Quoted ibid., 110.

39. Ibid., 121.

40. Quoted ibid., 111.

41. Ibid., 116.

42. Quoted in Clinton Bennet, *Victorian Images of Islam* (London: Grey Seal, 1992), 109.

43. Quoted ibid., 28.

44. Quoted ibid., 111.

45. Quoted ibid., 115.

46. Quoted ibid., 120–121.

47. Charles Forster, *Mahometanism Unveiled* (London: J. Duncan and J. Cochran, 1859), 1: 34.

48. Ibid., 104.

49. Ibid., 108–109.

50. Frederick Quinn, *To Be a Pilgrim: The Anglican Ethos in History* (New York: Crossroads, 2001), 191–194.

51. Quoted in Jane I. Smith, "Christian Missionary Views of Islam in the Nineteenth and Twentieth Centuries," *Islam and Christian–Muslim Relations* 9.3 (1998): 359.

52. Frederick Denison Maurice, *The Religions of the World and Their Relations to Christianity* (Boston: Gould and Lincoln, 1857), 251.

53. Quoted in Albert Hourani, *Islam in European Thought* (Cambridge: Cambridge University Press, 1991), 20.

54. Maurice, *Religions of the World and Their Relations to Christianity*, 40–41.

55. Hourani, *Islam in European Thought*, 22.

56. Maurice, *Religions of the World and Their Relations to Christianity*, 168.

57. Ibid.

58. Dane Keith Kennedy, *The Highly Civilized Man: Richard Burton and the Victorian World* (Cambridge, Mass.: Harvard University Press, 2005), 85.

59. Ibid., 74.

60. Ibid., 79.

61. Ibid., 227.

62. Ibid., 221.

63. Quoted in Abdur Raheem Kidwai, *Orientalism in Lord Byron's "Turkish Tales"* (Lewiston, N.Y.: Mellen University Press, 1995), 37.

64. Quoted ibid., 69.

65. Ibid., 71–127.

66. Quoted ibid., 45.

67. Ibid., 165–166.

68. Quoted in Stevens, *Orientalists*, 18.

69. Mancoff, *David Roberts*.

70. Katharine Sim, *David Roberts R.A., 1796–1864: A Biography* (New York: Quartet Books, 1984), 197.

71. Timothy Mitchell, *Colonising Egypt* (Berkeley: University of California Press, 1991), 28–29.

72. Bar-Yosef, *Holy Land in English Culture*, 132–133.

73. Hugh Casson, "Foreword," in Stevens, *Orientalists*, 13.

74. Jeffrey Richards, *Imperialism and Music: Britain 1876–1953* (Manchester: Manchester University Press, 2001), 25.

75. Quoted ibid., 386.

76. Georges Bizet, *Djamileh*, 1988. Orfeo CD C174881A.

77. John Davis, *The Landscape of Belief: Encountering the Holy Land in Nineteenth-Century American Art and Culture* (Princeton: Princeton University Press, 1996), 5.

78. Ibid., 9–10.

79. Quoted ibid., 95.

80. Quoted ibid., 87.

81. Quoted ibid. See John Heyl Vincent and James W. Lee, *Earthly Footsteps of the Man of Galilee, Being Four Hundred Original Photographic Views and Descriptions of the Places Connected with the Earthly Life of Our Lord and His Apostles, Traced with Note Book and Camera, Showing where Christ was born, brought up, baptized, tempted, transfigured, and crucified, Together with the scenes of his prayers, tears, miracles and sermons, and also places made sacred by the labors of his Apostles, from Jerusalem to Rome* (St. Louis, Mo.: Thompson, 1894).

82. Samir Khalaf, "Protestant Images of Islam: Disparaging Stereotypes Reconfirmed," *Islam and Christian–Muslim Relations* 8.2 (1997): 223.

83. Hymn 55, *The New English Hymnal* (Norwich: Canterbury Press, 2002).

84. Bayard Taylor, *The Lands of the Saracen: or, Pictures of Palestine, Asia Minor, Sicily and Spain* (New York: Putnam, 1855).

85. John Davis, *Landscape of Belief*, 43.

86. Paul Baepler, "The Barbary Captivity Narrative in American Culture," *Early American Literature* 39.2 (2004): 219–220.

87. Samuel Eliot Morison, *The Oxford History of the American People* (New York: Oxford University Press, 1965), 74.

88. Thomas A. Bailey, *A Diplomatic History of the American People*, 6th edition (New York: Appleton-Century-Crofts, 1968), 64.

89. Frank Lambert, *The Barbary Wars: American Independence in the Atlantic World* (New York: Hill and Wang, 2005), 82–84.

90. Baepler, "Barbary Captivity Narrative in American Culture," 217.

91. Robert J. Allison, *United States and the Specter of Islam: The Early Nineteenth Century*, 7. Council on Middle East Studies, Yale University Web site, http://128.36.236.77/workpaper/pdfg/MEEV3-1.pdf.

92. Quoted in Reeves, *Muhammad in Europe*, 238.

93. *Washington Irving's Life of Mohammed*, ed. Charles Getchell, with an introduction by Raphael Patai (Ipswich, Mass.: Ipswich Press, 1989), 205–206.

94. Quoted in Suzan Jameel Fakahani, "Islamic Influences on Emerson's Thought: The Fascination of a Nineteenth-Century American Writer," *Journal of Muslim Minority Affairs* 18.2 (1998): 291.

95. Ibid., 292.

96. Quoted ibid., 293.

97. Quoted ibid.

98. Quoted ibid., 294.

99. Quoted in John Davis, *Landscape of Belief*, 44.

100. Andrew Delbanco, *Melville: His World and Work* (New York: Alfred A. Knopf, 2005), 255–256.

101. Quoted in John Davis, *Landscape of Belief*, 46. See William McClure Thomson, *Land and the Book*, 2 vols. (London: Darf, 1985); William Cooper Prime, *Tent Life in the Holy Land* (New York: Harper, 1857; New York: Arno, 1977); and Samuel Clemens, *Innocents Abroad; or, The New Pilgrim's Progress* [c. 1869] (New York: Library of America, 1984).

102. Quoted in John Davis, *Landscape of Belief*, 50.

103. Quoted in Fred Kaplan, *The Singular Mark Twain: A Biography* (New York: Random House, 2005), 207.

104. Quoted in John W. Hollenbach, "The Image of the Arab in Nineteenth-Century English and American Literature," *Muslim World* 63.3 (July 1972): 205.

105. Quoted in Hilton Obenzinger, *American Palestine: Melville, Twain, and the Holy Land Mania* (Princeton: Princeton University Press, 1999), 190.

CHAPTER 4

1. A few European writers continued to hold the view that Muslim incursions over the centuries had destroyed the beauty and order of the Roman past, and only British and French imperialism had built a protective wall between civilized Europeans and barbarian Muslims. The French-born English novelist Hilaire Belloc championed such a view in his quickly written polemic *Esto Perpetua: Algerian Studies and Impressions* (1906), dashed off as a book to pay his bills after several months spent in Algeria to recover from pneumonia. His work is a paean to the French presence in Algeria, which he saw as restoring the former Roman province to its rightful place. Clash-of-civilizations proponents might find Belloc an embarrassing ally: "This is how it will end: they shall leave us our vineyards, our statues, and our harbor towns, and we will leave them to their desert here and beyond the hills, for it is their native place." Quoted in Benchérif, *Image of Algeria in Anglo-American Writings*, 144–145.

2. Two useful volumes in this regard are John L. Esposito and John O. Voll, *Makers of Contemporary Islam* (New York: Oxford University Press, 2001), and John L. Esposito, ed., *Voices of Resurgent Islam* (New York: Oxford University Press, 1983).

3. Bar-Yosef, *Holy Land in English Culture*, 247–249.

4. James L. Gelvin, *The Modern Middle East: A History* (New York: Oxford University Press, 2005), 257–260.

5. Michael J. Cohen, *Fighting World War Three from the Middle East: Allied Contingency Plans, 1945–1954* (London: Frank Cass, 1997), 42, 327.

6. Stephen Kinzer, *All the Shah's Men: An American Coup and the Roots of Middle East Terror* (New York: John Wiley & Sons, 2003), 221.

7. Gelvin, *Modern Middle East*, 287. While claiming to lead a full-fledged revolution, Khomeini never supported popular sovereignty and, despite his claims to be leading an Islamic republic, there were no examples of a republic or nationalistic government in the Koran or haddith.

8. Jean Lacouture, *Nasser, a Biography* (New York: Alfred A. Knopf, 1973), 128.

9. Quoted in William L. Cleveland, *A History of the Modern Middle East*, 3rd edition (Boulder, Co.: Westview, 2004), 313. The Asian-African Conference in Bandung, Indonesia, gathered leaders (most from recently independent nations) to discuss mutual cooperation and opposition to neocolonialism.

10. Operations Coordinating Board, Washington, D.C., *Inventory of U.S. Government and Private Organization Activity Regarding Islamic Organizations as an Aspect of Overseas Operations*, May 3, 1957. Declassified June 18, 1991. The document is

discussed in Bulliet, *Case for Islamo-Christian Civilization*, 99–117. I am grateful to Professor Bulliet for sending me a copy of the document.

11. Bulliet, *Case for Islamo-Christian Civilization*, 7.

12. Daniel Lerner, *The Passing of Traditional Society: Modernizing the Middle East* (Glencoe, Ill.: Free Press, 1958), and Walt W. Rostow, *The Stages of Economic Growth: A Non-Communist Manifesto* (London: Cambridge University Press, 1960).

13. Bulliet, *Case for Islamo-Christian Civilization*, 107. The author discusses this "modernization" phase of modern Islamic studies on pages 102–112.

14. Albert Hourani, *A History of the Arab Peoples* (Cambridge, Mass.: Harvard University Press, 1991), 434.

15. Hourani, *Islam in European Thought*, 67–69.

16. Lockman, *Contending Visions of the Middle East* 121–128.

17. Jean-Jacques Waardenburg, *L'Islam dans le miroir de l'occident* (The Hague: Mouton, 1962), 11–18, 125–127, 239–245, 265–270.

18. Hourani, *Islam in European Thought*, 35–42.

19. Waardenburg, *L'Islam dans le miroir de l'occident*, 18–27, 97–104, 127–129, 245–249, 270–273, 293–295.

20. The German sociologist Max Weber (1864–1920) left some scattered impressions about Islam, memorable less for their content than for the simple fact that they were part of his output. He was primarily interested in establishing models of various religions around ideal types, and wrote only a few pages on Islam. Nevertheless, he was one of the few leading scholars of his era to raise questions about the possible relationships among world religions, their sources of conflict, and the relationship between religion and political society. See Toby E. Huff and Wolfgang Schluchter, eds., *Max Weber and Islam* (New Brunswick, N.J.: Transaction, 1999).

21. Constance Padwick, *Temple Gairdner of Cairo*, 2nd ed. (London: Society for Promoting Christian Knowledge, 1930).

22. W. H. T. Gairdner, *The Reproach of Islam* (London: Church Missionary Society, 1909), 75.

23. Ibid., 28.

24. Ibid., 172.

25. Quoted in Michael T. Shelley, "Temple Gairdner of Cairo Revisited," *Islam and Christian–Muslim Relations* 10.3 (1999): 265.

26. Quoted ibid., 172.

27. Jane I. Smith, "Some Contemporary Protestant Theological Reflections on Pluralism: Implications for Christian–Muslim Understanding," *Islam and Christian–Muslim Relations* 8.1 (1997): 68–69.

28. Ibid., 69. On Zwemer, see also Jane I. Smith, "Christian Missionary Views of Islam," 361–363.

29. Quoted in Jane I. Smith, "Christian Missionary Views of Islam," 362.

30. Ibid., 362.

31. Thomas W. Arnold, *The Preaching of Islam: A History of the Propagation of the Muslim Faith*, 2nd ed. (London: Archibald Constable, 1896), 333.

32. Ibid., 39–41, 341–342, 347–348.

33. The Earl of Cromer, *Modern Egypt* (New York: Macmillan, 1908), 2: 565–570.

34. Quoted in Roger Owen, *Lord Cromer: Victorian Imperialist, Edwardian Proconsul* (Oxford: Oxford University Press, 2004), 353.

35. Quoted ibid., 245.

36. Quoted ibid., 345.

37. Quoted ibid., 363.

38. Ibid., 381.

39. T. E. Lawrence, *Seven Pillars of Wisdom: A Triumph* (Garden City, N.Y.: Doubleday, 1937).

40. Lowell Thomas, *With Lawrence of Arabia* (New York: Century, 1924).

41. John E. Mack, *A Prince of Our Disorder: The Life of T. E. Lawrence* (Boston: Little, Brown, 1976).

42. Quoted ibid., 208.

43. Quoted ibid., 189.

44. Quoted ibid., 251.

45. Duncan Black Macdonald, *Development of Muslim Theology, Jurisprudence and Constitutional Theory* ([1903] Beirut: Khayats, 1965), 286. See also J. Jermain Bodine, "Magic Carpet to Islam: Duncan Black Macdonald and the Arabian Nights," *Muslim World* 67.1 (January 1977): 1–11. *The Arabian Nights* were widely distributed as copiously illustrated children's literature in England and America. Their structure or subject matter were known to or employed by generations of British authors, including William Wordsworth, Walter Scott, Charles Dickens, the Brontës, and possibly C. S. Lewis.

46. Quoted in Bodine, "Magic Carpet to Islam," 4.

47. Quoted in Muhsin Jassim Ali, *Scheherazade in England: A Study of Nineteenth-Century English Criticism of the Arabian Nights* (Washington, D.C.: Three Continents Press, 1981), 88.

48. Macdonald, *Development of Muslim Theology*, 215.

49. Duncan Black Macdonald, *Aspects of Islam* (New York: Macmillan, 1911), 2.

50. Ibid., 14.

51. Ibid., 26.

52. David Samuel Margoliouth, *Mohammed* (London: Blackie & Son, 1939), vi–vii.

53. David Samuel Margoliouth, *Mohammed and the Rise of Islam,* 3rd ed. (New York: G. P. Putnam's Sons, Knickerbocker Press, 1905), 472.

54. Ibid., 460–461.

55. David Samuel Margoliouth, *Mohammedanism* (London: Williams and Norgate, [1911]), 14.

56. Ibid., 93–94.

57. Hourani, *Islam in European Thought*, 33.

58. James Thayer Addison, *The Christian Approach to the Moslem, A Historical Study* (New York: Columbia University Press, 1942).

59. Ibid., 284.

60. Ibid., 287.

61. Ibid., 294.

62. Quoted in Reeves, *Muhammad in Europe*, 278.

63. http://www.oxford.dnb.com/articles/31/31143—article.html?back=.

64. Hourani, *Islam in European Thought*, 118.

65. Lockman, *Contending Visions of the Middle East*, 108.

66. Quoted in Albert Hourani, "H. A. R. Gibb: The Vocation of an Orientalist," in Hourani, *Europe and the Middle East*, 53.

67. W. Montgomery Watt, "Muhammad in the Eyes of the West," *Boston University Journal* 2.3 (Fall 1974): 61.

68. W. Montgomery Watt, *Muhammad: Prophet and Statesman* (Oxford: Oxford University Press, 1961), 232–233, 240.

69. Years later, Pope John Paul II said that Christians and Muslims in general had "badly misunderstood each other," and that this resulted in "polemics and in wars." A new era of respect and cooperation was called for because God was inviting Christians to change their old practices. While the pope did not deviate from fundamental Roman Catholic theological premises, he was willing to encourage a much greater openness than the Church had exhibited until then for open dialogue on issues as wide ranging as human rights and interreligious cooperation.

70. See Hourani, *Islam in European Thought*, 43–49.

71. France's other major interpreter of Islam in this period was the sociologist Jacques Becque. Born in Algeria of parents who had long lived in North Africa, Becque served as a colonial administrator, UNESCO expert in Egypt, professor of the Collège de France, and author of several detailed works on Egypt, North Africa, and social and cultural aspects of Arab and North African Islamic society.

72. Quoted in Guilio Basetti-Sani, *Louis Massignon (1883–1962): Christian Ecumenist, Prophet of Inter-Religious Reconciliation*, ed. and trans. Allan Harris Cutler (Chicago: Franciscan Herald Press, 1974), 43.

73. Mary Louise Gude, *Louis Massignon: The Crucible of Compassion* (Notre Dame: University of Notre Dame Press, 1996), 25.

74. Quoted in Basetti–Sani, *Louis Massignon (1883–1962)*, 9.

75. Quoted ibid., 92.

76. Quoted ibid., 108.

77. For Tahar Ben Jelloun, see www.brainyquote.com/quotes/authors/t/tahar_ben_jelloun.html; Albert Camus is quoted in Frederick Quinn, *The French Overseas Empire* (Westport, Conn.: Praeger, 2000), 250.

78. *The Garden of Allah*, MGM Home Entertainment, Santa Monica, Calif.

79. Robert Hichens, *The Garden of Allah* (Bath, U.K.: Cedric Chivers, 1971), 6. See also http://www.oxford.dnb.com/articles/33/32851-nav.html?back=.

80. Quoted in Matthew Bernstein and Gaylyn Studlar, eds., *Visions of the East: Orientalism in Film* (New Brunswick, N.J.: Rutgers University Press, 1997), 17.

81. Some representative titles in videotape or DVD format are *The Sheik* and *The Son of the Sheik*, Image Entertainment, Chatsworth, Calif.; *The Thief of Bagdad*, Alpha Video Distribution, Narberth, Pa.; *Algiers*, Alpha Video, Narberth, Pa.; *Lawrence of Arabia*, Columbia Pictures, Culver City, Calif.; *Khartoum*, MGM Home Entertainment, Santa Monica, Calif.; *Aladdin*, Buena Vista Home Entertainment,

Burbank, Calif.; *Indiana Jones and the Temple of Doom,* Timhers Video, North Hollywood, Calif.

82. Quoted in Ella Shohat, "Gender and Culture of Empire: Toward a Feminist Ethnography of the Cinema," in Bernstein and Studlar, *Visions of the East,* 48–49.

83. *Rules of Engagement,* Paramount Home Video, Hollywood, Calif.

84. Brian Whitaker, "Arabs Accuse U.S. Filmmakers of Racism over Blockbuster," August 11, 2000, http://www.al-bab.com/media/cinema/rules.htm.

85. Quinn, *French Overseas Empire,* 253–254.

86. Timothy M. Renick, "Crusades Revisited," *Christian Century* 122.12 (June 14, 2005): 11.

87. Richards, *Imperialism and Music,* 495–524.

88. Espe de Metz, "La Sidi Ferruch," in Alain Ruscio, *Que la France était belle aux temps des colonies: Anthologie de chansons colonials et exotiques françaises* (Paris: Maisonneuve et Larose, 2001), 245–246. Also useful is Lionel Risler, "Chansons colonials et exotiques, 1906–1942" (2 CDs), 1995, E. P. M. Paris.

89. Risler, "Chansons colonials et exotiques, 1906–1942," 57 in accompanying text.

90. Steven C. Caton, "The Sheik: Instabilities of Race and Gender in Transatlantic Popular Culture of the Early Nineties," in Edwards, *Noble Dreams, Wicked Pleasures,* 224; Ruscio, *Que la France était belle,* 224–226. Like Lowell Thomas, the journalist Harold Lamb (1892–1962) helped create a heightened popular American interest in the Middle East. As a young writer, Lamb traveled widely in the Middle East and wrote numerous magazine articles, while acquiring fluency in French, Persian, and Arabic. Titles like "Beyond the Veil" and "The Mystery of the Middle East" suggest the content of his early works. Two of his most lasting works were *The Crusades: Iron Men and Saints* (1930) and *The Crusades: The Flame of Islam* (1931). Lamb was, above all, a storyteller and drew resourcefully from a spread of medieval chronicles. Although Lamb was a figure of his times, modern readers would find his appraisals of Islamic societies amazingly comprehensive, a harbinger of future generations of social scientists and mature journalists who sought to unravel a complex subject with balance and fairness.

91. Edwards, *Noble Dreams, Wicked Pleasures,* 192–198, 204–205.

92. Ibid., 197–198.

CHAPTER 5

1. Hentsch, *Imagining the Middle East,* 113.

2. Quoted in Byron Porter Smith, *Islam in English Literature,* 70.

3. Quoted ibid., 221.

4. John Henry Newman, *Lectures on the History of the Turks in Its Relation to Christianity* (Dublin: J. Duffy, 1845); Maurice, *Religions of the World and Their Relations to Christianity.*

5. Quoted in John Davis, *Landscape of Belief,* 5, 9–10.

6. Two useful volumes on the most recent period are Esposito and Voll, *Makers of Modern Islam,* and Esposito, *Voices of Resurgent Islam.*

7. David Edgar, *Pentecost* (London: Hern Books and the Royal Shakespeare Co., 1994). I am grateful to Professor Wade Jacoby, director of the Center for the Study of Europe, Brigham Young University, for calling my attention to this work.

8. Ibid., 104.

9. Associated Press, "Pope 'Deeply Sorry' for Comment on Islam," Internet version, September 17, 2001.

10. Ibid.

11. "Pope: Our Future Depends on Dialogue with Islam," Rome: ANSA Press, Internet version, September 25, 2006.

12. Raghidah Durgham, "Islam Is Innocent of Violence Committed in Its Name," *al-Hayah* (London), Internet version, September 29, 2006.

13. Jalal Duwaydar, "He Had to Apologize," *al-Akbar* (Cairo), Internet version, September 18, 2006.

14. "Instrumental Use of the Pope," *Jomhuri-ye Eslami* (Tehran), Internet version, September 19, 2006.

15. Haya al-Mani, "The Pope's Slip," *al-Riyad* (Riyad), Internet version, September 20, 2006.

16. Anthony Shadid, "Remarks by Pope Prompt Muslim Outrage, Protests," *Washington Post,* Internet version, September 16, 2006.

17. Giacome Galeazzi, "Italy's Islamic Communities, For Us, the Case Is Closed," *La Stampa* (Turin), Internet version, September 26, 2006.

18. *Singapore Strait Times,* Internet version, October 8, 2006.

19. "Spanish Cathedral Shuns Muslim Plea," BBC News: http://news.bbc.co.uk/go/pr/fr/-/2/hi/europe/6213665.stm.

20. Associated Press, "Congressman Criticized for Muslim Letter," *Washington Post,* Internet version, Wednesday, December 20, 2006.

21. James Zogby, "Celebrate Koran Oath as an all-American moment," *New York Daily News,* Internet version, January 5, 2007.

22. Middle East News Agency, Cairo, "Prince Charles Calls for Restoring Mutual Respect between Faiths," Internet version, March 21, 2006.

APPENDIX

1. Kenneth Cragg, *Muhammad and the Christian: A Question of Response* (Oxford: Oneworld, 1999), 136.

2. Kenneth Cragg, *Am I Not Your Lord? Human Meaning in Divine Question* (London: Melisende, 2003), 231.

3. Kenneth Cragg, *The Call of the Minaret,* 3rd ed. (Oxford: Oneworld, 2000), 30.

4. Cragg, *Muhammad and the Christian,* 31–52.

Selected Bibliography

Abulafia, David. *Frederick II: A Medieval Emperor*. London: Allen Lane, Penguin, 1988.

Ackerman, Gerald M. *American Orientalists*. Paris: ACR, 1994.

———. *La vie et l'oeuvre de Jean-Léon Gérôme*. Paris: ACR, 1986.

Acts and Monuments of John Foxe: With a Life of the Martyrologist, and Vindication of the Work, by the Rev. George Townsend, M.A., of Trinity College, Cambridge, Prebendary of Durham; and Vicar of Northallerton, Yorkshire. Vol. 4. New York: AMS, 1965.

Addison, James Thayer. *The Christian Approach to the Moslem, A Historical Study*. New York: Columbia University Press, 1942.

Agius, Dionisius A., and Richard Hitchcock, eds. *The Arab Influence in Medieval Europe*. Reading, U.K.: Ithaca, 1994.

Akbari, Suzanne Conklin. "The Rhetoric of Antichrist in Western Lives of Muhammad." *Islam and Christian–Muslim Relations* 8.3 (1997): 297–307.

Al-Da'mi, Muhammed. *Arabian Mirrors and Western Soothsayers: Nineteenth-Century Literary Approaches to Arab-Islamic History*. New York: Peter Lang, 2002.

Al-Disuqi, Rasha. "Orientalism in Moby Dick." *American Journal of Social Science* 4.1 (1987): 117–125.

Ali, Muhsin Jassim. *Scheherazade in England: A Study of Nineteenth-Century English Criticism of the Arabian Nights*. Washington, D.C.: Three Continents Press, 1981.

Alloula, Malek. *The Colonial Harem*. Edited by Myrna Godzich and Wlad Godzich, introduction by Barbara Harlow. Minneapolis: University of Minnesota Press, 1986.

Almond, Philip. "Western Images of Islam, 1700–1900." *Australian Journal of Politics and History* 49.1 (2003): 412–424.

Althaus, Horst. *Hegel, An Intellectual Biography*. Translated by Michael Tarsh. Malden, Mass.: Blackwell, 2000.

Arberry, A. J. *Oriental Essays: Portraits of Seven Scholars*. London: George Allen & Unwin, 1960.

Arnold, Thomas W. *The Preaching of Islam: A History of the Propagation of the Muslim Faith*. 2nd edition. London: Archibald Constable, 1896.

Arnold, Thomas W., and Alfred Guillaume, eds. *The Legacy of Islam*. Oxford: Oxford University Press, 1952.

Asbridge, Thomas. *The First Crusade: A New History. The Roots of Conflict between Christianity and Islam*. Oxford: Oxford University Press, 2004.

Asin, Miguel. *Islam and the Divine Comedy*. Translated by Harold Sunderland. London: John Murray, 1926.

Atil, Esin, Charles Newton, and Sarah Searight. *Visions: Nineteenth-Century European Images of the Middle East from the Victoria and Albert Museum*. Smithsonian Institution Traveling Exhibition Service and the Victoria and Albert Museum, London. Seattle: University of Washington Press, 1995.

Badir, Magdy Gabriel. "Voltaire et l'Islam." *Studies on Voltaire and the Eighteenth Century*, Vol. 125, edited by Theodore Betterman. Banbury, U.K.: Voltaire Foundation, 1974.

Baepler, Paul. "The Barbary Captivity Narrative in American Culture." *Early American Literature* 39.2 (2004): 217–246.

Ballaster, Ros, ed. *Fables of the East, Selected Tales, 1662–1785*. Oxford: Oxford University Press, 2005.

———. *Fabulous Orients: Fictions of the East in England, 1662–1785*. Oxford: Oxford University Press, 2005.

Bar-Yosef, Eitan. *The Holy Land in English Culture 1799–1917: Palestine and the Question of Orientalism*. Oxford: Clarendon Press, 2005.

Barbour, Richmond. *Before Orientalism: London's Theatre of the East, 1576–1626*. Cambridge: Cambridge University Press, 2003.

Basetti-Sani, Guilio. *Louis Massignon (1883–1962): Christian Ecumenist, Prophet of Inter-Religious Reconciliation*. Edited and translated by Allan Harris Cutler. Chicago: Franciscan Herald Press, 1974.

———. *Mohammed et Saint François*. Ottawa: Commissariat de Terre-Saint, 1959.

Baudrillars, Henri. J. *Bodin et son temps, tableau des théories politiques et des idées économiques au seizème siècle*. New York: Burt Franklin, 1969 (reprint of 1853 edition).

Beaulieu, Jill, and Mary Roberts, eds. *Orientalism's Interlocutors: Painting, Architecture, Photography*. Durham, N.C.: Duke University Press, 2002.

Beaumont, Daniel. *Slave of Desire: Sex, Love, and Death in the 1001 Nights*. Cranbury, N.J.: Associated University Presses, 2002.

Beckett, Katharine Scarfe. *Anglo-Saxon Perceptions of the Islamic World*. Cambridge: Cambridge University Press, 2003.

Benchérif, Osman. *The Image of Algeria in Anglo-American Writings, 1785–1962.* Lanham, Md.: University Press of America, 1997.

Benjamin, Roger. *Orientalist Aesthetics: Art, Colonialism, and French North Africa, 1880–1930.* Los Angeles: University of California Press, 2003.

Bennet, Clinton. *In Search of Muhammad.* New York: Cassel, 1998.

———. *Victorian Images of Islam.* London: Grey Seal, 1992.

Bernstein, Matthew, and Gaylyn Studlar, eds. *Visions of the East: Orientalism in Film.* New Brunswick, N.J.: Rutgers University Press, 1997.

Berque, Jacques. *The Arabs.* Translated by Jean Stewart, foreword by Sir Hamilton Gibb. New York: Frederick A. Praeger, 1964.

———. *Cultural Expression in Arab Society Today.* Translated by Robert W. Stookey. Austin: University of Texas Press, 1978.

———. *Egypt, Imperialism and Revolution.* Translated by Jean Stewart. New York: Frederick A. Praeger, 1972.

———. *French North Africa: The Maghrib between Two World Wars.* Translated by Jean Stewart. New York: Frederick A. Praeger, 1967.

Birks, Herbert. *The Life and Correspondence of Thomas Valpy French, First Bishop of Lahore.* 2 vols. London: John Murray, 1895.

Bisaha, Nancy. *Creating East and West: Renaissance Humanists and the Ottoman Turks.* Philadelphia: University of Pennsylvania Press, 2004.

Blanch, Lesley. *Pierre Loti: Travels with the Legendary Romantic.* Introduction by Philip Mansel. New York: I. B. Tauris, 2004.

Blanks, David, ed. *Images of the Other, Europe and the Muslim World before 1700.* Cairo: American University in Cairo Press, 1996.

Blanks, David, and Michael Frassetto, eds. *Western Views of Islam in Medieval and Early Modern Europe: Perception of Other.* New York: St. Martin's, 1999.

Bohrer, Frederick N. *Orientalism and Visual Culture: Imagining Mesopotamia in Nineteenth-Century Europe.* Cambridge: Cambridge University Press, 2003.

Briquet, Pierre-E. *Pierre Loti et l'orient.* Neuchatel: Éditions de la Baconnière, 1945.

Bulliet, Richard W. *The Case for Islamo-Christian Civilization.* New York: Columbia University Press, 2004.

Burrell, David B. "Thomas Aquinas and Islam." In Jim Fodor and Frederick Christian Bauerschmidt, eds., *Thomas for the Twenty-First Century.* Malden, Mass.: Blackwell, 2004, 67–83.

Caracciolo, Peter L., ed. *The Arabian Nights in English Literature: Studies in the Reception of the Thousand and One Nights into British Culture.* New York: St. Martin's, 1988.

Carboni, Stefano, ed. *Venice and the Islamic World, 828–1797.* New York: Metropolitan Museum of Art, 2007.

Carnoy, Dominique. *Représentations de l'Islam dans la France du XVIIe siècle: La ville des tentations.* Paris: L'Harmattan, 1998.

Cervantes, Miguel de. *Don Quixote de la Mancha.* Translated by Charles Jarvis. edited with introduction by E. C. Riley. Oxford: Oxford University Press, 1998.

Champion, J. A. I. *The Pillars of Priesthood Shaken: The Church of England and Its Enemies, 1669–1730.* Cambridge: Cambridge University Press, 1992.

Chateaubriand, François René. *Itinéraire de Paris à Jérusalem*. Vol. 1, edited by Emile Malakis. Baltimore, Md.: Johns Hopkins University Press, 1936.

Chaybany, Jeanne. *Les voyages en Perse et la pensée française au XVIIIème siècle*. Teheran: Ministère de l'Information, 1971.

Chew, Samuel C. *The Crescent and the Rose: Islam and England during the Renaissance*. Oxford: Oxford University Press, 1937.

Clancy-Smith, Julia. *North Africa, Islam, and the Mediterranean World: From the Almoravids to the Algerian War*. London: Frank Cass, 2001.

Coco, Carla. *Secrets of the Harem*. New York: Vendome, 1997.

Cohen, Michael J. *Fighting World War Three from the Middle East: Allied Contingency Plans, 1945–1954*. London: Frank Cass, 1997.

Coles, Paul. *The Ottoman Impact on Europe*. London: Thames and Hudson, 1968.

Cracknell, Kenneth. *Justice, Courtesy, and Love: Theologians and Missionaries Encountering World Religions, 1846–1914*. London: Epworth, 1995.

Cragg, Kenneth. *The Arab Christian: A History in the Middle East*. Louisville, Ky.: Westminster/John Knox Press, 1991.

———. *The Call of the Minaret*. 3rd edition. Oxford: Oneworld, 2000.

Cromer, Earl of, (Evelyn Baring). *Modern Egypt*. Vols. 1 and 2. New York: Macmillan, 1908.

Croutier, Alev Lytle. *Harem: The World behind the Veil*. New York: Abbeville, 1989.

Daniel, Norman. *The Arabs and Mediaeval Europe*. 2nd edition. London: Longman, 1979.

———. *Islam, Europe, and Empire*. Edinburgh: Edinburgh University Press, 1966.

———. *Islam and the West: The Making of an Image*. Edinburgh: Edinburgh University Press, 1960; revised edition, Oxford: Oneworld, 1993.

Davis, John. *The Landscape of Belief: Encountering the Holy Land in Nineteenth-Century American Art and Culture*. Princeton: Princeton University Press, 1996.

Davis, Natalie Zemon. *Trickster Travels: A Sixteenth-Century Muslim between Worlds*. New York: Hill and Wang, 2006.

Davis, Robert C. "Counting European Slaves on the Barbary Coast." *Past and Present* 172 (August 2001): 87–124.

Dean, Vera Micheles. *The Nature of the Non-Western World*. New York: Mentor, New American Library, 1963.

Dedouvres, L. *Le Père Joseph, polémiste: Ses premiers écrits, 1623–1626*. Paris: Alphonse Picard, 1895.

Delbanco, Andrew. *Melville: His World and Work*. New York: Alfred A. Knopf, 2005.

De Nerval, Gérard. *Journey to the Orient*. Translated with an introduction by Norman Glass. New York: New York University Press, 1972.

Djaït, Hichem. *Europe and Islam*. Translated by Peter Heinegg. Berkeley: University of California Press, 1985.

Doughty, C. M. *Passages from Arabia Deserta*. Selected by Edward Garnett. New York: Penguin Books, 1983.

Draper, John W. *Orientalia and Shakespeareana*. New York: Vantage, 1978.

Dufrenoy, Marie-Louise. *L'orient romanesque en France, 1704–1789*. Montreal: Éditions Beauchemin, 1946.

Edwards, Holly. *Noble Dreams, Wicked Pleasures: Orientalism in America, 1870–1930*. With essays by Brian T. Allen, Steven C. Caton, Zeynep Çelik, and Oleg Grabar. Princeton: Princeton University Press, 2000.

Embassy to Constantinople: The Travel Letters of Lady Mary Wortley Montagu. Edited and compiled by Christopher Pick, introduction by Dervla Murphy. London: Century, 1988.

Finucane, Ronald C. *Soldiers of the Faith: Crusaders and Moslems at War*. London: Phoenix, 2004.

FitzGerald, Edward. *Rubáiyát of Omar Khayyám: A Critical Edition*. Edited by Christopher Decker. Charlottesville: University of Virginia Press, 1997.

Flaubert, Gustave. *The Desert and the Dancing Girls*. London: Penguin Books, 1972.

Fletcher, Richard. *The Cross and the Crescent: Christianity and Islam from Muhammad to the Reformation*. New York: Viking, 2004.

Forster, Charles. *Mahometanism Unveiled*. Vol. 1. London: J. Duncan and J. Cochran, 1859.

Franklin, Julian H. *Jean Bodin and the Sixteenth-Century Revolution in the Methodology of Law and History*. New York: Columbia University Press, 1963.

Frassetto, Michael, and David R. Blanks. *Western Views of Islam in Medieval and Early Modern Europe: Perception of Other*. New York: St. Martin's, 1999.

Friedenthal, Richard. *Goethe: His Life and Times*. Cleveland: World Publishing, 1963.

Gairdner, M. D., ed. *W.H.L.T. to His Friends*. London: Society for Promoting Christian Knowledge, 1929.

Gairdner, William Henry Temple. *The Reproach of Islam*. London: Church Missionary Society, 1909. The 5th edition (1920) was entitled *The Rebuke of Islam*.

Gelvin, James L. *The Modern Middle East: A History*. New York: Oxford University Press, 2005.

Gerhardt, Mia I. *The Art of Story-Telling: A Literary Study of the Thousand and One Nights*. Leiden: E. J. Brill, 1963.

Ghareeb, Edmund, ed. *Split Vision: The Portrayal of Arabs in the American Media*. Washington, D.C.: American-Arab Affairs Council, 1983.

Gibbon, Edward. *The History of the Decline and Fall of the Roman Empire*. Vol. 3. Edited by David Womersley. New York: Penguin, 1995.

Gobineau, Joseph. *Essai sur l'inégalité des races humaines*. Paris: Firmin-Didot, 1853.

Goddard, Hugh P. *A History of Christian–Muslim Relations*. Chicago: New Amsterdam Books, 2000.

———. *Muslim Perceptions of Christianity*. London: Grey Seal, 1996.

Goodman, Susan. *Gertrude Bell*. Dover, N.H.: Berg, 1985.

Graham-Brown, Sarah. *Images of Women: The Portrayal of Women in Photography of the Middle East, 1860–1950*. New York: Columbia University Press, 1988.

Grimmelshausen, H. J. C. von. *The Adventurous Simplicissimus*, Translated by A. T. S. Goodrick, preface by Eric Bentley. Lincoln: University of Nebraska Press, 1962.

Gude, Mary Louise. *Louis Massignon: The Crucible of Compassion.* Notre Dame: University of Notre Dame Press, 1996.

Guenther, Alan M. "The Image of the Prophet as Found in Missionary Writings of the Late Nineteenth Century." *Muslim World* 90.1, 2 (Spring 2000): 43–71.

Gunny, Ahmed. *Images of Islam in Eighteenth Century Writings.* London: Grey Seal, 1996.

Haddad, Yvonne Y., and Wadi Z. Haddad, eds. *Christian–Muslim Encounters.* Gainesville: University Press of Florida, 1995.

Hamilton, Alastair. *Arab Culture and Ottoman Magnificence in Antwerp's Golden Age.* Oxford: Arcadian Library and Oxford University Press, 2001.

———. *Europe and the Arab World: Five Centuries of Books by European Scholars and Travelers from the Libraries of the Arcadian Group.* Dublin: Arcadia Group and Oxford University Press, c. 1994.

———. *William Bedwell, the Arabist: 1563–1632.* Leiden: Sir Thomas Browne Institute / E. J. Brill / Leiden University Press, 1985.

Hamilton, Alastair, and Francis Richard. *André du Ryer and Oriental Studies in Seventeenth-Century France.* Oxford: Arcadian Library and Oxford University Press, 2004.

Hammerbeck, David William. "Orientalism, Islam and the Other in Seventeenth and Eighteenth-Century French Theatre." Ph.D. dissertation, University of California at Los Angeles, 2002.

Harvey, Leonard Patrick. *Islamic Spain, 1250 to 1500.* Chicago: University of Chicago Press, 1990.

———. *Muslims in Spain, 1500 to 1614.* Chicago: University of Chicago Press, 2005.

Hentsch, Thierry. *Imagining the Middle East.* Translated by Fred A. Reed. New York: Black Rose Books, 1992.

Herold, J. Christopher. *Bonaparte in Egypt.* New York: Harper & Row, 1992.

Hichens, Robert. *The Garden of Allah.* Bath, U.K.: Cedric Chivers, 1971.

Hillgarth, J. N. *Ramon Lull and Lullism in Fourteenth-Century France.* Oxford: Clarendon Press, 1971.

Hindley, Geoffrey. *The Crusades: A History of Armed Pilgrimage and Holy War.* New York: Carroll & Graf, 2003.

Hodgson, Marshall G. S. *The Venture of Islam: Conscience and History in a World Civilization.* Chicago: University of Chicago Press, 1974.

Holt, P. M. *A Seventeenth-Century Defender of Islam, Henry Stubbe (1632–76) and His Book.* London: Dr. Williams's Trust, 1972.

Hopwood, Derek. "Albert Hourani: Islam, Christianity, and Orientalism." *British Journal of Middle Eastern Studies* 30.2 (November 2003): 127–137.

Houlgate, Stephen, ed. *The Hegel Reader.* Malden, Mass.: Blackwell, 1998.

Hourani, Albert. *Europe and the Middle East.* Berkeley: University of California Press, 1980.

———. *Islam in European Thought.* Cambridge: Cambridge University Press, 1991.

Huff, Toby E., and Wolfgang Schluchter, eds. *Max Weber and Islam.* New Brunswick, N.J.: Transaction, 1999.

Husayn, Muhammad Kamil. *The City of Wrong: A Friday in Jerusalem.* Translated by Kenneth Cragg. Oxford: Oneworld, 1994.

Irving, Washington. *Life of Mahomet.* London: Henry G. Bohn, 1856.

Irwin, Robert. *The Arabian Nights: A Companion.* London: Allen Lane, 1994.

Johnson, Galen. "Muhammad and Ideology in Medieval Christian Literature." *Islam and Christian–Muslim Relations* 11.3 (2000): 333–346.

Jones, Eldred. *Othello's Countrymen: The African in English Renaissance Drama.* London: Oxford University Press, 1965.

Jones, Norman L. "The Adaptation of Tradition: The Image of the Turk in Protestant England." *East European Quarterly* 12.2 (1978): 161–175.

Kamalipour, Yahya R., ed. *The U.S. Media and the Middle East: Image and Perception.* Forward by George Gerbner. Westport, Conn.: Greenwood, 1995.

Kaplan, Fred. *The Singular Mark Twain: A Biography.* New York: Random House, 2005.

Karabell, Zachary. *Parting the Desert: The Creation of the Suez Canal.* New York: Alfred A. Knopf, 2003.

Kennedy, Dane Keith. *The Highly Civilized Man: Richard Burton and the Victorian World.* Cambridge, Mass.: Harvard University Press, 2005.

Kerr, David. "The Prophet Muhammad in Christian Theological Perspective." In Daniel Cohn-Sherbok, ed., *Islam in a World of Diverse Faiths.* Basingstoke, U.K.: Macmillan, 1991, 119–134.

Keylor, William R. *The Twentieth Century World and Beyond: An International History since 1900.* New York: Oxford University Press, 2005.

Khalaf, Samir. "Protestant Images of Islam: Disparaging Stereotypes Reconfirmed." *Islam and Christian–Muslim Relations* 8.2 (1997): 211–229.

Kidwai, Abdur Raheem. *Orientalism in Lord Byron's "Turkish Tales."* Lewiston, N.Y.: Mellen University Press, 1995.

Kinzer, Stephen. *All the Shah's Men: An American Coup and the Roots of Middle East Terror.* New York: John Wiley & Sons, 2003.

Klausen, Jytte. *The Islamic Challenge: Politics and Religion in Western Europe.* New York: Oxford University Press, 2005.

Kontje, Todd. *German Orientalisms.* Ann Arbor: University of Michigan Press, 2004.

Kritzeck, James. *Peter the Venerable and Islam.* Princeton: Princeton University Press, 1964.

Kuklick, Bruce. *Puritans in Babylon: The Ancient Near East and American Intellectual Life, 1880–1930.* Princeton;: Princeton University Press, 1996.

Lacouture, Jean. *Nasser, a Biography.* New York: Alfred A. Knopf, 1973.

Lamb, Christopher. *The Call to Retrieval: Kenneth Cragg's Christian Vocation to Islam.* London: Grey Seal, 1997.

Lambert, Frank. *The Barbary Wars: American Independence in the Atlantic World.* New York: Hill and Wang, 2005.

Lamoreaux, John C. "Early Christian Responses to Islam." In *Medieval Christian Perceptions of Islam, A Book of Essays,* edited by John Victor Tolan. New York: Garland, 1996, 3–31.

Langland, William. *Piers Plowman*. Translated and introduced by A.V.C. Schmidt. Oxford: Oxford University Press, 2000.

Lapidus, Ira M. *History of Islamic Societies*. Cambridge: Cambridge University Press, 1988.

Lawrence, T. E. *Seven Pillars of Wisdom: A Triumph*. Garden City, N.Y.: Doubleday, 1937.

Leask, Nigel. *British Romantic Writers and the East: Anxieties of Empire*. Cambridge: Cambridge University Press, 1992.

Lessing, Gotthold E., *Nathan the Wise*. Translated by Bayard Quincy Morgan. New York: Frederick Ungar, 1955.

Lewes, George Henry. *The Life of Goethe*. Introduction by Victor Lange. New York: Frederick Ungar, 1965.

Lewis, Bernard. "Gibbon on Muhammad." In G. W. Bowersock, John Clive, and Stephen R. Graubard, eds., *Edward Gibbon and the Decline and Fall of the Roman Empire* (Cambridge, Mass.: Harvard University Press, 1977), 61–73.

Lewis, Bernard, and Peter M. Holt, eds. *Historians of the Middle East*. London: Oxford University Press, 1962.

Llewellyn, Briony. *The Orient Observed Images of the Middle East from the Searight Collection*. London: Victoria & Albert Museum, 1989.

Lockman, Zachary. *Contending Visions of the Middle East: the History and Politics of Orientalism*. Cambridge: Cambridge University Press, 2004.

Loti, Pierre. *Aziyadé*. Translated by Marjorie Laurie. New York: Kegan Paul, 1989.

Lowe, Lisa. *Critical Terrains: French and British Orientalisms*. Ithaca, N.Y.: Cornell University Press, 1991.

Maalouf, Amin. *The Crusades through Arab Eyes*. Translated by Jon Rothchild. New York: Schocken Books, 1984.

MacCulloch, Diarmaid. *The Reformation: A History*. New York: Viking, 2004.

Macdonald, Duncan Black. *Aspects of Islam*. New York: Macmillan, 1911.

———. *Development of Muslim Theology, Jurisprudence and Constitutional Theory*. [1903] Beirut: Khayats, 1965.

Macfie, Alexander Lyon, ed. *Orientalism: A Reader*. New York: New York University Press, 2000.

Mack, John E. *A Prince of Our Disorder: The Life of T. E. Lawrence*. Boston: Little, Brown, 1976.

Mack, Robert L., ed. *Arabian Nights' Entertainments*. Oxford: Oxford University Press, 1995.

MacKenzie, John M. *Orientalism: History, Theory, and the Arts*. Manchester: Manchester University Press, 1995.

Mahdi, Muhsin. *The Thousand and One Nights*. New York: E. J. Brill, 1995.

Mancoff, Debra N. *David Roberts: Travels in Egypt and the Holy Land*. San Francisco: Pomegranate, 1999.

Margoliouth, David Samuel. *Mohammed*. London: Blackie & Son, 1939.

———. *Mohammed and the Rise of Islam*. 3rd edition. New York: G. P. Putnam's Sons, Knickerbocker Press, 1905.

——. *Mohammedanism*. London: Williams and Norgate, [1911].

Martino, Pierre. *L'orient dans la littérature française au XVIIe au XVIIIe siècle*. Geneva: Slatkine Reprints, 1970.

Mason, Herbert. *Memoir of a Friend, Louis Massignon*. Notre Dame: University of Notre Dame Press, 1988.

Massignon, Louis. *L'hospitalité sacrée*. Preface by René Voillaume. Paris: Nouvelle Cité. 1987.

——. *La passion de Husayn ibn Mansur, martyr mystique de l'Islam*. 4 vols. Paris, 1975. English translation by H. Mason, *The Passion of al-Hallj: Mystic and Martyr of Islam*. 4 vols. Princeton: Princeton University Press, 1982.

Matar, Nabil. *Islam in Britain, 1558–1685*. Cambridge: Cambridge University Press, 1998.

Maurice, Frederick, ed. *The Life of Frederick Denison Maurice*. Vols. 1 and 2. London: Macmillan, 1884.

Maurice, Frederick Denison. *The Religions of the World and Their Relations to Christianity*. Boston: Gould and Lincoln, 1857.

Mazower, Mark. *Salonica: City of Ghosts, Christians, Muslims, and Jews, 1430–1950*. New York: Harper Perennial, 2004.

McAuliffe, Jane Dammen. *Qur'anic Christians: An Analysis of Classical and Modern Exegesis*. Cambridge: Cambridge University Press, 1991.

Melman, Billie. *Women's Orients: English Women and the Middle East, 1718–1918*. Ann Arbor: University of Michigan Press, 1992.

Menocal, María Rosa. *The Ornament of the World*. Foreword by Harold Bloom. Boston: Little, Brown, 2002.

Metlitzki, Dorothee. *The Matter of Araby in Medieval England*. New Haven: Yale University Press, 1977.

Michelmore, Christina. "Old Pictures in New Frames: Images of Islam and Muslims in Post World War II American Political Cartoons." *Journal of American and Comparative Cultures* 23.4 (2000): 37–50.

Miller, Gregory J. "Holy War and Holy Terror: Views of Islam in German Pamphlet Literature, 1520–1545." Ph.D. dissertation, University of Michigan, 1994.

Milton, Giles. *White Gold: The Extraordinary Story of Thomas Pellow and North Africa's One Million European Slaves*. London: Hodder & Stoughton, 2004.

Mitchell, Timothy. *Colonising Egypt*. Berkeley: University of California Press, 1991.

Montagu, Lady Mary Wortley. *Letters from the Levant during the Embassy to Constantinople 1716–18*. New York: Arno Press and New York Times, 1971.

——. *Turkish Embassy Letters*. Introduction by Anita Desai, text edited by Malcolm Jack. Athens: University of Georgia Press, 1993.

Morton, H. V. *Through Lands of the Bible*. New York. Dodd, Mead, 1938.

Neill, Michael, ed. *Othello, The Moor of Venice* by William Shakespeare. Oxford: Clarendon Press, 2006.

Nerval, Gérard de. *Journey to the Orient*. Translated by Norman Glass. New York: New York University Press, 1972.

Newman, John Henry. *Lectures on the History of the Turks in Its Relation to Christianity*. Dublin: J. Duffy, 1845.

Obeidat, Marwan Mohammad. "The Muslim East in American Literature: The Formation of an Image (Middle East)." Ph.D. dissertation, Indiana University, 1985.

Obenzinger, Hilton. *American Palestine: Melville, Twain, and the Holy Land Mania*. Princeton: Princeton University Press, 1999.

Oren, Michael. *Power, Faith, and Fantasy: America in the Middle East, 1776 to the Present*. New York: W. W. Norton, 2007.

Oueijan, Naji B. *A Compendium of Eastern Elements in Byron's Oriental Tales*. New York: Peter Lang, 1999.

———. *The Progress of an Image: The East in English Literature*. New York: Peter Lang, 1993.

Owen, Roger. *Lord Cromer: Victorian Imperialist, Edwardian Proconsul*. Oxford: Oxford University Press, 2004.

Oxford Dictionary of National Biography. Edited by H. C. G. Matthew and Brian Harrison. Oxford: Oxford University Press, 2001.

Padwick, Constance. *Temple Gairdner of Cairo*. 2nd edition. London: Society for Promoting Christian Knowledge, 1930.

Pearson, Roger. *Voltaire Almighty: A Life in Pursuit of Freedom*. London: Bloomsbury, 2005.

Pinault, David. *Story-Telling Techniques in the Arabian Nights*. New York: E. J. Brill, 1992.

Porter, Bernard. *The Absent-Minded Imperialists: What the British Really Thought about Empire*. Oxford: Oxford University Press, 2004.

———. *The Lion's Share: A Short History of British Imperialism, 1850–2004*. Oxford: Oxford University Press, 2004.

Prime, William Cooper. *Tent Life in the Holy Land*. New York: Harper, 1857; New York: Arno, 1977.

Quinn, Frederick. *The French Overseas Empire*. Westport, Conn.: Praeger, 2000.

———. *To Be a Pilgrim: The Anglican Ethos in History*. New York: Crossroads, 2001.

Qureshi, Emran, and Michael A. Sells, eds. *The New Crusades: Constructing the Muslim Enemy*. New York: Columbia University Press, 2003.

Rawashdeh, Moh'd Ahmed. "England in Disguise: The Orient on Restoration and Eighteenth-Century Stage." Ph.D dissertation, Purdue University, 2001.

Reeves, Minou. *Muhammad in Europe*. With biographical contribution by P. J. Stewart. New York: New York University Press, 2000.

Renan, Ernest. *L'Islamisme et la science: Conférence faite à la Sorbonne le 29 Mars 1883*. Paris: Calmann Lévy, 1883.

———. *Studies of Religious History and Criticism*. Translated by O. B. Frothingham. New York: Carleton, 1864.

Renwick, John, ed. *L'invitation au voyage: Studies in Honour of Peter France*. Oxford: Voltaire Foundation, 2000.

Richards, Jeffrey. *Imperialism and Music: Britain 1876–1953*. Manchester: Manchester University Press, 2001.

Riley-Smith, Jonathan. *The Crusades: A History*. 2nd edition. New Haven: Yale University Press, 2005.

Robinson, Edward. *Later Biblical Researches in Palestine and in the Adjacent Regions*. [1856] New York: Arno, 1977.

Rodinson, Maxime. *Europe and the Mystique of Islam*. Translated by Roger Veinus. Seattle: University of Washington Press, 1987.

Ropes, Arthur R. *Lady Mary Wortley Montagu*. New York: Charles Scribner's Sons, n.d.

Rouillard, Clarence Dana. *The Turk in French History, Thought, and Literature (1520–1660)*. Paris: Boivin, 1938.

Ruscio, Alain. *Que la France était belle aux temps des colonies: Anthologie de chansons colonials et exotiques françaises*. Paris: Maisonneuve et Larose, 2001.

Sahas, Daniel J. *John of Damascus on Islam: The "Heresy of the Ishmaelites."* Leiden: E. J. Brill, 1972.

Said, Edward. *Orientalism*. New York: Pantheon, 1978.

———. *Reflections on Exile and Other Essays*. Cambridge, Mass.: Harvard University Press, 2000.

Schacht, Joseph, and C. E. Bosworth, eds. *The Legacy of Islam*. Oxford: Oxford University Press, 1979.

Schildgen, Brenda Deen. *Dante and the Orient*. Chicago: University of Illinois Press, 2002.

———. *Pagans, Tartars, Moslems, and Jews in Chaucer's Canterbury Tales*. Gainesville: University Press of Florida, 2001.

Schwab, Raymond. *The Oriental Renaissance: Europe's Rediscovery of India and the East, 1680–1880*. Translated by Gene Patterson-Black and Victor Reinking, foreword by Edward Said. New York: Columbia University Press, 1984.

———. *La renaissance orientale*. Preface by Louis Renou. Paris: Payot, 1950; New York: AMS, 1977.

Schwobel, Richard. *The Shadow of the Crescent: The Renaissance Image of the Turk, 1453–1517*. Nieuwkoop: B. De Graff, 1967.

Shaban, Fuad. *Islam and Arabs in Early American Thought: Roots of Orientalism in America*. Durham, N.C.: Acorn Press, 1991.

Shaheen, Jack G. *Reel Bad Arabs: How Hollywood Vilifies a People*. New York: Olive Branch Press, 2001.

———. *The TV Arab*. Bowling Green, Ohio: Bowling Green State University Press, 1984.

Shelley, Michael T. "Temple Gairdner of Cairo Revisited." *Islam and Christian–Muslim Relations* 10.3 (1999): 261–278.

Sherrington. *Three Novels by Flaubert: A Study of Techniques*. Oxford: Clarendon Press, 1970.

Sim, Katharine. *David Roberts R.A., 1796—1864: A Biography*. New York: Quartet Books, 1984.

Simon, Reeva S. *The Middle East in Crime Fiction: Mysteries, Spy Novels, and Thrillers from 1916 to the 1980s.* New York: Lilian Barber, 1989.

Smith, Byron Porter. *Islam in English Literature.* Edited by S. B. Bushrui and Anahid Melikian. 2nd ed. Delmar, N.Y.: Caravan Books, 1939.

Smith, George. *Henry Martyn, Saint and Scholar: First Modern Missionary to the Mohammedans, 1781–1812.* London: Religious Tract Society, 1892.

Smith, Jane I. "Christian Missionary Views of Islam in the Nineteenth and Twentieth Centuries." *Islam and Christian–Muslim Relations* 9.3 (1998): 357–373.

———. "French Christian Narratives Concerning Muhammad and the Religion of Islam from the Fifteenth to the Eighteenth Centuries." *Islam and Christian–Muslim Relations* 7.1 (1996): 47–61.

Southern, Richard William. *Western Views of Islam in the Middle Ages.* Cambridge, Mass.: Harvard University Press, 1962.

Steegmuller, Francis, ed. *Flaubert in Egypt: A Sensibility on Tour.* London: Bodley Head, 1972.

Stevens, Mary Anne, ed. *The Orientalists: Delacroix to Matisse, European Painters in North Africa and the Near East.* London: Royal Academy of Arts, 1984.

Stoddard, John L. *John L. Stoddard's Lectures.* Boston: Balch Borthers, 1897.

Stoddard, Lothrop. *The New World of Islam.* London: Chapman & Hall, 1921.

Strickland, Debra Higgs. *Saracens, Demons, and Jews: Making Monsters in Medieval Art.* Princeton: Princeton University Press, 2003.

Stubbe, Henry. *An Account of the Rise and Progress of Mahometanism with the Life of Mahomet.* Edited by Hafiz Mahmud Khan Shairni. London: Luzac, 1911.

Tabachnick, Stephen E., ed. *Explorations in Doughty's Arabia Deserta.* Athens: University of Georgia Press, 1987.

Taraud, Christelle. *La prostitution coloniale: Algérie, Tunesie, Maroc (1830–1962).* Paris: Payot, 2003.

Tasso, Torquato. *Jerusalem Delivered (Gerusalemme liberata).* Edited and translated by Anthony M. Esolen. Baltimore, Md.: Johns Hopkins University Press, 2000.

Taylor, Julie. *Muslims in Medieval Italy: The Colony at Lucera.* New York: Lexington Books, 2003.

Thomson, Ann. *Barbary and Enlightenment: European Attitudes towards the Maghreb in the 18th Century.* New York: E. J. Brill, 1987.

Thomson, William McClure. *The Land and the Book.* 2 vols. [1877] London: Darf, 1985.

Thorne, Susan. *Congregational Missions and the Making of an Imperial Culture in Nineteenth-Century England.* Stanford, Calif.: Stanford University Press, 1999.

Thornton, Lynne. *Les orientalistes: peintres voyageurs, 1828–1908* [The Orientalists: Painters-Travelers, 1828–1908]. Paris: ACR, 1983.

Tolan, John Victor, ed. *Medieval Christian Perceptions of Islam: A Book of Essays.* New York: Garland, 1996.

———. *Saracens: Islam in the Medieval European Imagination.* New York: Columbia University Press, 2002.

Toynbee, Arnold. *Civilization on Trial.* New York: Meridian Books, 1958.

————. *The World and the West*. New York: Oxford University Press, 1953.

Trevor-Roper, Hugh. *Archbishop Laud, 1573–1645*. 2nd edition. London: Phoenix Press, 2000.

Turner, Bryan S. *Weber and Islam: A Critical Study*. London: Routledge & Kegan Paul, 1974.

Tyerman, Christopher. *God's War: A New History of the Crusades*. Cambridge, Mass.: Belknap Press of Harvard University Press, 2006.

Vitkus, Daniel J., ed. *Piracy, Slavery, and Redemption*. Introduction by Nabil Matar. New York: Columbia University Press, 2001.

————, ed. *Three Turk Plays from Early Modern Europe: Selimus, A Christian Turned Turk, The Renegado*. New York: Columbia University Press, 2000.

————. *Turning Turk: English Theater and the Multicultural Mediterranean, 1570–1630*. New York: Palgrave Macmillan, 2003.

————. "Turning Turk in Othello: The Conversion and Damnation of the Moor." *Shakespeare Quarterly* 48.2 (Summer 1997): 145–176.

Volney, Constantin-François Chassebeuf. *Voyage en Egypte et en Syrie*. Edited by Jean Gaulmier. Paris: Mouton, 1959.

Waardenburg, Jean-Jacques. *L'Islam dans le miroir de l'occident*. The Hague: Mouton, 1962.

————. *Muslim Perceptions of Other Religions: A Historical Survey*. Oxford: Oxford University Press, 1999.

————. "Muslims and Christians: Changing Identities." *Islam and Christian–Muslim Relations* 11.2 (2000): 149–162.

Wardman, H. W. *Ernest Renan: A Critical Biography*. London: Athlone, 1964.

Weiss, Daniel H., and Lisa Mahoney, eds. *France and the Holy Land: Frankish Culture at the End of the Crusades*. Baltimore: Johns Hopkins University Press, 2006.

White, Joseph. *Sermons Preached before the University of Oxford in the Year 1784 at the Lecture Founded by the Rev. John Bampton*. 4th edition. London: G.G.J. and J. Robinson, 1792.

Womersley, David. *Gibbon and the "Watchmen of the Holy City": The Historian and His Reputation, 1776–1815*. Oxford: Oxford University Press, 2002.

Yeğenoğlu, Meyda. *Colonial Fantasies Towards a Feminist Reading of Orientalism*. Cambridge: Cambridge University Press, 1998.

Zwemer, Samuel M. *The Disintegration of Islam*. New York: Fleming H. Revell, 1916.

Index